MAY WE FOREVER STAND

THE JOHN HOPE FRANKLIN SERIES IN
AFRICAN AMERICAN HISTORY AND CULTURE

Waldo E. Martin Jr. and Patricia Sullivan, *editors*

MAY
WE
FOREVER
STAND

A History of the Black National Anthem

IMANI PERRY

The University of North Carolina Press
Chapel Hill

*This book was published with the assistance of the William R. Kenan Jr. Fund
of the University of North Carolina Press.*

Manufactured in the United States of America
Designed and set in Adobe Text Pro by Rebecca Evans
The University of North Carolina Press has been a member of the
Green Press Initiative since 2003.

Cover photograph: Carver Negro School chorus singing at the 1957
Florida Folk Festival, White Springs, Florida. Photograph by Jim Stokes,
courtesy of the State Archives of Florida.

Library of Congress Cataloging-in-Publication Data
Names: Perry, Imani, 1972– author.
Title: May we forever stand : a history of the black national anthem /
  Imani Perry.
Other titles: John Hope Franklin series in African American history and culture.
Description: Chapel Hill : The University of North Carolina Press, [2018] |
  Series: The John Hope Franklin series in African American history and
  culture | Includes bibliographical references and index.
Identifiers: LCCN 2017037709 | ISBN 9781469638607 (cloth : alk. paper) |
  ISBN 9781469638614 (ebook)
Subjects: LCSH: Johnson, J. Rosamond (John Rosamond), 1873–1954. Lift
  every voice and sing. | African Americans—Music—History and criticism. |
  Anthems—United States—History and criticism. | African Americans—
  United States—History.
Classification: LCC ML3561.L54 P37 2018 | DDC 782.25089/96073—dc23
  LC record available at https://lccn.loc.gov/2017037709

For my mother,
THERESA A. PERRY,
who taught me
to know and love
my people

Contents

Illustrations

Preface

O black and unknown bards of long ago,
How came your lips to touch the sacred fire?
How, in your darkness, did you come to know
The power and beauty of the minstrel's lyre?

—JAMES WELDON JOHNSON

Oh, Black known and unknown poets, how often have your auctioned
pains sustained us? Who will compute the lonely nights made less lonely
by your songs, or by the empty pots made less tragic by your tales?

—MAYA ANGELOU

There he was, busily moving about his toys and happily humming.

"Do you know what that song is?" I asked him.

"Yes, it's the Black National Anthem!"

"Where did you learn it?"

"At school."

He walked away. I was surprised. My eldest son was then in kindergarten at a predominantly white, mostly upper-middle-class Quaker elementary school. Like many other middle-class black parents I lived with a quiet nervousness about whether my child would grow up to have an adequate appreciation for black culture given his environment. But here he was, singing our precious song.

Even I, thirty-one years older than him, hadn't learned the song in school. I'd picked it up at countless Martin Luther King Jr. memorial events, at churches, reading *Ebony Jr.* magazine,[1] and in black youth groups. It was in the ether. My academic experience was much like that of my children: flies in rich buttermilk. But in the time between my childhood and theirs, racial dynamics and my family's trajectory had changed. I was always, to some extent, a guest in the prep school world, much more identified with the red dirt of my birth state of Alabama than my clipped New England speech superficially attested. But my children were something much closer to being "to the manor born." It hadn't quite occurred to me just how much I worried about the losses entailed in privilege until I felt jubilant that my son knew "Lift Every Voice and Sing." His childhood might have passed without it.

Every Thanksgiving we travel to Birmingham, Alabama, to celebrate the holiday with our extended family. Dozens of us gather in the den, huddled close together on a wraparound sofa, a few chairs, and some of us on the floor. That fall when my first born was in kindergarten and my baby was two years old we were grieving the loss of my grandmother. She was my family's guiding force. Sadness lingered. Spontaneously, I asked my son to share the song he'd been learning in school. He stood and began to sing. Before he finished the first line, everyone in my mother's generation stood up with him and raised their right arms with solid black power fists. His eyes widened like saucers and mine filled with tears.

I wondered how my grandmother, who was born in 1917, would have responded in that moment. What would she have remembered about the song if she had been there with us in the flesh? Four generations of my family, at least, have lived with this anthem. Each generation, each individual, knows this song in a distinctive manner. We discovered it in our coming of age and in the varied orbits of our lives. I thought of a great aunt of mine whom I never met named Avie Kibble Lovely. Avie served in World War II, against her husband's wishes, and she collapsed and died while out canvassing for the NAACP in 1963, back when it was both illegal and treated like a seditious organization in Alabama. For years I wished I had known her, but I now know enough to recognize that I stand in her legacy just as I stand in that of my grandmother and the other women and men of that generation and the one before in my family; people to whom I owe not just my existence but my way of being in the world. My ancestors took in laundry and cleaned others peoples' houses for a pittance, then dragged themselves home to tend to their own. They pushed ploughs, canned vegetables, and hung meat on ceiling hooks in the smokehouse, aproned and exhausted. They sent their children on long walks to one-room schoolhouses to learn and dream, all the while scrubbing floors and picking cotton and serving. They donned their Sunday best to begin each week and loved and lived a grace that those who were white and powerful tried to steal away. This song, that I know, coursed through all the details of their lives that I will never know. It rang through lives out of which I have been made. The words connect them to me, and me to them. In this, I am not alone. The contemporary jazz artist Jason Moran described his decision to record the song to me in this way:

"I recorded the song because I was coming out of a focus on the blues. My album *Same Mother* was about that, and the recording *Artist in Residence* was mainly a catalog of commissions. So, the song actually didn't really have a place, but I felt compelled to record it because I thought it connected the materials. On the recording it follows 'Rain,' which was a commission centering on the 'ring shout.' So, how to connect these songs that reflect our past and our possibility? Does that make sense? I also like that the song was written for one reason, the assignment on Lincoln, and then 50 years later, the song gains a totally new context. It's a piece that doesn't sit still, and in that way, defines it as a brilliant composition."

In other words, it is our common thread.

By the time my younger son was in kindergarten and also came home singing "Lift Every Voice and Sing,"[2] I had finally committed to writing a history of the song. It came in fits and starts; I put down the project twice, knowing that other smart people had written or were planning to write about it. Those other works are each meaningful in their own way:[3] in particular Shana Redmond's careful consideration of the efforts to use the song as a form of cultural policy in relations with Japan and her brilliant analyses of its compositional features and relationship to other anthems; Timothy Askew's historical analysis and thoughtful rendering of the political conservativism of the song's lyricist, poet James Weldon Johnson, and Johnson's assertions of American patriotism regarding its use; and Keith Cartwright's captivating account of the diasporic cultural resonances and genealogy of the Johnson brothers, James Weldon and John Rosamond, who wrote the song's music. All these books are well researched and insightful, and I recommend them eagerly. Particularly useful for my purposes was a collection of memories of the song published by Julian Bond in 2000 in honor of its 100th anniversary. However, upon reading all of these works, I realized that the story I planned to tell hadn't yet been told. The research completed by the late literary scholar Rudolph Byrd, who also founded the James Weldon Johnson Institute at Emory University, and who wrote introductory essays for the reprints of a number of James Weldon Johnson's publications, provided a key roadmap for me, especially as he focused on both the details of the poet's life as well as the context in which he and his brother developed. But the story I have chosen to tell is less concerned with the authors of the song, although they do appear here and there, especially James Weldon Johnson. It is far more a story about the collective embrace of the song as an anthem, as well as the social and cultural history that is revealed by following its trajectory.

Only roughly chronological, this story is one of black civic and institutional life and political imaginings under hostile and even captive conditions, with the song woven throughout. Over the course of these pages I discuss the significance of the song in black life over the course of the twentieth and the beginning of the twenty-first century. The reader will also encounter vignettes that show how the song was situated in the midst of varying social and political moments, as well as individual lives. A picture will also emerge of black civic, educational, and political life. Although not comprehensive, it should give a rich picture of the world and people the anthem described.

When I first began telling people what I was doing with this book, more than a few editors and scholars questioned whether I would have enough to write about. But I wasn't frustrated that so many others didn't get it. It simply indicated to me how little people understood of the robust history of this song, and the culture in which it was situated. Their doubt fueled my commitment to write this story. Rather than "not enough," I had too much, over 9,000 documented references, very few of which had ever been discussed in scholarly literature, to pore over in order to write this book. I have tried to organize the story they revealed, and to streamline it by choosing representative examples and stories of how "Lift Every Voice and Sing" was used and embraced throughout the book. This song was part of a wide range of various political, cultural, and social moments and historical currents.

The ways we tell history often make transitions from one period to the next seem permanent and strict. But in truth every moment and movement bleeds with the ink of a previous era. This truth emerged dramatically as I researched the history of "Lift Every Voice and Sing." It was the epic anthem embraced by black institutions as well as black and multiracial social movements. Although the tides shifted, and ideologies and tactics rose and fell, the anthem kept people afloat. "Lift Every Voice and Sing" moved with social history, but it also always stands as a sign of a particular racial identity and culture. Even as it was embraced by widely divergent political actors, some aspects of its meaning were and are resilient. It tells the singer to see herself or himself as emerging magnificently through struggle. It nurtures an identity rooted in community. It is a song that moves regionally and internationally, yet holds fast to a sense of particular belonging. It has had a remarkable longevity due to both its beauty and its vision. Perhaps most important, it was and is the song of a people, *my* people. In the following pages I will trace its journey and with it I will trace a story of African American life over 115 years.

LIFT EVERY VOICE AND SING

Lift every voice and sing,
Till earth and heaven ring,
Ring with the harmonies of Liberty;
Let our rejoicing rise
High as the list'ning skies,
Let it resound loud as the rolling sea.
Sing a song full of the faith that the dark past has taught us,
Sing a song full of the hope that the present has brought us;
Facing the rising sun of our new day begun,
Let us march on till victory is won.

Stony the road we trod,
Bitter the chast'ning rod,
Felt in the days when hope unborn had died;
Yet with a steady beat,
Have not our weary feet
Come to the place for which our fathers sighed?
We have come over a way that with tears has been watered.
We have come, treading our path through the blood of the slaughtered,
Out from the gloomy past,
Till now we stand at last
Where the white gleam of our bright star is cast.

God of our weary years,
God of our silent tears,
Thou who hast brought us thus far on the way;
Thou who hast by Thy might,
Led us into the light,
Keep us forever in the path, we pray.
Lest our feet stray from the places, our God, where we met Thee,
Lest our hearts, drunk with the wine of the world, we forget Thee;
Shadowed beneath Thy hand,
May we forever stand,
True to our God,
True to our native land.

—JAMES WELDON JOHNSON
  (set to music by John Rosamond Johnson)

CHAPTER ONE

I'll Make Me a World
Black Formalism at the Nadir

The beginnings of "Lift Every Voice and Sing" can be found in the lives of its lyricist, James Weldon Johnson, and its composer, John Rosamond Johnson. The building blocks were, of course, their imaginations and intellects. But how they came of age, the social fabric in which they lived, and the culture to which they belonged (and the many others of which they partook) are essential contexts for understanding how and why their song became the anthem of black America.

James was born in 1871, just six years after black Americans, baptized by a horrific war, had begun the transition from the status of chattel to citizens. His brother John, known as Rosamond throughout his life, arrived in 1873. Their early years buzzed with a family, a community, and a people desperately yearning, learning, organizing, and striving for freedom. The Johnson brothers were born to two seekers. Their father, James Johnson, was a freeborn man from Richmond, Virginia, who had traveled to New York as a young adult seeking his fortune. There he met their mother, Helen Louise Dillet, a young Bahamian singer who had immigrated to New York as a girl. Helen's paternal lineage could be traced back to late eighteenth-century Haiti. Her father, Stephen Dillet, had served as the postmaster of Nassau, making him one of the few black Bahamians with a high-status government job. The Johnson brothers were sons of the black diaspora. Their roots were wide and varied. But they also came of age in a period of black dispersal across the globe, overwhelmingly under subjugated conditions. As sons of the diaspora, wherever they went and no matter how deeply connected they felt to the land, the laws of the places they inhabited usually denied them full citizenship and full membership. Accordingly, identity and culture, for them and for their peoples from Virginia to Nassau, were things bigger and more amorphous than patriotism or nationalism.

Helen Louise Dillet and James Johnson married in 1864 in the Anglican Christ Church Cathedral of Nassau, an imposing gothic edifice built of smoky gray stone gathered from a local quarry. Although the church dated to

1670, when they married, it had only been designated a cathedral, and Nassau had only been declared a city, three years earlier. Helen and James had left New York a few years prior, together. They feared the rumors that if the South won the Civil War, slavery would be reestablished in New York, and their freedom would be at risk. So they made their way to Helen's homeland.[1]

In New York, although slavery had finally been abolished in 1827 after an emancipation process that lasted many decades, black people continued to suffer second-class status. The Bahamas proved little better in this regard. Under the British Crown, it had its own Caribbean predecessor to what would be known as Jim Crow in the United States nearly a century later. Black Bahamians in the mid-nineteenth century had very limited opportunities to be educated and were overwhelmingly excluded from politics and many public places, as well as coerced into exploitative labor conditions. A white oligarchy ruled the chain of small islands.[2]

After the Civil War ended, the Johnson couple moved again, to Jacksonville, Florida, which like the rest of the South was under the military authority of the Radical Republicans. This meant that despite the legacy of slavery in their midst, there was a sense of possibility that came along with emancipation and the Reconstruction-era promises of civil and legal equality.

Jacksonville, in particular, was an appealing migration destination for many African Americans. Homesteading in Florida allowed black people to acquire property more easily than in many other parts of the South.[3] And Jacksonville's burgeoning tourist industry offered numerous employment opportunities. James landed a position at the St. James Hotel, a luxury resort that catered to wealthy white Americans. This job was both more lucrative and safer than many. Tourism often seemed to mediate the worst forms of racist violence. Too much violence was bad for business, particularly from northerners seeking relaxing vacations.

But perhaps the most important attraction Jacksonville held for the Johnson family was that Florida, unlike all other southern states, had a public school system before the Civil War. In 1839 the Florida legislature first established a public school system, whereas elsewhere in the South public education systems were introduced in the 1860s and 1870s, only as a result of African Americans' and Radical Republican legislators' impassioned efforts. Florida was different. With the Reconstruction-era promises of equality and citizenship, it was clear that the Florida public school system would have to include the newly emancipated black population. In 1868, black residents of Jacksonville established the Education Society, with the goal of building a school. With the assistance of the Freedmen's Bureau, by the end of the year they had established the first public school for black children in the state, the Edwin McMasters Stanton School, named for Abraham Lincoln's secretary of war. Although the faculty was initially comprised of northern white women, Helen Louise Dillet Johnson became the first black public school teacher in the city, and her two exceptional sons' first teacher as well.[4]

By the time these teacher's sons learned to read, Reconstruction, with its promises of political and legal equality for black citizens, faced a horrific backlash. Violence was the handmaiden of the "redemption" of white supremacy, and black southerners were routinely terrorized. In Florida, one of the last states to remain under Republican control, Reconstruction ended formally in 1876. Seven years later, in 1883, the Supreme Court hammered the final nail in Reconstruction's coffin with the "Civil Rights Cases" that declared the Civil Rights Act of 1875 unconstitutional.[5] The ironically titled cases granted southern businesses the license to systematically exclude black people from train cars, eating establishments, hotels, clothing stores, and virtually all commercial life. And they did. This was the first large step toward a de jure Jim Crow society. Attack on the vote soon followed, as all-white primaries established a "democratic" process that effectively excluded black citizens from participation in government "by the people, for the people." A new brutality came along with these exclusions. Between 1882 and 1902 over 2,000 black people were lynched.[6] Southern state legislatures all rewrote their constitutions to explicitly and boldly assert their commitment to white supremacy. And in 1896, in *Plessy v. Ferguson*,[7] the Supreme Court declared that Louisiana could mandate legal segregation, which became the foundation upon which Jim Crow white supremacy rested and grew.

While James, in recollection, considered Jacksonville to be kinder and more equitable for African Americans than the rest of the South, it was unquestionably subject to the post-Reconstruction Jim Crow order. However, he and his brother were middle class and relatively privileged, although certainly not spoiled, according to James's memories. In their youth, they achieved a great deal in the tradition of black strivers across the globe who, with every little bit of opportunity, worked diligently to transcend the color line that nevertheless circumscribed their lives. Both brothers attended the Stanton School for Negroes through eighth grade and, there being no public high school for black students in Jacksonville, both departed in order to further their educations. James enrolled at Atlanta University for high school and college, and Rosamond at the New England Conservatory, after which he studied music in London.

After his graduation from Atlanta University, James returned home and took a position as a teacher at the Stanton School; he also studied law in preparation for the Florida bar examination. In 1897, James sat for the two-hour oral examination before three attorneys and a judge.[8] He later recalled that one of the examiners, disgusted by the prospect of a black attorney, left the room. Despite this affront, James passed and became the first African American admitted to the bar in Florida since Reconstruction.

James soon thereafter was made principal of the Stanton School. At the time, Rosamond was an educator as well. He served as a music teacher at the neighboring Florida Baptist Academy, one of a number of black boarding schools scattered throughout the South. It was while they taught at these institutions that they penned "Lift Every Voice and Sing." They'd go on to many other musical collaborations, but this was to be their most famous and enduring coauthored work.

In 1900, when they wrote the song, Jacksonville was the largest city in Florida, with a population of 28,429. The black population of 16,236 comprised over half of the city.[9] It was a robust community but one that lived under the thumb of a racially unjust system. This period in history was described by the historian Rayford Logan (who would become both a friend and protégé of James) as the "nadir" of American race relations in his 1954 book *The Betrayal of the Negro: Rutherford B. Hayes to Woodrow Wilson.*[10]

> The last decade of the nineteenth century and the opening of the twentieth century marked the nadir of the Negro's status in American society. The continued decline in the recognition of his political and legal rights cannot be attributed entirely to the emergence of new issues that shunted the Southern question further into the background. To be sure the tariff, the free and unlimited coinage of silver, federal regulation of interstate commerce and of corporations, the "closing of the frontier" reform of the civil service and of municipal governments—these and other domestic questions, diverted attention from the treatment of the Negro. . . . The nadir was reached however not by lack of attention. On the contrary, the plight of the Negro worsened precisely because of the efforts made to improve it. The Republicans, once more in the White House and with a majority in both houses for the first time since 1875, introduced two major pieces of legislation to

protect the right to vote and to provide expanded educational facilities. The resurgent South, supported by old allies in the North and by new allies in the West, not only defeated both measures but launched a counter attack that further curtailed the already diminishing rights of Negroes. The questions of the tariff and of free silver served less to divert attention from the deterioration of the Negro's status, especially in the South, than to buttress the deliberate relegation of Negroes to the role of an inferior class. At the turn of the century it seemed, indeed, that they might become a caste.[11]

Rayford Logan chose his symbolism effectively. A nadir is the lowest point in an orbit. It is the location directly below the gaze. The heavenward hopeful eyes of black Americans had shifted down as America broke the promise of Reconstruction, a betrayal that reached sickening depths under Jim Crow. The Johnson brothers and their contemporaries experienced this transition from the hope of Reconstruction to the devastation of the nadir as they came of age. They were called to both mourn dashed dreams and dream anew in their adulthoods as a pigmentocracy took hold where citizenship had been promised.

In response to the rise of Jim Crow, black Americans turned inward and organized. One of the principal signs of this organization was the rise of the black press. In the last thirty-five years of the nineteenth century more than 1,200 black newspapers were founded, and at the dawn of the twentieth they served a vital function in black life and letters.[12] James himself had founded a newspaper in Jacksonville, the *Daily American*, in 1895. It covered black American life in the region. Due to financial difficulties, however, it lasted only eight months. But the Johnson brothers were part of the collective black aspirations of this period in other ways too, as educators and musicians. Black schools, from elementary to college, were steadily opening and growing across the country. Black musicians were pursuing formal training, publishing their compositions, and applying notation to traditional folk tunes. Additionally, black musicians were creating new musical forms and expanding the scope of traditional ones. Black writers were publishing novels, essays, short stories, and plays, and activists described their output as an important tool for racial uplift. And black organizations—religious, political, and civic—were on the move, incorporating, meeting, and developing agendas for "the Negro." Hence, the nadir can be remembered as a time not simply of exclusion and racist violence but also of blossoming.

These activities fit into what Alexis de Tocqueville described as the distinctly American practice of "associational life," that is, the forming and joining of associations for nearly every venture, from entertainment and education to religion and commerce.[13]

Black associationalism was likewise robust, though behind the veil.[14] The organizations created by black Americans in the Jim Crow era numbered in the thousands. As Nina Mjagkij writes, "Throughout American history, African Americans have established a multitude of religious, professional, business, political, recreational, educational, secret, social, cultural and mutual aid societies."[15] For black Americans, however, associationalism was often explicitly political, even with respect to organizations that had no explicitly political purpose. For example, members of social clubs, Greek letter organizations, fraternal lodges, and teachers organizations all at various points and in varying branches were involved in civil rights organizing.

Like many of their peers, the Johnson brothers were "race men." This meant the work they did was not pursued for mere personal achievement or acclaim. Race men and women understood that each accomplishment was meaningful for the aspirations of the race as a whole. Their pursuits were attached to the needs and hopes of black people generally. James and Rosamond were artists and intellectuals who pursued their particular passions, but they also would have long careers in service of black people, as educators, activists, and archivists of black literature, sermons, and music.

"Lift Every Voice and Sing" was initially imagined by James as a poem to celebrate the February 12 birthday of late president Abraham Lincoln, but on the page it came to be something else. What James created with his lyrics stood in the tradition of a different February-born leader, the abolitionist author Frederick Douglass. Douglass, like most enslaved children, hadn't had his birth date recorded. However, he'd chosen February 14 as the day on which he would celebrate his birth. Not incidentally this was two days after Lincoln's. Frederick Douglass's narratives told the story of his journey from slavery to freedom with drama, passion, breathtaking emotion, and stunning brilliance. James's poem did something quite similar: he told the story of black life in terms that were epic, wrenching, and thunderous:

A group of young men decided to hold on February 12th a celebration in honor of Lincoln's birthday. I was put down for an address, which I began preparing, but I wanted to do something else also. My thoughts began buzzing round a central idea of writing a poem about Lincoln

but I couldn't net them. So I gave up the project as beyond me. . . .
My central idea, however, took on another form. I talked over with my
brother the thought I had in mind and we planned to write a song to be
sung as part of the exercises. We planned better still to have it sung by
school children, a chorus of 500 voices.[16]

The children of the Stanton School sang "Lift Every Voice and Sing" (published under the title "Lift Ev'ry Voice and Sing," but intoned as "every") at
the Lincoln's birthday celebration. They delivered it with a special dedication to Booker T. Washington: the preeminent (albeit controversial) black
leader at the turn of the century and the founder of Tuskegee Institute. It was
quite common for black institutions to honor Washington. Washington had
greater fundraising capacity and access to powerful people than any other
black leader of his era. He could be a rainmaker or a destroyer of opportunity.
Washington's attractiveness to white leaders rested heavily upon the fact that
he did not advocate for black political power or the full exercise of their civil
rights. Rather, he focused on economic development by means of vocational
education that trained black people to be farmers or to work in semiskilled
and skilled labor rather than the professions. It was strategically wise for the
Johnsons to honor Washington with "Lift Every Voice and Sing," despite the
fact that their own journeys had pushed beyond the circumscribed role for
black Americans that Washington embraced.

The song proved to be, both then and soon thereafter, much bigger than
an ode to any one leader or icon. It was a lament and encomium to the story
and struggle of black people. The Johnsons at once wrote black history and
wrote black people into the traditions of formal Western music with their
noble song.

"Lift Every Voice and Sing" would become an important feature of a cultural
practice that I refer to as "black formalism." Black formalism emerged in the
late nineteenth-century United States. It is a term I am using here to describe
the performance and substance within black associations and institutions.
Black formalism includes ritual practices with embedded norms, codes of
conduct, and routine, dignified ways of doing and being. It includes greetings, sartorial practices (e.g., wearing one's Sunday best with a slip underneath and a hat on one's head, or a fresh handkerchief and a button-down
shirt), and ideals of appropriate behavior for certain times and places, as well

as oratory, homiletics, traditional songs, and standard ways of structuring events and special occasions. It is, in its symbolic meaning, an articulation and expression of grace and identity that existed in refuge from the violence of white supremacy.

Though black formalism was engaged in by "the folk," poor and working-class African Americans, it is not what one would term a "folk" practice. Rather it was the formal rituals and habits that exist in virtually all cultures, marking a sense of propriety that depends upon time and place. Stated simply, what one would do on Saturday night at the juke joint was different from the starched and straight-backed expectations of the church on Sunday or the classroom on Monday.

Historian Evelyn Brooks Higginbotham astutely described "the politics of respectability" of the same period as a practice of striving black women's organizations that used "being respectable" according to middle-class white Christian norms and ideals of virtue.[17] I argue that black formalism is distinct from the politics of respectability. Black formalism describes practices that were primarily internal to the black community, rather than those based upon a white gaze or an aspiration for white acceptance. It was engaged in across class lines rather than being rooted in a belief in white and middle-class superiority and pushed from the middle class top down to the poor, as was the politics of respectability. The source material for my account of black formalism is made up of thousands of documents—school and church programs, graduation ceremonies, works of literature, oral histories, material culture and images—that revealed a captivating cultural landscape within black communities from the late nineteenth century on, which included not only a striking vernacular culture of spirituals, blues, and the like but also a similarly compelling formal culture of pageantry, oratory, and ritual.

The late nineteenth century was a remarkable period in black American life, because it allowed black people to fashion civic life like never before. While black religious, musical, and family culture existed within enslavement, the establishment of formal institutions and associational life was largely new in the South. As these institutions and associations were developed, norms of "black formalism" emerged therein. Although the period of Reconstruction, during which black Americans were able to exercise their constitutional rights and participate fully in politics and economics, was rather short, and the brutality of Jim Crow, which entailed not just segregated facilities but extralegal violence, agricultural labor domination, and the rise of the convict lease system, began within twelve years after the end of slavery, black civic and social organizing continued to grow.

Certainly, the formal rituals of the southern gentry and the overwhelmingly American culture of associational life played a role in the development of black formalism. These were deeply American people. But the expression of black formalism in particular was distinct from mainstream culture in both form and political content. An example is found in the concluding ceremony of a black dressmaker's school organized in New York City in the summer of 1921 by a Madame Katherine of Savannah, Georgia. That July afternoon, "Mrs Edith Turnage, who rendered a piano selection," was accompanied by Miss Pauline V. Ferguson "in a most thrilling vocal solo." Mrs. Turnage also "rendered the music for the class song 'Negro National Anthem'" (by 1921 "Lift Every Voice and Sing" was known as such). The graduation ceremony featured the students' work, including a salmon satin evening gown by Mrs. Lonis Savor, and both a black-and-white taffeta bathing suit and a dinnergown of peacock blue taffeta and pink crepe de chine, by the aforementioned singer of the anthem, Pauline Ferguson. Additionally, Mrs. Ella La Nair produced a blue broadcloth coat suit and an afternoon dress of sand-color crepe de chine trimmed with brown satin, and Alice L. Ferguson created a "brown chiffon velvet street costume trimmed with brown lace."[18] For these young black women, making beautiful clothing was not simply an adoption of traditional Western feminine conventions. It was a means by which elegance and formal attire symbolized a refusal of the degradations heaped upon black women and their bodies. They were better than the inferior lot the world assigned to them. To be a seamstress was a working-class profession, one that many black women held. Hunching over a sewing machine all day was debilitating and exhausting physical work, often underpaid. But nevertheless it held creative power and the possibility of self-definition, as exemplified by their designs.[19] In this instance, and throughout this book, you can see how the singing of "Lift Every Voice and Sing" would become a consistent element of the ritual behaviors that were part of black formalism.

But the song was situated in a rich mix of performance and mastery. Ralph Ellison's description of the May Day celebrations of his youth in 1920s Oklahoma presents a striking picture of this cultural milieu:

On May Day children from all the Negro schools were assembled on the playing field of the old Western League baseball stadium, the girls in their white dresses and the boys in blue serge knickers and white shirts, and there to the music of the Douglass High School Band, we competed in wrapping dozens of maypoles and engaged in the mass dancing of a variety of European folk dances . . . in learning such dances we were gaining an appreciation of the backgrounds and cultures of our fellow Americans whose backgrounds lay in Europe. . . . And while there were those who thought that we were stepping out of the role assigned Negroes and were expressing a desire to become white, we ignored them. For we knew that dancing such dances would no more alter our racial identity or social status than would our singing of Bach chorales.

Ellison admires the lesson his teacher imparted through these performances:

Thanks to Mrs. Breaux, we were being introduced to one of the most precious of American freedoms, which is our freedom to broaden our personal culture by absorbing the cultures of others. Even more important was the fact that we were being taught to discover and exercise those elements of freedom which existed unobserved (at least by outsiders) within our state of social and political unfreedom. And this gift, this important bit of equipment for living, came through the efforts of a woman educator who by acting as agent of the broader American culture was able to widen our sense of possibility and raise our aspirations.[20]

It is also important to note that black formalism doesn't follow the schema of what critics in the West conventionally describe as high- or low-status identities, nor does it adhere to the traditional Western rules of high and low culture, where rarified and exclusive tastes are deemed "high culture" and popular and relatively simplistic tastes are part of "low culture." The formalism in black formalism came from the structure of the rituals and the regard for their seriousness, and not whether the work of a classical European composer or a vernacular poet like Paul Laurence Dunbar was part of a given program or event. Ellison goes on to say of the teacher who introduced him to black formalism,

It was Mrs. Breaux who introduced me to the basic discipline required of the artist. And it was she who made it possible for me to grasp the basic compatibility of the classical and vernacular styles which were part of our musical culture. She was one of the owners of what for many years was the only Negro theater in Oklahoma City. . . . In her Aldridge Theater one could see and hear the great blues singers, dancers and comedians, the famous jazz orchestras and such repertory drama groups as the Lafayette players. In other words, just as she taught the Negro spirituals along with Bach and Handel, she provided a cultural nexus in which the vernacular art forms could be encountered along with the classical.[21]

In this vignette, Ellison captures something important about the order of black formalism and its departure from the conventions of "high" and "low." Mrs. Breaux's theater was a community institution, and the education she provided and the formal rituals her students performed as part of it were rich and varied.

By asserting the cross-class and multigenre and style collage of black formalist rituals, I, like Ellison, am disagreeing with a good deal of African American studies criticism. A distinction has sometimes been made by such critics that treats art (or behaviors) deemed vernacular or "folk" as the only truly authentic forms of black expression, while the classical (e.g., European concert music) is simply seen as a mimicry of European cultural forms. That distinction is largely erroneous. Instead, the archive and artistry show something quite different. Hortense Spillers uses the same term "black formalism" to describe black artistic production. Her use is highly related albeit distinct from my own use of the term. Spillers's black formalism refers to the aesthetics and technical form of black American arts. And according to her, complexity and creolization exist across the board. She thereby refutes a distinction often drawn between "authentic folk" and "imitative classical." Rather she identifies a "black classical" that is of the folk and voraciously and beautifully creolized. Here, I am describing what could be termed the *social* corollary to this classical black expression.[22] I am referring to rituals and performance, whereas Spillers brilliantly describes artistic content. As Spillers asserts for composition, I am arguing that the rituals of black formalism—that is, social graces and rules of engagement—were not the property of elites. This is evidenced in the range of stories that appear in this book. Formalism was deeply rooted in the communities that black folks imagined and carefully crafted from the late nineteenth century through most of the twentieth century, and that continue in more modest form today. In particular, I'm interested in black formalism as part of the culture attached to institutions like schools, churches, and civic organizations. Appropriately, given the creole forms of black life in the Americas, black formalism included elements of European cultural forms, though in its constitution it became something distinctly black American. For example, performances in black schools or before black civic associations at the turn of the century often included spirituals and black vernacular poems by Paul Laurence Dunbar alongside operatic singing and Western classical music and oratory. This collage of "high" and "low," Western and African, Southern and European, reflected the matrix of black life in the West. Moreover, the black community forged, by dint of these ritual practices, a means of articulating who they were and aspired to become.

Black formalism, then, was not based upon hierarchical ideas of culture that marked some cultures as more worthy than others. Rather, the distinctions made were about time and place appropriateness. Gutbucket blues and shake dancing were not part of black formalist endeavors. But black language and art of other sorts were. It was not an exercise in asserting cultural superiority or hierarchies, like so much formal culture of the West. Rather it was a ritual engagement in performative, musical, literary, institutional, and social culture with practiced seriousness. It did not compete with vernacular form. It was simply another dimension of the spectrum of cultural life in which most black Americans participated.

Although black formalism was engaged in across the lines of socioeconomic class and education, the increased access to formal education, literacy, and property that emerged in the postbellum period unquestionably aided the development of black formalism. To be able to record the community's doings, in the form of written language,[23] and to own property in which to perform (schools, churches, clubs, homes) was essential to the development of institutions in which exercises of black formalism would take place. After the Civil War southern black Americans created a public culture and institutional life that had previously been denied. In addition to rebuilding family ties and pursuing political participation and literacy, freedpeople sought, passionately and early, to develop their civic life. It is within this vision and effort that formalism grew.

Singing "Lift Every Voice and Sing" was not simply one aspect of black formalism, it was one of the most fundamental elements of it. Soon after its composition, the song would become a definitive part of ritual practices in schools and churches and civic gatherings. But how? According to James, the song quickly became popular among young people in Jacksonville and spread from there.[24] However, neither James nor Rosamond remained in Jacksonville long enough to directly witness that growing popularity. Their departure the year after writing the song was precipitated by a devastating event. In 1901, a fire started in a mattress factory in their neighborhood, LaVilla, and destroyed much of Jacksonville. "We met many people fleeing," James recounted. "From them we gathered excitedly related snatches: the fiber factory catches afire—the fire department comes—fanned by a light breeze, the fire is traveling directly east and spreading out to the north, over the district where the bulk of Negroes in the western end of the city live—the firemen spend all their efforts saving a low row of frame houses just across the street on the south side of the factory, belonging to a white man named Steve Melton."[25]

But the fire chief allowed black-owned homes to burn. After a mere eight hours, 10,000 people were homeless and 2,368 buildings were gone. The brothers, undoubtedly heartbroken at the cruelty of Jim Crow and enticed by the hub of opportunity up north, departed for New York. Many other black Jacksonville residents departed in the next couple of years as well, hoping to begin somewhere else anew.[26]

In New York, James and Rosamond took up work in the musical theater. Almost immediately successful, they collaborated on such hits as "Tell Me, Dusky Maiden" and "Nobody's Looking but the Owl and the Moon," for which James wrote the lyrics and Rosamond the music. They also established a prolific partnership with another black musician, Bob Cole. When James dropped out to pursue his careers as an activist and writer, Rosamond and Bob, known as "Johnson and Cole," continued to write another string of hits.

Those who remained in black Jacksonville after the fire gradually put the pieces of their lives back together. They rebuilt buildings and homes, stung by or raging quietly with the memory of cruel neglect. "Lift Every Voice and Sing," a song of endurance, lament, and supplication, suited their moment, and the cruelties experienced by so many others in the black world. It resonated deeply with the heartache of second-class citizenship. It's no surprise, then, that the song also grew in popularity by means of one of the most important black organizations of the period, the National Association of Colored Women's Clubs (NACW).

The NACW was founded in July 1896, two months after the *Plessy v. Ferguson* decision. It was the product of a merger between two black women's activist organizations: the National Federation of Afro-American Women and the League of Colored Women. One of its leaders, and a founding member, Victoria Earle Matthews, was a former slave, born in Fort Valley, Georgia. So light-skinned that she could have easily passed for white yet born in bondage, her body and history served as evidence of the blunt instrument of white supremacy. As an adult under the tutelage of journalist and activist Ida B. Wells, Matthews became an antilynching activist and the president of the Woman's Loyal Union, an organization that compiled data about the status of black people nationwide by sending questionnaires to black ministers, teachers, and other community leaders across the country. Its goal was to correct common misperceptions about the race as well as to aggregate information that could facilitate collective efforts to develop skills and resources among the black population, which remained overwhelmingly poor and subject to aggressive racism. Although club women like Matthews have often been described as elitist and classist by scholars, and that characterization was often warranted, it bears noting that the great majority of them, no matter how elite they were, were just a generation or two from enslaved family members. Very few were totally removed from the condition of "the least of these." Even those who descended from free people came from a freedom that was so tightly circumscribed by racism that it barely qualified as such. And even the beneficiaries of a color hierarchy, the lightest and often the wealthiest among them, carried for the world to see on their flesh the evidence of how stringent the color line was (they were not to think of themselves as white as long as they were "stained" by blackness). Black Americans grew in the seventeenth, eighteenth, and nineteenth centuries to be a multiracial population, with a phenotypic spectrum as wide as that of the entire globe, in large part because of the routine sexual assault of black women by white men during slavery and Jim Crow. Any room filled with black people, and their many colors, reveals this history. To be elite in this group was a modest privilege at best.

Matthews's mother, Caroline, had run away from Georgia to New York soon after her daughter was born. Caroline hoped that in New York she would be able to earn enough money to buy the freedom of Victoria and her older daughter. She never was able to make enough to do so. However, after the war, in 1869, Caroline returned to Georgia to find her daughters and reclaim custody by bringing a lawsuit in Georgia state court. She became the first black women to be granted standing before the court and to succeed in a custody case in the state of Georgia, and soon thereafter returned with her daughters to New York.[27] Victoria Matthews and her sister were born to an independent and courageous woman, and Victoria followed in her footsteps as a race woman working in the nadir of American race relations.[28]

In 1901, she wrote an article on the Johnson brothers for *Colored American*. The placement of this first journalistic appreciation of the song is important. *Colored American* was the first monthly magazine in the United States devoted to African American culture and was an important publication in the thriving black print culture at the turn of the century. In her piece, Matthews wrote that "Lift Every Voice and Sing" was "not only an anthem. It is a revelation leading to and ending in prayer. It is based upon what we as a people have come from, a saddened sense of what we are, and a trembling fear of what we might be, ending in a pain drawn, sob like prayer to God. The music is endearing, it soothes as it inspires. Like the real heart-songs of our mothers it affects the singer as deeply as the listener, by a certain weirdly plaintive melody that lingers and lingers, like a subdued memory picture, long after the sounds have rolled away. From the beginning to the end, words and music blend in tender pathos."[29]

That Matthews, one of the most prominent black thinkers and activists of the turn of the century, referred to "Lift Every Voice and Sing" as an *anthem* merely a year after it was written foreshadowed its future impact. Matthews went on to say, "James W. Johnson, known best as the author of 'Lift Every Voice and Sing,' is the elder. He is very quiet, almost grave, just the opposite extreme to his brother Rosamond, the composer. . . . If he had done no more than produce the music of 'Lift Every Voice and Sing,' he would have endeared himself to us all."

In the following decade and a half, the historical record shows the slow but steady proliferation of "Lift Every Voice" in various segments of black life and culture. In 1903, it concluded the Emancipation Day program of the Negro Literary and History Society of Atlanta, held at Ebenezer Baptist Church.[30] The ceremony celebrated the fortieth anniversary of Abraham Lincoln's signing of the Emancipation Proclamation. Emancipation Day was an annual holiday in black America, although it was held on varying dates depending upon when freedom was granted or first heard about by the formerly enslaved in that particular state. Like the early nineteenth-century freedom celebrations of black communities in the North, this postbellum southern holiday provided a ritual occasion for the recall of history, the celebration of freedom, and the assertion of identity.[31] In the late nineteenth and early twentieth centuries Emancipation Day became one of the most important black formalist occasions in African American communities, and singing "Lift Every Voice and Sing" was a ritualistic part of the celebration. By 1905, "Lift Every Voice" was also being sung as part of graduation programs, as was the case for the Douglass Colored High School (named after Frederick Douglass) in El Paso, Texas, where the hymn opened the May 6 commencement.[32] The program also included an instrumental of Franz von Suppé's "Overture to Poet and Peasant," and the chorus singing Eben H. Bailey's march "On the Move." The formalism of the event thus included both European and African American music. The von Suppé selection, which is a musical love story featuring a peasant youth who, notwithstanding his low social status, has exceptional literary gifts that attract the adoration of the young woman he loves, along with the robust hopefulness of Bailey's march and the newly beloved Johnson brothers' anthem, together proffer a portrait of a ritual intended to foster resilience, struggle, and greater attainment out in the world. Formalism was functional. It nourished the spirit and bolstered future endeavors.

For these reasons, and more, club women circulated the song and encouraged their communities to embrace it. The NACW published the lyrics in its newsletter *National Notes* a number of times and sang it at the gatherings of both the state organizations and the national organization in the early years of the twentieth century.

The women who belonged to the NACW were highly influential in black communities. They were members of a thick and developing network of black associational life. They were teachers, social workers, church matrons, community activists, and civic association members as well as mothers, daughters, wives, aunts, and cousins. That Matthews, along with the rest of her colleagues in the NACW, asserted the sanctity of this anthem ensured that it would become fully ensconced in black life. When they chose it, black America writ large was choosing it as well. Further evidence of this choice is found in how the song circulated throughout black print culture. The lyrics were published in newspapers as various as *Lutheran Women's Work*; the *Topeka Plain Dealer*; and the organ of the National Association for the Advancement of Colored People, the *Crisis*.

As an anthem, "Lift Every Voice and Sing" was easy to embrace. It is an enchanting composition. Contemporary critic Keith Cartwright writes that "its patriotism and piety can seem utterly conventional. There is however, in 'Lift Every Voice' a yearning for integration of sacral inheritances that does not reduce to paths of assimilation into Anglo-American national norms. For the God and native land of this countercultural anthem of modernity differ from the God and native land of the republic's imaginary. . . . It seeks to produce a utopian space of nativity in the congregational labor of lifting voice and moving beyond fixed boundaries."[33]

Cartwright interprets the song's patriotism as not belonging to the United States. Rather, he sees it as a patriotism that belonged to an alternative imagined community, one built of the stuff of black experience here on these shores but reaching for something or somewhere else where freedom would be truly possible. He describes the song as one of contemplation and meditation upon the theme of freedom. Musically, as well as linguistically, the repetitions and the way the composition plays with time make it feel like a meditation upon a theme. And while it is emotionally uplifting, it is also challenging. Remembering her many years of playing the song as part of a children's band in the mid-twentieth century, Evelyn Fairbanks wrote, "The official Negro national anthem was requested the most. . . . The song has everything for a musician. It's full bodied, with important parts for all the instruments. The rhythm and tempo are varied, the shading and phrasing are intricate, the figuring is difficult, requiring the purest tones, and you never quite get it right. Nothing pleases musicians more than finding music that constantly presses them to play better the next time."[34] What the Johnson brothers did was both complex and effective. James's lyrics borrowed elements from political, classical, and liturgical prose and music. British writer Rudyard Kipling's "Recessional" was one direct influence. Kipling wrote "Recessional" in 1897 for Queen Victoria's Jubilee. When preparing for the occasion, at first he wrote an ode to imperialism titled "White Man's Burden," but he decided to set that aside (he would pick it up again two years later) and wrote "Recessional" instead. Like "Lift Every Voice," "Recessional" is hymn-like. It celebrates the glories of empire but anticipates its tragic demise. ("White Man's Burden," in contrast, is a more joyful and destructive poem, imagining the United States as picking up the responsibility of empire and white supremacy as the British Empire declined.) "Recessional" reads as follows:

> *God of our fathers, known of old,*
>   *Lord of our far-flung battle-line,*
> *Beneath whose awful Hand we hold*
>   *Dominion over palm and pine—*
> *Lord God of Hosts, be with us yet,*
> *Lest we forget—lest we forget!*

The tumult and the shouting dies;
*   The Captains and the Kings depart:*
Still stands Thine ancient sacrifice,
*   An humble and a contrite heart.*
Lord God of Hosts, be with us yet,
Lest we forget—lest we forget!

Far-called, our navies melt away;
*   On dune and headland sinks the fire:*
Lo, all our pomp of yesterday
*   Is one with Nineveh and Tyre!*
Judge of the Nations, spare us yet,
Lest we forget—lest we forget!

If, drunk with sight of power, we loose
*   Wild tongues that have not Thee in awe,*
Such boastings as the Gentiles use,
*   Or lesser breeds without the Law—*
Lord God of Hosts, be with us yet,
Lest we forget—lest we forget!

For heathen heart that puts her trust
*   In reeking tube and iron shard,*
All valiant dust that builds on dust,
*   And guarding, calls not Thee to guard,*
For frantic boast and foolish word—
Thy mercy on Thy People, Lord!

Like Kipling, James stated this was not his first effort. He began by trying to compose for Lincoln just as Kipling tried to compose for the queen, but then was moved in another direction, away from simple celebration and toward telling and making a people's history.

In style, it is also immediately apparent that James borrowed from Kipling's work. He repeats many of Kipling's short phrases and words: "God of our," "Drunk with the," and "lest we forget." Johnson also adopts some of Kipling's concepts: a shared caution, sense of inheritance, legacy, and faith as responsibility and not mere endurance. Kipling, however, is looking backward, ruing the end of Western domination. James is moving both back and forth constantly throughout his piece, seeking the promise of freedom. Perhaps James's choices reflect how the imaginative possibility and dreams of citizenship during Reconstruction, and the violently dashed hopes of

Reconstruction's demise, were smashed together wildly in the decade of his birth. It is heroic and epic verse. But the hero of "Lift Every Voice and Sing" is not singular. It is a collective: black people. Perhaps we ought to consider "Lift Every Voice" as a *processional* in contrast to Kipling's "Recessional," in terms of both substance and form.

The formal aspects of the poem also stand as an interesting departure from, and a means of signifying upon, Kipling. Kipling uses the English sestet form for his rhyme scheme: ababcc, as well as the iambic tetrameter meter form (with four iambs in each stanza), while Johnson uses the Spanish sestet, as well as the six- or seven-syllable lines characteristic of Spanish poetry, and specifically Spanish sonnets. Over many subsequent years Johnson would frequently use those six- or seven-syllable lines in his poetry. This choice was indicative of Johnson's fluency in Spanish and the influence of the multiculturalism of Jacksonville, a city with a significant Latin American Caribbean population, on his creative work. But it also reveals Johnson's aesthetic priorities, and the imaginative world of African American letters and politics at the turn of the century in general. Johnson and his fellow race men and women were building black institutional life and black formal culture in the aftermath of slavery and in light of Jim Crow. In so doing they looked for distinction and distinctiveness, and they drew from a vast archive of earlier and global styles as they attempted to capture black life, sensibilities, and beauty. Johnson's use of the aesthetics of Spanish poetry, his subversion of Kipling's sense of grand purpose, and even his manner of playing with the sonnet form (the poem is eleven lines long or maybe thirteen depending on whether you count the internal rhymes) at once suggests both a searching and experimentation in his work as well as a rigorous attention to form and formalism in the creative process.

Textually, the song is filled with his political imagination. It is a procession toward liberation. The three stanzas have often been described as praise, lament, and prayer. But even within each one, they move in time between past, present, and future possibilities. Jason Moran describes the composition in the following manner:

There are two parts that drive me wild. The first four notes, LIFT, EV, RY, VOICE. . . . It ramps up you with the ascension of the melody. The second part is during the bridge, the second time we say "SING A SONG," we switch to a minor version of the SING A SONG that was just a few measures earlier. It always made the song a little odd to me, even as a child. Like, hmmm, why do that? But on those two phrases alone, I could spend all day playing, listening and reconfiguring them. The most emotional part of the song is on the lyrics, "facing the rising sun of our new day begun." The melody rises and it falls, and if I play it right, I always feel like I'm about to lose it emotionally in the middle of performing it. I am always on the search for measures of music that pack weight, and that phrase packs weight. It pulls us all back in out of the cold.[35]

For James Weldon Johnson "Lift Every Voice" was "a hymn for Negro people." We should understand this designation, proffered by a man who declared himself agnostic, as an acknowledgment of the importance of hymnody in black cultural life. To speak to black life by using a devotional frame made perfect sense, given that churches were the earliest black American institutions, and given that at the core of black American culture was the distinct form of Christianity that black Americans created on these shores. In particular the idea of faith as a practical repository, and as an intellectual and ideological orientation looking toward freedom that stood in the face of enslavement and Jim Crow and all manner of violence faced by black America, was deeply rooted in black life during the late nineteenth century.[36] It was organic philosophy as well as devotion. The sense of obligation and piety that always attended to black religious devotion grew to also be demanded in the singing of "Lift Every Voice."

The substance of that demand with respect to "Lift Every Voice" might be described as a form of collective resilience as well as devotion. I speak of black people rather than African Americans here quite deliberately. Although, as previously stated, the Johnson brothers had ancestry in both the Bahamas and the United States, as well as Haiti, Europe, and of course Africa, the point I am making extends beyond the multinational origins of the brothers. The words *America*, *Negro*, and *colored* do not appear in the song. However, the story of the song traces in specific detail the experience of black people in the New World, including all of the Americas, through both slavery and freedom. It was written with so large a scope, I would argue, precisely because racial consciousness at that time for people of African descent in the diaspora was not tied as tightly to the individual nation-state as it would be in the anticolonial and anti–Jim Crow period midcentury. Though geographically spread out and culturally diverse, there was a sense of "linked fate" across islands, coasts, and interior mainlands of the New World. Though the song itself never became broadly embraced throughout the diaspora, and remained overwhelmingly associated with black people in the United States, it was written as part of a sense of racial membership that extended beyond the borders of the nation.

A year before "Lift Every Voice," the Johnson brothers had produced a satirical opera, *Toloso*, that spoofed and criticized U.S. imperialism writ broadly. That work was a sign that they understood racial domination to be a global phenomenon and not merely a local one. This understanding was echoed in the black press, which consistently and comprehensively covered both local and global diasporic as well as continental African news. At the turn of the century black people were, to paraphrase Gwendolyn Brooks, a nation on no map.[37] Or perhaps they were a nation on many maps.

Musically, the song reflects how black people were part of the West and yet excluded from so many parts of the lifeworlds of the West. It goes "in and out" and "up and down" as it were. Rosamond wrote it in a major key, but he shifts to a minor key toward the end of each verse, moving the spirit from high to low, from hope to despair. In the first line, the pitch ascends progressively, upward with each word, depicting the aspirations of black America.

Rosamond paired sadness with triumph and resilience. The highest notes of the "Lift" are found on the words "rise," "beat," and "might," giving, again, the sensibility of a march, if not the compositional form. It is slower than a march. The time signature is a 6/8, moving more like a dance. And yet it has more gravitas and plodding than what we generally hear in "war anthems." The "break" that begins in the first verse with "sing a song" has one word for one beat. James's use of anapestic stresses in the break of each verse ("Sing a song," "We have come") also suggests a march, literally if not sonically. It gives the sense of moving in lock step, also marching forward. Also, as Rosamond was classically trained, it is worthwhile to note that this one word–one beat form is reminiscent of an operatic recitative.[38] In making that section speech-like, the song moves from sounding like an anthem to feeling like a mantra. It then finishes with an extended note on the third-to-the-last line of each stanza: "us," "slaughtered," and "Thee" in reference to God. Over the course of all the stanzas, then, there is a posture of supplication, with "us . . . the slaughtered" appealing to God.

In a 1909 article for *Colored American* titled "Why They Call American Music Ragtime," Rosamond described how the music of Spain always consists of the direct or indirect emotions of the Spanish peasantry, and how, similarly, American music is the product of the American peasant class: the Negro. Rosamond goes on to describe how the foot-tapping and hand-clapping origins of ragtime—its syncopation—are similar to the rhythm of the Spanish bolero. He argues further that his formal training in music at the New England Conservatory and in England did not and could not erase the haunting of that "spirit of melody" found in black people and black folk music. "Lift Every Voice" is anticipatory evidence of this argument: "If the baby laughs today we soon forget it until he laughs again. But if the baby dies today we never forget for it has struck the chord of the heart. Just so with lively music, we think of it while we hear it, and enjoy it as we do the pleasing things in life. But when we hear the minor strains in music we call up the sad memories we can never forget. Therefore dissonant chords are used to express the tragedies in life which are far more impressive than our moments of pleasure, which we so soon forget."[39] In "Lift Every Voice," Rosamond merged the tragedy of the minor strain with the major aspirations, hopes, and even joys of black people.

The song encapsulated the complex fabric of black life, and it grew to be part of the complex fabric of black life. The formalism of "Lift Every Voice and Sing" was born into, and existed alongside, a broader and rich tradition of vernacular music and social culture. Jacksonville was one of the homes of the blues. In fact the word *blues* was early on used to describe a performance in Jacksonville's LaVilla on April 16, 1910. That very well may have been the first time the style of music that would be named the blues was designated as such.[40] Jacksonville was also the home of blues queen Ma Rainey and the popular Rabbit Foot's Company vaudeville troupe. For a time in the first decade of the twentieth century, John Robichaux, a key early jazz bandleader and composer from Louisiana, also lived there, and it was one of the childhood homes of Zora Neale Hurston, the anthropologist and novelist who would become one of the most important chroniclers of southern vernacular culture.

A mix of the vernacular and the formal as well as the sacred and profane were to be found in Jacksonville and other black communities throughout the nation and the Americas more broadly in the early 1900s. In this rich cultural milieu, "Lift Every Voice and Sing" was situated overwhelmingly in places specifically organized for political, educational, and social mobilization and uplift. For example, in 1905, the "hymn" or "anthem" (and debate would be coming in future years about which description was most apropos) was sung by the Williams and Walker Glee Club at the opening to Booker T.

Washington's National Negro in Business League (NNBL) conference.[41] The NNBL conferences were intended to operate like a think tank for the development of economic independence and racial uplift for African Americans. Although not ultimately successful in changing the staggering poverty and discrimination in employment and wages that black people faced, the NNBL did foster social networks where black small-business people and professionals shared information and resources. The song symbolized their aspiration. And the ethos of the organization, of sharing and collective uplift, was bolstered by the participants' singing their history and charge in unison.

However, it is in the second decade of the twentieth century that "Lift Every Voice" begins to appear routinely in accounts of both more regular and widespread formal occasions such as graduations, special events in churches, and meetings of civic associations. One such institution that would adopt the song for nearly its entire existence, and into the present day, was founded in September 1913. Comprised of a group of middle-class black women of Atlanta, the Chautauqua Circle was an offshoot of the national Chautauqua movement. The first Chautauqua was created in 1874 in southwest New York. It was initially conceived of as a place where Methodist Sunday school teachers could supplement their learning in a pastoral landscape during the summers. But it soon expanded into a broader "out-of-school" learning site for adults. Visitors to Chautauqua, New York, attended lectures and read books together in organized courses. In between they biked and picnicked throughout the verdant campus.[42] In the early twentieth century, correspondence courses were also formed by the organization, and smaller local Chautauquas developed in towns across the country.

Although liberal on race issues, the original Chautauqua was not particularly devoted to making itself welcoming to black participants, and the local versions were often explicitly hostile to black presence. However, black thinkers soon after its founding began to talk about creating "Negro Chautauquas."[43] In Atlanta, the African American Chautauqua Circle designated itself as a book club, but it might be better described as a comprehensive scholarly endeavor. The women of the Chautauqua Circle studied as well as read books together. They presented their research to one another, thereby amplifying and scaffolding the knowledge each acquired independently. Their concerns were global: they studied the Mexican and Bolshevik Revolutions as well as the creation of the Panama Canal and the history of the suffrage movement.[44] The circle's members included local activists in addition to intellectuals. Clara Pitts was a cofounder of a foster home. Selena

Sloan Butler founded the national black PTA, and several Chautauqua Circle members worked together to establish the Gate City Free Kindergarten Association.[45] This was the first kindergarten program for black children in Georgia, and by 1913 it served 200 children a year. Eventually they had five different sites in the city.

These women, who had their hands in so much of the community work in Georgia, gathered regularly as members of the Chautauqua Circle to learn, to work, and to share. And at every single meeting from 1918 to the present, they have joined hands to "Lift Every Voice and Sing." Their meetings have always been an elegant ritual. Whichever member hosted a particular meeting made sure the tables were covered in beautiful linens and fine china, crystal, and silver. The circle was and is a private organization and unquestionably elite. The ladies' gatherings were mentioned in the society pages of black newspapers with a good deal of pomp and circumstance. But the song they sang at each session was also sung in rural churches and one-room schoolhouses. Just as the Chautauqua Circle's work reached beyond members of their class, the song they sang ritualistically tied black communities of various sorts together. And no matter who sang it, by the 1910s it was being referred to in virtually every mention as the "Negro National Anthem." These women of the Chautauqua Circle, like the NACW (and some of them were also members of the NACW), held the song aloft through their service work and activism.[46] Ceremonially, whether at the beginning of the program as a sort of invocation or call to prayer, or at the conclusion of the program as a benediction, or as a gift to take with you into the world, "Lift Every Voice" became a spiritual shield against racial injustice, as well as a motivator. But perhaps most important, it drew a line of membership and shaped what sociologist Michael Dawson has termed "linked fate" for African Americans, referring to the sense of a common lot across the lines of class and culture that shapes both political beliefs and action.[47]

CHAPTER TWO

The Sound and Fury of a Renaissance

Art and Activism in the Early Twentieth Century

Oh, Kinsmen! We must meet the common foe;
Though far outnumbered, let us show us brave,
And for their thousand blows deal one deathblow!
What though before us lies the open grave?
Like men we'll face the murderous, cowardly pack,
Pressed to the wall, dying, but fighting back!

—CLAUDE MCKAY, "If We Must Die"

I have commonly found printed or typewritten copies of the words
pasted in the back of hymnals and the song books used in Sunday
schools, Y.M.C.A.s and similar institutions and I think that is the
manner by which it gets its widest circulation. . . . Nothing I have
done has paid me back so fully as being part creator of this song.

—JAMES WELDON JOHNSON

By shedding the old chrysalis of the Negro problem we are achieving
something like a spiritual emancipation. . . . With this renewed self-
respect and self-dependence, the life of the Negro community is bound
to enter a new dynamic phase, the buoyancy from within compensating
for whatever pressure there may be of conditions from without.

—ALAIN LOCKE, "Enter the New Negro"

Alain Locke's 1925 essay "Enter the New Negro" is a classic in African American letters.[1] In it, Locke describes a shift in black cultural and political life, a step toward greater boldness and unfettered imagination. But by the time the essay was published, black America was already a decade into the movement he described. During the years of World War I, and in its aftermath, black Americans, with their institutions now solidified, began mobilizing widely and creating more. Locke described this transition toward "the New Negro" by focusing on the work of artists and activists centered in Harlem, and in particular on black efforts to be included in American electoral politics, and

25

the rise of black modernist art and literature. But in truth, notwithstanding the brilliance of many of Locke's insights, the scope of the New Negro extended far beyond his account.

In the midst of this period of social, cultural, and political transformation, "Lift Every Voice and Sing" became even more deeply entrenched in black life. The song not only journeyed with migrants and strivers but it also gave voice to their aspirations and became a part of the canon upon which the artists and intellectuals drew as they boldly asserted their blackness. In particular, the embrace of "Lift Every Voice and Sing" as the official song of National Association for the Advancement of Colored People (NAACP), and its ultimate rejection by Marcus Garvey and other critics, signaled both the song's importance in the articulation of black politics and the fact that it was already cherished by the time new and expanding political organizations were grappling with what to do with it. Therefore it is unsurprising that in the art and public culture that were so critical in this period, the song was used as a universal signifier of black identity. This chapter will proceed by first providing a foundational account of the transformations of the New Negro era and then elaborating on how the anthem fit within that transformation—at times as a ground of contention and conflict—setting the stage for its role in black politics and culture through the subsequent decades.

Between 1910 and 1930, 1.6 million African Americans moved from the rural South to southern, midwestern, and northern cities.[2] The pace of this migration quickly accelerated at the beginning of World War I and stayed steady until the stock market crash of 1929. Black migrants were seekers, pushing past the roadblocks set up by Jim Crow injustice. Locke astutely noted that the New Negro wasn't all that dramatically different from preceding generations. Black people had always been strivers, resisters, and creators. But, he argued, now black Americans were assertively shedding the erroneous stereotypes that had been applied to the "Old Negro" (docility, complacency, obedience) and entering into public, political, and artistic arenas with heretofore unseen boldness. Migrants sought greater economic and political opportunity, and simply more freedom, all of which usually proved elusive. They nevertheless set off on faith and sought their fortunes in new places. And they kept searching when the promise of a destination didn't pan out. "The migrant masses," Locke wrote, "shifting from countryside to city, hurdle several generations of experience at a leap, but more important, the same thing happens spiritually in the life—attitudes and self-expression of the Young Negro, in his poetry, his art, his education and his new outlook, with the additional advantage, of course, of the poise and greater certainty of knowing what it is all about."[3]

Locke's anthology, which bore the same title as his featured essay, was an important document of the 1920s. But the age of the New Negro, which by some accounts dates as far back as the earliest years of the twentieth century, was an intellectual and political project articulated most powerfully through the black press. There were over 1,000 black newspapers and magazines in the United States by 1910.[4] This remarkable quantity reflects both the passionate struggle for literacy following emancipation, and its achievement.[5] In these papers the promises of migration were touted. But perhaps even more salient, black political life and thought, as revealed in their pages, was international in scope. Black Americans were encouraged to see themselves as part of a global racial community of people who were both Jim Crowed and colonized. They also saw themselves as being, overwhelmingly, exploited workers. Therefore, the Bolshevik Revolution of 1917 and the rise of leftist politics internationally were meaningful and instructive for readers.

Even the structure of capitalism was shifting, and so dedicated capitalists were as well. Western societies became less oligarchic in the wake of the second industrial revolution. That is to say that although the bosses of this gilded age were as exploitative as any economic elites, their leadership was volatile and fortunes were rapidly made and lost. As businesses rose and fell, even capitalism had a populist luster.

At the same time, while African Americans were witnessing the fall of European empires and the victory of the Mexican Revolution, they watched in horror as European powers grabbed the land of Africa. Between the 1870s and World War I, 85 percent of the globe was gobbled up by colonialism.[6] In a time at once harrowing and marked by change, it is no wonder that black political organizing thrived. The political imagination and the need and calls for black self-defense were heightened. Two organizations in particular became dramatically representative of the political energy of the period: Marcus Mosiah Garvey's United Negro Improvement Association (UNIA) and the NAACP.

As a young man, Garvey, a native of St. Ann's Bay, Jamaica, was inspired and influenced by Booker T. Washington's memoir *Up from Slavery*. Washington's gospel of economic development and self-improvement appealed to Garvey, who formed the UNIA in Jamaica in 1914. Finding the development of his organization challenging, he decided to travel to the United States to meet with Booker T. Washington. By the time he arrived in 1916, however, Washington had died (with a statesman-like funeral that featured the singing of "Lift Every Voice"). Garvey remained for a time and traveled around the United States. He was incensed to find that black soldiers who had served in the World War were not treated with appreciation or respect when they returned home but often encountered racist violence instead. He saw that Jim Crow was not simply a matter of southern racial domination but that it extended north as well, impacting where and how black people lived and worked all over the nation.[7] Garvey began to distinguish himself philosophically from Washington, skeptical that economic development and self-improvement by themselves would soften white racism against black people, or lead to full citizenship. He became nationalistic, more in the vein of Martin Delany than Washington.[8] Garvey built his platform touting the greatness of African culture and insisting that black people across the globe should pursue independence and the creation of a black empire. Under this philosophy, Garvey established the UNIA headquarters in New York in 1917. The ultimate goal of the organization was for the descendants of the African diaspora to return to Africa and build the great black nation. While this goal wasn't met, Garvey was incredibly successful in nurturing and developing explicit racial pride and cultural nationalism among people of the African diaspora. The UNIA grew rapidly and by the early 1920s had 700 chapters in thirty-eight U.S. states in addition to several in Canada and the Caribbean. Members were urban and rural, local and global. The UNIA claimed to have 6 million members by 1921. Even the more conservative estimate of 1 million members was extraordinary.[9]

Although ultimately they would share a commitment to return to Africa (though only one of the two was successful) and both placed a premium on economic development and cultural affirmation for people of African descent, Marcus Garvey and W. E. B. DuBois, the preeminent African American scholar and intellectual, had an antagonistic relationship in the 1910s and 1920s. Garvey made the first overture to DuBois by going to visit him at his NAACP office in New York, from which DuBois edited *The Crisis: A Record of the Darker Races*. Garvey was astonished and dismayed that the staff of the *Crisis* was overwhelmingly white.[10] He also didn't like the way DuBois rebuffed him. Garvey accused the NAACP and DuBois of being too white, and DuBois responded with nativist and colorist insults to Garvey's heritage and flesh. They went back and forth for years. DuBois ultimately exposed the UNIA's troubled and troublesome finances and, with his NAACP colleagues, worked to undermine Garvey's popularity.[11]

Beyond the personal attacks were substantive disagreements that give a sense of the era's politics. DuBois was becoming a Marxist, Garvey a capitalist. DuBois's racial logic considered the color line internationally, to include Asian and indigenous people. He saw the line, as sociologist Albert Memmi would later deem it, as one that distinguished between the colonizer and the colonized. Garvey was explicitly devoted to Africans, although he understood that term internationally as well. Within the NAACP, DuBois chafed under white leadership and was often at odds with the organization's moderate and cautious board.[12] Garvey's charges regarding the NAACP's "whiteness" unquestionably struck a nerve. That said, there is some irony in the fact that while Garvey saw himself following in the footsteps of Washington, and DuBois had always been to the political left of Washington, Garvey's work resonated more deeply with the black everywoman and everyman.

Garvey's reaction to the racial composition of the NAACP was, in fact, shared by many black organizers and activists.[13] The organization's reluctance to invite politically radical and outspoken black people to serve in key positions increased general black skepticism of the NAACP. However, the organization changed in the 1910s in some critical ways. The *Crisis*, a monthly magazine first published by the NAACP in 1910, began with a circulation of 1,000. A year later, the circulation was 9,000. By 1912 it was 27,000, and by 1918 it was 100,000.[14] While the numbers of NAACP members and *Crisis* subscribers were dwarfed by those of the UNIA, the *Crisis* had immense influence on black sociopolitical thought. Its circulation, in fact, is likely to have been several times greater than the number of issues sold, because issues were widely shared within communities. In its pages DuBois and his fellow authors offered passionate critiques of Jim Crow, economic exploitation, and colonialism, as well as white supremacy generally. The *Crisis* established a network of knowledge, as well as a common body of written work, that was both creative and journalistic for black Americans. Further, it deepened the information provided by local or regional black newspapers. The *Crisis* documented the work of its parent organization as well. Writings recounted how the NAACP challenged segregation in the Woodrow Wilson administration and effectively lobbied against segregationist bills in D.C. This activism, which produced tangible results, elicited approval and increased interest from black people.

In 1916, the NAACP issued a call for a conference of black leaders in the aftermath of Booker T. Washington's death. The goal was to unite activists who had too often fallen into two camps: pro- or anti-Washington. The conference was held from August 24 to 26 in Troutbeck, New York, at Joel Spingarn's estate, "Amenia." The fifty attendees adopted what they termed a "Unity Platform" that focused upon both education and political rights. They pledged to undo old hurts and enmities.[15] Garvey, still new to black American politics, was not present at Amenia and probably would have demurred even if he had been invited, as it was held at the home of one of the white NAACP founders and there were many white people in attendance. However, there were also many notable African Americans present, including the president of Morehouse college, John Hope; lawyer, journalist, and novelist Charles Waddell Chestnut; NACW and YWCA activist Addie Hunton (one of only two black women assigned to work with American troops during World War I); NACW president and NAACP cofounder Mary Church Terrell; and antilynching activist and suffragist Mary B. Talbert. DuBois would write in retrospect, "I doubt if ever before so small a conference of American Negroes had so many colored men [sic] of distinction who represented at the same time so complete a picture of all phases of Negro thought. Its very completeness was its salvation."[16]

That number also included James Weldon Johnson. Over the weekend Johnson and Dubois bonded as friends and brothers in struggle, so much so that they talked of forming their own secret civil rights organization.[17] Johnson was one of those who had once been associated with Booker T. Washington, but his political writings over the twenty years preceding the Amenia meeting had been closer to DuBois. Johnson once commented wryly that Washington, who advocated industrial education for African Americans, had himself benefited from a liberal education.[18] And as an Atlanta University graduate, Johnson knew firsthand the benefits of a classical education. Moreover, over the years he had developed a strong critique of colonialism, particularly during his years as an ambassador. He was not willing to leave politics to whites and merely focus on economic development like Washington. However, he also knew that a good part of the reason he was granted consular positions in Venezuela and Nicaragua was due to Washington's advocacy for him with the State Department, and so he acted with appropriate gratitude. However, Washington's 1915 death opened up space for Johnson to emerge fully as a political activist.

After Amenia, Johnson was hired as a field secretary for the NAACP. At that point, he'd already had a distinguished career. He had served as U.S. ambassador to Puerto Caballo, Venezuela, beginning in 1906, with a salary of $2,000, when many black men and women, trapped in cycles of debt peonage, were making nothing and the average annual salary across the races was between $200 and $400. In 1909 he was promoted to a post in Corinto, Nicaragua, with a salary of $3,000. In 1912 Johnson was nominated to a post in the Azores by President Howard Taft, but when the Woodrow Wilson administration took over, with its notoriously racist practices, he was denied the post. Johnson and Grace Nail Johnson, whom he had married in 1909, then went back to Jacksonville for a while, before returning in 1914 to New York, where he served as the director of the editorial staff of the *New York Age*, the city's oldest black newspaper. His work for the *Age*, as well as his poetry and prose, are what drew him to the attention of the NAACP in the first place.

In 1916, having taken a position as an NAACP field secretary, Johnson began an organizing tour of the South. He addressed conferences in every major city to which he traveled, and he started NAACP branches in black communities large and small. Walter White, one of his colleagues, described an Atlanta meeting where Johnson gave one of his organizing speeches as "so packed with eager faced Negroes and even a few whites that we had difficulty wedging the platform party through the crowd to enter the auditorium. Mr. Johnson, calm, slender, and immaculate, stood hazardously between the footlights and a painted backdrop. . . . There was none of the sonorous flamboyant oratory of that era in the meeting . . . only the quiet irrefutable presentation of the facts and the need to wipe out race prejudice before the hate."[19]

The steady pace at which Johnson and his colleagues pursued organizational growth would effectively change the racial composition and even the character of the NAACP. Between Johnson and others in the field and DuBois at the *Crisis*, the NAACP effectively became a black organization rather than simply an organization advocating for black people. By 1919 there were 155 southern branches.[20]

The work they faced was daunting. Black servicemen returning from war had been met with racist violence, with 1919 the bloodiest year in recent history: seventy black people were lynched, and eleven were burned to death. For black Americans, it was also their 300th year on American shores, and their 300th year of exclusion. White mobs attacked African Americans in over three-dozen American cities. Johnson referred to it as the "Red Summer."

In the midst of that summer, DuBois and Ida Gibbs Hunt organized the second Pan-African Congress in Paris (the first had been held in 1900).

Hunt had taught at the M. Street School (soon to be known as the Dunbar School) in Washington, D.C., as well as Florida A&M College, and was living in Paris at the time with her husband, the diplomat William Henry Hunt.[21] She and DuBois brought together leaders from across the black world. Their congress was scheduled to coincide with the Versailles Peace Conference, a gathering of the allied powers in the aftermath of World War I. The Pan-African Congress delegates planned to petition the Allies to begin a process of allowing "home rule" for Africans. In Paris as well as New York, DuBois, Johnson, and their collaborators strategized about how to resist the expansion of European domination, how to escape being made pawns in the struggle over global hegemony, how to achieve black self-determination, and how to end the bloodshed.

That year, the NAACP declared "Lift Every Voice and Sing" its official song. And in 1920, Johnson was named the organization's executive secretary, the highest staff position in the NAACP. His appointment coincided with the NAACP's publishing copies of "Lift Every Voice" to be nationally distributed with "The Battle Hymn of the Republic," another beloved song in African American communities, printed on the reverse side. It was a brilliant move, serving as an assertion that the NAACP was a black organization—that is, one that claimed the popularly recognized black American anthem as its own. New chapters, new leadership, a robust publication, and a new song combined to enable the NAACP to refashion itself as an institution that would be controlled and developed by black political actors and black agency.

In August 1920, several weeks after the Pan-African Congress, Garvey's UNIA and the African Communities League held their first International Convention of the Negro Peoples of the World at Madison Square Garden in New York. The month-long convention assembled approximately 2,000 delegates from twenty-two countries. They held regular sessions throughout the month. Halfway through the gathering, the red, black, and green flag (a symbol of black nationalism) and the Universal Ethiopian Anthem "Ethiopia, Land of Our Fathers" were introduced and ratified by delegates as symbols of the UNIA and the black world. Throughout the convention, huge parades were held in the streets of Harlem. One, on August 3, featured UNIA officers in full regalia reminiscent of the French military, riding in floats while the "Black Star Line Band and Choir" played marches. The UNIA Motor Corps, the African Legion, and the Black Cross nurses, along with various national contingents, marched behind them.[22] This pageantry was a heightened performance of black formalism, an effort to bring those community rituals into an imagined international community forged of a common political and racial identity. The UNIA anthem's reference to "Ethiopia," the biblical term for Africa, was explicit about race and nation in a manner that "Lift Every Voice and Sing" was not. And representatives of the entire black world marched to it together.

The audience for Garvey's inauguration as "president of Africa" at the end of the month was estimated at 25,000.[23] The hall in which he spoke that day was decorated in the flags of the many nations represented by convention delegates, including flags of the Caribbean, Africa, and the United States. On the platform, the officers sat in their bright attire, and the audience was decked out in fine Sunday dress. As Garvey stepped onstage to begin his address, the band played "Ethiopia, Land of Our Fathers." In recording this moment, UNIA reports referred to the song as "the Negro National anthem."[24] This wasn't an altogether surprising designation, given that Garvey imagined the African continent as a single nation. But it was, somewhat provocatively, the same term almost always exclusively applied to "Lift Every Voice and Sing." On previous occasions, Garvey had in fact used "Lift Every Voice and Sing" to rally listeners. In 1917, while responding to the riots in East St. Louis,[25] in a speech delivered at Lafayette Hall in Harlem, Garvey made subtle reference to the anthem by saying that it was "a time to lift one's voice against the savagery of a people who claim to be the dispensers of democracy." The East St. Louis riots had begun when 470 African American workers were hired to replace white workers who had gone on strike against the Aluminum Ore Company. Angry white workers complained loudly about black migration into East St. Louis at a local city council meeting. After the meeting, an unsubstantiated rumor started that an armed black man had attempted to rob a white man. In response, white mobs took to the street and savagely assaulted any black person they encountered. Mobs barricaded streetcars and trolleys, dragging black passengers into the street and beating them. The governor, Frank O. Lowden, eventually called in the National Guard and the mobs dispersed for four days, only to return with a vengeance on July 2. This time the crowds beat and shot at black children as well as adults. In the evening they began setting the homes of black people on fire; when the residents ran out to escape the flames, they were shot at. The National Guard and police arrived but did little to stop the violence.[26]

The NAACP responded by staging a silent protest march in New York

City. Ten thousand well-dressed African Americans marched down Fifth Avenue. Garvey's response was louder. "Millions of our people in slavery gave their lives that America might live," he said. "From the labors of these people the country grew in power, until her wealth today is computed above that of any two nations. With all the service that the Negro gave he is still a despised creature in the eyes of white people, for if he were not to them despised, the whites of this country would never allow such outrages as the East St. Louis massacre. . . . This is a massacre that will go down in history as one of the bloodiest outrages against mankind for which any class of people could be held guilty."[27]

In some sense East St. Louis revealed the appeal and even necessity of a black nationalist politics. Although the white working classes were economically exploited, just as black people were, the most vicious racists were often among that group. Garvey tapped into the deep distrust of all white people, not simply those with concentrated economic and political power, that black Americans generally and appropriately held. At times when Garvey spoke to this distrust, and to the necessity of a black empire, he did so with "Lift Every Voice" as his pomp and circumstance. He approached the podium to the sound of the anthem in 1919 when he gave a speech at the Harlem Casino,[28] for example. So, in 1920, when Garvey declared a new anthem, he was betting upon his extraordinary success in rallying black people. He had given them a vision, an imagined independent nation, and was naming and authorizing this imagined national community by declaring "Ethiopia, Land of Our Fathers" to be its anthem. In contrast, the NAACP used "Lift Every Voice" as a way for the organization to assert its fidelity to the people it sought to serve.

"Ethiopia, Land of Our Fathers" is not a particularly well-composed song: its lyrics are repetitive and not terribly poetic or narrative in form (it mainly consists of a series of claims rather than a story), and the music is plodding without the coloratura and emotion of "Lift Every Voice and Sing" (at least not until the 1970s reggae versions began to be produced). Perhaps that's why it never really took hold. Moreover, regardless of the excitement and commitment generated by the UNIA, by 1920 black Americans had already committed to their song, and it was "Lift Every Voice and Sing." It was embedded in so many aspects of life—church services, civic organization meetings, school assemblies, and celebrations—that even the majesty of the

UNIA processions, for those who witnessed them, couldn't possibly rival its impact. The regularity of the rituals associated with black formalism meant that changing the dearly held anthem would have required much more. Moreover, as Garvey came under attack, the UNIA suffered alongside him. In 1919, J. Edgar Hoover, head of the Bureau of Investigation (which became the Federal Bureau of Investigation in 1935), already had officers reporting on the UNIA in numerous cities. In 1925 Garvey was charged and convicted of federal mail fraud. Soon the UNIA began to fray, with factionalism across regions unsettling the unity it had enjoyed under Garvey's leadership. In 1927 Garvey was deported. He spent a few years in Jamaica before moving to London, where he died in 1940. It bears repeating that despite the acrimony between the UNIA and the NAACP, the two groups shared some common sensibilities and some common weaknesses. They both had an international scope, as did the black press and many other black civic organizations. They both rejected colonialism. In August 1920, James Weldon Johnson published an article in the *Nation* titled "Self-Determining Haiti." A book by the same title would soon follow. Johnson opened his essay with a denunciation of U.S. colonialism:

> To know the reasons for the present political situation in Haiti, to understand why the United States landed and has for five years maintained military forces in that country, why some three thousand Haitian men, women, and children have been shot down by American rifles and machine guns, it is necessary, among other things, to know that the National City Bank of New York is very much interested in Haiti. It is necessary to know that the National City Bank controls the National Bank of Haiti and is the depository for all of the Haitian national funds that are being collected by American officials, and that R. L. Farnham, vice president of the National City Bank, is virtually the representative of the State Department in matters relating to the island republic. Most Americans have the opinion—if they have any opinion at all on the subject—that the United States was forced, on purely humane grounds, to intervene in the black republic because of the tragic coup d'état which resulted in the overthrow and death of President Vilbrun Guillaume Sam and the execution of the political prisoners confined at Port-au-Prince, July 27–28, 1915; and that this government has been compelled to keep a military force in Haiti since that time to pacify the country and maintain order. . . . The

independence of a neighboring republic has been taken away, the people placed under foreign military domination from which they have no appeal, and exposed to foreign economic exploitation against which they are defenseless. All of this has been done in the name of the Government of the United States; however, without any act by Congress and without any knowledge of the American people.

The law by which Haiti is ruled today is martial law dispensed by Americans. There is a form of Haitian civil government, but it is entirely dominated by the military occupation.[29]

Even as Garvey's organization declined in membership and prestige in the late 1920s, members of the NAACP and other organizations kept alive a global vision of black liberation. Even though the NAACP maintained an integrationist philosophy in the United States, contrary to Garvey's nationalism, this was an argument for full inclusion of black Americans into the body politic, and the NAACP supported anticolonialism and racial equality abroad. Both the UNIA and the NAACP, however, had the unfortunate limitation of assuming that those in the diaspora had greater capacity to do this work than Africans on the continent, and they often maintained paternalistic assumptions about what Africa ought to do, and some presumptuousness regarding their claims to Africa as "theirs." Despite this shortcoming, they did nurture and follow the will of the "people": black folks who saw their lot in terms of "the race" and not simply in terms of the nation where they lived.

The people—that varied, large, and complex group who fell under the designation "Negroes"—found themselves politically much more often in the interstices of these and other organizations rather than explicitly identified with one or another. In fact, black institutional life and civic life was so robust that many black Americans belonged to a number of political, religious, and civic organizations devoted to the well-being and uplift of black people, with distinct models and approaches.

As we have seen, their ritual programs, events, discussions, and celebrations of all sorts organized by these associations usually began or concluded with the singing of "Lift Every Voice and Sing." Emancipation Day gatherings on January 1, Frederick Douglass's birthday gatherings in February, May Day celebrations on May 1, and Juneteenth ceremonies (the summertime emancipation ritual of the Southwest) were among the principal holidays when people sang "Lift Every Voice," in addition to graduation ceremonies and church celebrations. Carrie Allen McCray, a civil rights activist from

Lynchburg, Virginia, describes an Emancipation Day program circa 1919: "The congregation stood to sing James Weldon Johnson's 'Lift Every Voice and Sing,' a song Negroes back then sang at the beginning of almost every important program. We knew every word growing up."[30] It should be noted, however, that at the time the NAACP referred to "Lift Every Voice" not as an "anthem" but instead, more cautiously, as the national Negro *hymn*. However, its stature as an anthem was proved by the angry response of those who thought an anthem specifically designated for black Americans was anathema to the goals of full citizenship. Interestingly, this objection began to be raised well before the United States adopted "The Star-Spangled Banner" as its anthem in 1931.

Ernest Lyons, a black Honduran African Methodist Episcopal minister and professor at Morgan College who had served as consul to Liberia in 1903, directed his anger about a "Negro Anthem" at James Weldon Johnson in the June 19, 1926, edition of the *Baltimore Afro-American*:

> The anthem has been going the round of schools and colleges and
> without serious thought is being adopted as an appropriate thing for
> the youth of our group. We are persuaded to inquire from its author,
> by reason of its title, what it can really mean, what it is intended to
> accomplish, and for what class or group to which it can be applied. . . .
> There are only two independent sovereign Negro Nations of African
> origin. They are the republics of Hayti and Liberia. . . . It is our judg-
> ment that neither one of these would be willing to discard their own
> inspirational national anthem for one arranged by a subdued group,
> whose social status in their own land is somewhat nondescript. . . .
> If we need a national anthem, then we will also need a negro national
> flag which will carry us on the verge of Garveyism. We need neither.
> We are American citizens.[31]

Johnson replied in the same issue:

> There is nothing in "Lift Every Voice and Sing" to conflict in the slight-
> est degree with use of "Star-Spangled Banner" or "America" ["My
> Country 'Tis of Thee"] or other patriotic songs. It is fully as patriotic,
> among possibilities are that it may grow in general use among white as
> well as colored Americans. . . . Music of "America" is that of the British
> National Anthem. Music of "Star-Spangled Banner" is derived from old
> foreign drinking songs, difficult to sing; in addition the sentiments are

boastful and bloodthirsty. Words of "Lift Every Voice" are more elevated in spirit. I do not hesitate to say my brother's music is better than either of these imported songs.[32]

Johnson's defense, that the song was home-grown and not exclusive, was perhaps effective argumentation, but it was also a bit of an obfuscation. Whatever he intended, his song was in fact an anthem and in particular black America's anthem, and he knew it. In March 1926 W. E. B. DuBois wrote a letter to James Weldon Johnson asking him to provide an account of how the song came to be written, presumably because of its clear status in the cultural life of black Americans. Over the years, Johnson would be repeatedly asked to recount the story of how he and Rosamond came to write and compose the song. There was some variation in his tellings. As a result, some scholarly accounts have the brothers writing and composing it at the same time, while others say the lyrics came before the words. Some accounts have "Lift Every Voice" sung first at Florida Baptist Academy, where Rosamond worked, but most have its premiere at Stanton, where James was principal. And some reports say the song was adopted by the NAACP in 1919 (as my research suggests), but others say 1920. Despite the variance in these details, one constant in every version of the story Johnson shared is this: Communities carried forward the popularity and significance of the song, not its authors. And communities chose it as the anthem. That was beyond the power of Johnson or Lyons to dictate or dismantle.

Critics continued to complain about this community embrace of "Lift Every Voice" over the years. An editorial in the Kansas *Plaindealer* from 1949 praised the song but rejected its designation as an anthem: "We believe that every Negro should know and have a copy of the words to a song that yet causes many of us mental anguish whenever a group rises to sing it. Too, an effort to correct an impression will be made. There is NO Negro National Anthem. The correct title, we believe, is LIFT EVERY VOICE AND SING. . . . Do you know all three verses, just one or none at all? Anyway, here is the whole song, clip it out and learn it, teach it to your children!"[33]

Even people from outside the community acclaimed the song. Reform Rabbi Stephen S. Wise, who founded the Free Synagogue of New York, wrote to Johnson after hearing the song performed at Morehouse College: "Your national anthem, text and music alike, is the noblest anthem I have ever heard. It is a great upwelling of prayer from the soul of a race long wronged but with faith unbroken. I wish that 'Lift Every Voice and Sing' might be substituted for some of the purely martial and unspiritual so-called anthems which are sung by the people."[34]

Regardless of the designation, singing this song together, repeatedly, had a profound impact on black communities. Cultural critic Benedict Anderson referred to the emotion produced by collective anthem singing as "unisonance."[35] Unisonance is a way of feeling in one's body, resonating through one's breath and flesh, membership in a community bigger than simply those in the room. For singers of "Lift Every Voice," it is a physical realization of belonging to the black world.

That sense of membership was on display when the Circle for Peace and Foreign Relations, an African American women's group, organized the 1927 Pan-African Congress in New York City. They raised $3,000 to hold the conference, whose sessions took place in Harlem churches. The conference was opened by delegates singing "Lift Every Voice and Sing." Then Addie Hunton, who had attended the NAACP's Amenia weekend in 1916, delivered the opening address and articulated a vision of international solidarity. Other activists and intellectuals present included the Philadelphian novelist and essayist Jessie Fauset; William Leo Hansberry, a Howard University professor who specialized in African history; Melville Herskovits, an anthropologist remembered for his work establishing the African retentions present in African American culture; and J. E. Caseley Hayford, founder of the National Congress of West Africa and author of what has been called the first Pan-African novel, *Ethiopia Unbound*. DuBois chaired the proceedings and put together an elaborate exhibit that displayed replicas and drawings of the black world, with attention to both political formations and economic conditions. The resulting manifesto called for the immediate withdrawal of U.S. troops from Haiti, the end of economic exploitation in Haiti, and the restoration of local control. It also explicitly condemned the growing racial segregation and subjugation of black Africans in South Africa, as well as Western imperial ventures in Egypt and Ethiopia.

If the Pan-African congresses, and the everyday reporting of black newspapers, conceived of the black world to which African Americans belonged as vast and politically complex, this was enhanced by a remarkable depth in the telling of black history, in ways that were broad, epic, and creative. There was no better evidence of this practice than what we find in the historical record about the popularity of African American historic chronicle pageants. In the words of DuBois, author of the early and influential 1911 *Star of Ethiopia* pageant, "It seemed to me that it might be possible with such a demonstration to get people interested in this development of Negro drama to teach . . . the colored people themselves the meaning of their history and their rich emotional life through a new theatre." DuBois, as imaginative as he was analytically brilliant, used virtually all of his own music, composed with the assistance of Rosamond, in the *Star of Ethiopia*. Like Garvey, DuBois reached for the symbolism of biblical Ethiopia to articulate a contemporary black identity. Representations of African culture and symbols would continue to resonate with dramaturges, and they appeared throughout subsequent pageants. However, most later pageant authors didn't compose new music but instead looked to "Lift Every Voice and Sing" for the musical climax and conclusion of their productions.

By the 1920s, these traveling events often included hundreds of untrained actors performing pieces written and directed by women dramaturges. As Soyica Diggs Colbert argues, these pageants focused on education, democracy, and uplift, yet "the pageant's ability to entertain coincided with its ability to garner an emotional and spiritual reaction, similar to the affect that produces the shout of the church revival."[36] The appropriateness of the anthem's repeated appearance in the pageants is evident. It was a song that had spiritual significance and moved black people when sung in unison, but it was also a song of uplift and possibility, one that itself rested upon learnedness, of music and of history.

One of the pageant dramaturges of this era, Ada Crogman, was an Atlanta native and the daughter of William Crogman, a Latin and Greek professor and later the first black president of Atlanta University. Ada attended Atlanta University and went on to study theater at Emerson College in Boston, after which she was a professor at both Alabama State College and Tennessee State University. Later, while working at the National Playground and Recreational Association of New York, Crogman wrote a pageant depicting African American history titled *Milestones of a Race*. Crogman traveled to various cities, setting up productions of the pageant with local casts in each city, which she both trained and directed.[37] *Milestones* had nine scenes and consisted of folk dances, tableaux, announcers, and decorative scene setting as well as song.[38] The first scene in Egypt depicted black people in "Ancient Life." The second showed animism in West Africa by means of a ritual devotion to the crocodile. The third scene featured daily life in West Africa. The fourth represented a slave market in the United States, during which the actors sang traditional spirituals. "Swing Low, Sweet Chariot" was featured in scene 5, set in the cotton fields, along with "Old Time Religion," "Old

Black Joe," and "Steal Away" during the prayer meeting scene of scene 6. At the conclusion to the sixth scene, Abraham Lincoln appeared to declare the enslaved people free, and in response to this joyful event, the freed-people sang the spiritual "Free at Last." Scene 7 depicted the ascent of black American people through a showcase of distinguished figures, including Booker T. Washington, Bert Williams, and Charles Young. The final scene, "Progress," brought together the entire cast, nearly 100 trained voices, singing "Lift Every Voice and Sing." Although the pageant was generally directed at black Americans, at times audiences were integrated, as during a 1922 performance at Memorial Hall in Dayton, Ohio. Due to its popularity with black patrons, it continued to be performed regularly throughout the 1920s.

Like many pageants, Crogman's echoed the structure of biblical history even as it traced African and African American history. Theatergoers and performers traveled from pre–transatlantic slave trade "innocence" to the suffering of slavery, and finally to striving and ascent. The invocation was of a precolonial past, and the benediction in song carried them into the future. Moreover, the structure of the pageant also mirrored the cycles repeated within the anthem: past, present, and future; suffering, hope, and promise.

Another chronicle pageant, *Temple of Progress*, was written and directed by Topeka Kansas native Lillian J. Craw and performed in various cities over the 1920s. It begins with African American history on these shores: The first scene is on a plantation, with enslaved people singing and picking cotton, and contrasts that arduous labor of the day, to nighttime festivities when the enslaved could enjoy themselves and socialize with music and laughter. *Temple* moves on to an account of the process of emancipation, and finally the emergence of the contemporary "Queen of Progress" as a symbol of the "New Negro" striving. A newspaper account of the pageant when it was performed at Lowther Junior High in Emporia, Kansas, described it as "review[ing] the history of the Negro race ... wherein the historical picture of the race was constructed scene by scene, through the unhappy events of slave importation and auctioning; through colonial days and the death of the first Negro who fought for America; through the nineteenth century, artistic, religious and educational and professional achievements, and the eighth scene was a tableau of the nations of the world, including the entrance of the New Negroes." *Temple of Progress* was written for some 200 performers, and it also concluded with "Lift Every Voice and Sing." Again, the conclusion of the pageant with the anthem underscores the social purposes these pageants served, to both educate and inspire.

In contrast to Crogman's, Dorothy Guinn's 1924 chronicle pageant, *Out of the Dark*, did not begin with Africa but rather ended with it, in the form of a tableau replica of Meta Fuller's *Ethiopia Awakening* (1910), a model of a woman who looks something like a female pharaoh with her hand over her heart, a patriot to the black imagined community. At its conclusion, the chronicler of the pageant states in summation, "Out of the dark and into the light I have brought this record for you, May you have courage, Oh people, to press onward and upward to the very throne of beauty and truth." The cast concluded the performance with "Lift Every Voice and Sing."[39] The use of Fuller's sculpture at the conclusion is a sign of the early twentieth-century historical Pan-Africanism in black American communities that sought to recover an illustrious pre–transatlantic slave trade past. There is a subversion, the African past is not "dark"; instead, the pageant brings viewers from the darkness of slavery "into the light" of African iconography built by the hands of an African American woman. "Lift Every Voice," with its cyclical time and nationalism bound to a racial identity rather than a nation-state, echoes the themes of Guinn's pageant.

Instructive as well as uplifting, these pageants were forms of political theater. Through them, black Americans could rehearse their identities as members of a transnational and modern people, with an epic history—one of endurance—while at the same time the participants in each show forged bonds with fellow members of the cast who were often neighbors, as the casts were almost always comprised of local talent. Pageants provided occasions to act out the freedom that was being sought. And for both audience and actors they were an opportunity to assert one's worthiness. In the performances "Lift Every Voice" operated as at once a recessional and a processional. Pageants were a charge of sorts, encouraging people to leave the theater emboldened by the recollection of resilience in black history, and to proceed forward, ready to face the world.

Less widely popular, but no less critical to African American artistic development, was the work of writers shaped by "Lift Every Voice" during the New Negro Era. This is due both to James Weldon Johnson's parental influence in the Harlem Renaissance and to the mandate for artists to effectively capture black expression, culture, and aesthetics in the "New Negro" movement. For example, Langston Hughes, who was known for his vernacular genius, nevertheless drew upon the form and formalism embedded in the anthem. His poem "Youth," which appeared under this title in his collection *Dreamkeepers* (1932), was first published untitled in the *Crisis* in 1924:

We have tomorrow
Bright before us
Like a flame

Yesterday
A night-gone thing
A sun-down name

And dawn-today
Broad arch above the road we came

We march![40]

The movement through time across the stanzas—"tomorrow," "yesterday," and "today"—mirrors the temporal movement in the verses of "Lift Every Voice." Likewise, the references to light ("bright," "flame," "sun-down," "dawn") and finally of course "the road" on which we are to "march," all hearken back to the anthem.

Gwendolyn Bennett dedicated her poem "To Usward," published in the *Crisis* in 1924, "to Negro Youth, known and unknown, who have a song to sing, a story to tell or a vision for the sons of earth. Especially dedicated to Jessie Fauset upon the event of her novel, *There Is Confusion*. Bennett draws on both "Lift Every Voice" and Paul Laurence Dunbar's poem "Sympathy" in a meditation upon both individual yearning and collective singing that yields collective strength.

Let us be still
As ginger jars are still
Upon a Chinese shelf.
And let us be contained
By entities of Self. . . .
Not still with lethargy and sloth,
But quiet with the pushing of our growth.
Not self-contained with smug identity
But conscious of the strength in entity.
If any have a song to sing
That's different from the rest,
Oh let them sing
Before the urgency of Youth's behest!
For some of us have songs to sing
Of jungle heat and fires,

And some of us are solemn grown,
With pitiful desires,
And there are those who feel the pull,
Of seas beneath the skies,
And some there be who want to croon
Of Negro lullabies.
We claim no part with racial dearth;
We want to sing the songs of birth!
And so we stand like ginger jars
Like ginger jars bound round
With dust and age;
Like jars of ginger we are sealed
By nature's heritage.
But let us break the seal of years,
With pungent thrusts of song,
For there is joy in long-dried tears
For whetted passions of a throng![41]

Bennett ends with a couplet that vaguely echoes the meter of the "sing a song" break in "Lift Every Voice." Throughout the poem, the lifted voice of song is the sound of hope and breaking through bonds to reach freedom. In sensibility, then, it mirrors "Lift Every Voice." What DuBois referred to as "the veil" in his classic 1903 book *The Souls of Black Folk* is Bennett's ginger jar, which will release a sweet fragrance when unsealed.

In a 1926 essay, Georgia Douglas Johnson (no relation to the lyricist and composer of "Lift Every Voice") was more explicit in her references. "The Gift of Song" appeared in the *Pittsburgh Courier* and reads like a praise poem to the anthem: "Song is a divine gift. When the chords about the heart are strung to the breaking point-sing. Sing your cares away. Soon the chords begin to loosen and tears may fall soothing the spirit like spring showers. James Johnson, who knows the long long night of sorrow, bide us 'Lift Every Voice and Sing' to be able to sing is a divine gift. Birds of prey never sing."[42] The testimonial, as to the spiritual benefits of song, also gives us a means of interpreting how "Lift Every Voice" entailed a philosophical argument of sorts about black humanity and existence. To sing is to be more than a work horse or a bird of prey. To create beauty is to refuse and refute efforts to degrade you.

In a simple couplet, Sterling Brown's poem "Salutamus," from his 1932 collection *Southern Road*,[43] does something similar. The lines "What though some roads wind through a gladsome land / it is a gloomy path that we must go" poignantly capture the promise and peril of this nation, so dependent upon the side of the color line on which one stood. The road is stony, but it must be taken nevertheless.

According to literary scholar Robert Stepto, Frederick Douglass initiated a tradition in African American letters of seeing movement and literacy as tied to freedom.[44] While they had quite literal reference points in the narrative: Douglass escaped from slavery and violated the laws against literacy for enslaved people, literacy and movement became symbolic modes of representing freedom throughout black aesthetics. Johnson uses movement multiple times in "Lift Every Voice": "let us march on," "stony the road we trod," "we have come over a way," and so on. Similarly, Brown depicts a path toward freedom that is treacherous yet necessary.

Countee Cullen, one of the most celebrated poets of the Harlem Renaissance, was one of the very few people who treated "Lift Every Voice and Sing" in a satirical rather than pious fashion. His only novel, *One Way to Heaven*, was published in 1932.[45] Although critically panned, mostly for ineffective plotting, it gave full display to Cullen's cutting wit. One character, based on Jessie Fauset, is named "Mrs. Harold De Peyster Johnson." Cullen lifted the name "Mrs. Harold De Peyster" from a 1904 book of manners,[46] a clever dig at Fauset's bourgeois unflappability. In describing Mrs. Harold de Peyster, Cullen wrote that her "race consciousness dated back some seven or eight years. She had, as it were, midwifed at the New Negro's birth, and had groaned in spirit with the travail and suffering of Ethiopia in delivering herself of this black enfant terrible, born, capped and gowned, singing 'The Negro National Anthem' and clutching in one hand a pen, in the other a paint brush. In the eyes of Mrs. De Peyster Johnson this youngster could do no wrong nor had his ancestors ever been guilty of a moral lapse."[47] Cullen's teasing about the perfectionism of a certain branch of New Negro ideology and aspiration presents "Lift Every Voice" as a part of a stodgy race woman and race man practice that could be stifling. Notwithstanding Cullen's impiousness and revelation that the era's "lifting as we climb" politics weren't unanimously embraced, it was standard in black communities in the early twentieth century to treat "Lift Every Voice" in near-religious fashion. Honor and fidelity to its substance characterized the overwhelming majority of references to it, and criticism was scattered and rare. Even Dubose Heyward, a white Charleston writer who wrote about black Gullah life, most famously in *Porgy and Bess*, treated the anthem reverently. His 1929 novel *Mamba's Daughters*, which was serialized in the *Baltimore Afro-American*, traced three generations of black women. The grandmother, Mamba, is a figure who works to ingratiate herself to Charleston's white elites by affecting a "Mammy" masquerade while in domestic service. Underneath her stereotypical role-playing are Mamba's hopes for her granddaughter Lissa. Lissa's mother, and Mamba's daughter, is depicted as monstrous: hulking, ignorant, and prone to violence although crudely protective of her child. Lissa is the repository of the family's future. Because Lissa is a gifted singer, Mamba's employer, a white Charlestonian named Saint Wentworth, pays for Lissa to study opera in New York. After years of study, Lissa has her debut at the Metropolitan Opera House in New York. At the conclusion of her performance, the audience "got to their feet and cheered. They kept the clamour going with a sort of mad persistence. After five minutes of it the curtain was seen to move, rising slowly on the bright vacant wings." Lissa returns to the edge of the stage. "She stopped where she was just out of the wings and unaccompanied commenced to sing the National Anthem of the American Negro." Wentworth, who is watching her performance, has never heard the song before. "From the first note he was aware of an absolutely new sensation. Against his perception beat the words of James Weldon Johnson's inspiring poem swept forward in the marching rhythm of Rosamond's music." As he listens, Wentworth "felt suddenly the impact of something tremendously and self-consciously racial; something that had done with apologies for being itself, done with imitations, reaching back into its own origin, claiming its heritage of beauty from the past."[48]

For Heyward, Wentworth is a semiautobiographical character, and his encounter with the song is a sort of baptism and reckoning with the complex and beautiful truth of blackness. Although not black, Heyward crafted a "New Negro" novel that repeated, like so many rituals within the black community, the idea that "Lift Every Voice and Sing" was a powerful articulation of the souls of black folk.

This sense that a spiritual renewal and reckoning with truth might take place by means of the mantra-like singing of the anthem is not limited to imaginative literature. Rather, the literature captured something about the spiritual dimension of the ritual of singing "Lift Every Voice." Frequently, the devotional singing of the song was part of church programs. Given the importance of churches in African American cultural and social life, this is unsurprising. Churches were places for people to gather, to organize, to socialize, and to celebrate, in addition to being sites of ritualized religious ceremonies. But even in moments that were explicitly and primarily religious, "Lift Every Voice and Sing" could be part of the program. When it was, it was usually the only song that was not gospel or a religious hymn. Furthermore, it was sometimes incorporated into moments of spiritual beckoning. Sylvia Woods, founder of the famous Sylvia's restaurant in Harlem, recalls of her childhood in South Carolina, "During the 1930s as a small child I would often sit on the floor near the fireplace (where there were invariably a few sweet potatoes roasting in the ashes) and listen to my mother, grandmother and other female relatives telling stories and singing their 'burden-lifting' songs as they quilted. As the women sang the lines 'God of our weary years / God of our silent tears' they would stop quilting. Then in unison, they'd rock their heads back and forth, pat their feet, and clap loudly."[49]

"Lift Every Voice and Sing" was a ritual bridge between the political and the spiritual dimensions of black social life that were so often deeply connected. Expressions of faith were intimately integrated into both politics and the social world of black Americans, and the placement of "Lift Every Voice and Sing" in church programs befit this dynamic. At the 1927 celebration in honor of the 110th birthday of Frederick Douglass at the Calvary Baptist Church of Topeka,[50] the choir sang "Lift Every Voice," and Frederick Douglass's granddaughter Fredericka Douglass Sprague Perry shared stories about her grandfather's home life and his kindness to children. She noted what a shame it was that black Americans didn't celebrate the birthday of John Brown like they did those of Douglass and Lincoln. Another speaker encouraged the young people in the congregation to read *The Narrative of Frederick Douglass*. "Lift Every Voice and Sing" was thereby ensconced spiritually, politically, and historically in black church life.

Every community has its fault lines, its points of internal distinction and dissension. Unquestionably, class and region were sometimes the bases for conflict between black people in the United States. Also, the sacred and the profane, or the church and the juke joint, were opposing zones of black life, distinct and sometimes in direct tension. Different forms of expression developed and were curated for each. In other words, Friday night demanded different things from community members than did Sunday morning, not to mention which hat one was to put on to go to work on Monday morning. Which music one listened to and where was part and parcel of these tensions. "Lift Every Voice and Sing" was a song of black formal life, both religious and civic, but the lovers of the song were also folks who hung out in the juke.

The father of the blues, W. C. Handy, was a contemporary of the Johnson brothers, musically trained and formally educated as they were. But he took a divergent path from theirs as both a musician and archivist. However, a consideration of Handy's life, work, and memory also reveals how central the Johnson brothers' anthem was to black America, from the secular to the sacred world.

Handy's father was a pastor in Guntersville, Alabama, and W. C.'s youthful experiences with the sounds and sites of poor and rural southern black culture were the raw material of his musical genius. Handy noticed, while working at a furnace company, "the music made by the workers as they beat shovels, altering the tone while thrusting and withdrawing the metal part against the iron buggies to pass the time while waiting for the overfilled furnace to digest its ore. With a dozen men participating, the effect was sometimes remarkable.... It was better ... than the music of a martial drum corps, and our rhythms were far more complicated."[51]

Handy was captivated by black culture's ability to make music everywhere and out of anything at hand, no matter how humble the circumstance. And although he was a composer and even held a post as a faculty member at Alabama A&M between 1900 and 1902, he was drawn primarily to exploring black music in the most vernacular settings. And so he went to the Mississippi Delta. There, he settled in Clarksdale and became the director of a band. During his six years in Mississippi he grew familiar with the repetitive wailing strings of the local guitarists and mandolin players. He noticed, among his many observations, that in the local square dances all the songs were called in the key of G.

> The primitive southern Negro, as he sang, was sure to bear down on the third and seventh tone of the scale, slurring between major and minor. Whether in the cotton field of the Delta or on the Levee up St. Louis way, it was always the same. Till then, however, I had never heard this slur used by a more sophisticated Negro, or by any white man. I tried to convey this effect ... by introducing flat thirds and sevenths (now called blue notes) into my song, although its prevailing key was major ..., and I carried this device into my melody as well. ...

This was a distinct departure, but as it turned out, it touched the spot in the folk blues the singer fills up occasional gaps with words like "Oh, lawdy" or "Oh, baby" and the like. This meant that in writing a melody to be sung in the blues manner one would have to provide gaps or waits.[52]

As a musician and composer, Handy was identifying the sophisticated and distinctive compositional forms of rural black social music and rejecting suppositions of its inferiority in comparison to the classical composers he'd also studied.

In 1912, Handy published "Memphis Blues," which initiated the classification of the twelve-bar blues as a genre in published and copyrighted music. Of the first time his most famous composition "St. Louis Blues" was played in 1914, Handy wrote, "The one-step and other dances had been done to the tempo of Memphis Blues. . . . When St. Louis Blues was written the tango was in vogue. I tricked the dancers by arranging a tango introduction, breaking abruptly into a low-down blues. My eyes swept the floor anxiously, then suddenly I saw lightning strike. The dancers seemed electrified. Something within them came suddenly to life. An instinct that wanted so much to live, to fling its arms to spread joy, took them by the heels."[53]

Handy had a lucrative career playing and writing the blues. While Rosamond, and to a lesser extent James, composed and collected some vernacular expressions, including the pop styles of their day—"coon songs" and "rag time," as well as traditional southern sermons and spirituals—they were not bluesmen like Handy. Several times, however, Handy worked with Rosamond, and even when they didn't work together, their paths frequently crossed. For example, Handy's one-time musical partner Henry Pace established Black Swan Records in 1921. It was the first African American–owned record company in the United States and would be identified as *the* music company of the Harlem Renaissance. Many greats of the 1920s and 1930s recorded for Black Swan, including William Grant Still, Ethel Waters, Fletcher Henderson, Nathaniel Dett, and Alberta Hunter.

Black Swan announced itself with an advertisement that read, "Every Time You Buy a Black Swan Record, you buy the only record made by colored people." Oftentimes in the *Crisis* the page advertising the sale of "Lift Every Voice and Sing" sheet music (which read, "The National Negro Hymn, Sung at Emancipation Day Exercises, Public Meetings and Conventions. Suitable for Choruses, Schools, Choirs, Etc.") came directly before the advertisement for Black Swan Records. It is appropriate, then, that Black Swan pressed the first recording of "Lift Every Voice and Sing" performed by a gospel quartet called the Manhattan Harmony Four. On the flip side of that record was the spiritual "Steal Away Jesus."

As is evidenced by these vignettes, the musical landscape available to black people in the first half of the twentieth century was wide, spanning from gospel and blues to jazz and concert music. The musicians, even if they specialized in one style or another, generally had deep knowledge across the spectrum, as their audiences experienced and appreciated it all. This was true of both Handy and the Johnson brothers, although their centers of gravity differed.

Arguably, Handy's most striking achievement was the 1929 two-reel film *St. Louis Blues*, which featured blues queen Bessie Smith in a Prohibition–era nightclub singing Handy's most famous song. Rosamond was the arranger and provided the choral background. For Smith, it was a reprisal of the hit she and Handy had in 1925. This story of a woman left by her philandering man had an all-black cast and is the only film recording of Smith.

Just two years after the film's release to great acclaim, Handy was honored in his adopted hometown of Memphis, where a public park was named for him at the end of Beale Street. A musical cavalcade processed to the park, with the local community cheering all along the route. They played some of Handy's greatest songs: "Memphis Blues," "Beale Street Blues," and "AfraAmerican Hymn," a march written for a military band. The only non-Handy song on the program was "Lift Every Voice and Sing."

At the podium, Handy recalls, "some of the most forceful speakers of both races began a flood of oratory covering every phase of achievement in Memphis relative to our race. Many speakers were veterans and others brilliant young men just out of their teens. Some were humorous, others serious, but all contributed to the greatest experience of my life."[54]

The program was dedicated to Handy, but it was also intended to honor the collective. Handy stood as a representative of black achievement. His gifts shone light on the entire populace. This was at a time when public parks, train stations, and stores in Memphis and throughout the South remained segregated. "Lift Every Voice and Sing" symbolized collective will, achievement, and endurance. But what makes Handy's commemoration an even more special setting for "Lift Every Voice" is the manner in which it rested, as part of that program, in the midst of a larger musical tradition alongside Handy's blues, gospel, and jazz, a tradition that was both sacred and profane, vernacular and classical. "Lift Every Voice and Sing" belonged to it, and yet within it, it remained distinctive and ceremonial.

Many critics have noted that music has been the primary art form of African American culture and has, as a result, influenced all other artistic forms in that tradition. While this may be true, the literary—textual, aural, and oral literature—has also been central to the African American artistic tradition and influenced other artistic forms. Even the man hailed as the father of the blues was first and foremost a composer. The music that would be called jazz is defined by improvisation yet rooted in the mastery of musical composition and notation. Part of what made "Lift Every Voice" work so well as an expression of black American identity is the synchronization of masterful musical notation, and masterful poetry, in song.

Far less attention has been paid, both historically and presently, to how visual artists fit within the African American aesthetic tradition. But while a smaller tradition, the visual arts are nevertheless substantial. Visual artists also found inspiration in "Lift Every Voice," and the substance of that inspiration reveals a great deal about the intimate experience, and the individual expression, of the collective singing voices that intoned the anthem.

Vivian Schuyler Key, an artist who provided paintings and drawings fairly regularly for the *Crisis*, was the first African American woman to pursue a program in art at the Pratt Institute in New York, from which she graduated in 1923. Key was less famous and less highly regarded than some of her fellow *Crisis* artists, such as Laura Wheeler Waring and Aaron Douglass. She was also poorer and therefore professionally hampered. She simply didn't have the resources to devote herself solely to art. Yet her legacy is still significant.

In August and September 1927, Vivian drew the maps that DuBois used for his display at the Pan-African Congress. She did so under difficult conditions. In response to his request that she take on the work, she wrote to him, "I would be glad to do the work of which you speak, that is the work on maps and charts. But I am handicapped in a way. I am working down near Northampton Beach. Although I am kept quite busy, I have three or four hours a day which I could devote to your work."[55]

Two months later, Schuyler learned that she'd won first prize in the cover illustration contest for the NAACP's popular theatrical group the Krigwa Players. This meant her work would grace the cover of the November 1927 issue of *Crisis*. Her winning piece was titled *Lift Every Voice and Sing*. The anchor of the image is a sultry Lady Liberty with her palms open in supplication and an impressionistic face that appears to be in distress. The title and the lyrics from the first verse are written to her right and reach behind her back. Key's placement of a woman at the center is striking and yet appropriate. Notwithstanding the fact that the ideals of masculinity and men leading the race toward freedom were widely embraced in black religious life and in the largest black political organizations, black women were central in black social and political leadership at all levels, and across the nation. Moreover, as we have seen, black women were primary figures, as educators and activists, in the process by which the song was adopted as an anthem, one endowed with political and spiritual purpose for black America.

Upon learning she had received the prize, Schuyler wrote to DuBois, "It is with great pleasure that I acknowledge receipt of your letter announcing the success of my crisis cover. I am proud and happy beyond description."[56] This prize, however, was to be a bittersweet victory, as her career soon fell on hard times. Within a few years she was divorced and became the single mother of three children. Schuyler spent most of the following years struggling to maintain a career despite those obstacles. She worked with the Works Progress Administration (WPA) and taught at the Merrick Community Center. However, she only occasionally was able to sell paintings. Much of the time she made a living doing the most common work for black women of her era: cleaning the homes of white people.[57]

During the interwar years, "Lift Every Voice and Sing" consistently captured the imagination of artists and political leftists (both black and white) despite the fact that according to mainstream aesthetic norms it would have registered as bourgeois "high culture." As a feature of black formal culture, it cut across class and was part of the broad panoply of black expression, ranging from the improvisational and vernacular to the formal and ceremonial. Perhaps more significant, Key's story and those of many others reveal that black life was overwhelmingly working class. In the first half of the twentieth century, even college-educated and professionally accomplished black Americans frequently found themselves in the position of being hand-to-mouth "working people." And so black formalism was in many ways a cultural expression of working-class people.

Black folks in America were, to the minds of many leftists, and communists in particular, America's peasant class. The Communist Party and various socialist groups grew in popularity in the 1920s and 1930s in the United States and made gains in recruiting black people with their willingness to

The cover of the November 1927 issue of the NAACP magazine The Crisis: A Record of the Darker Races *shown here featured a painting titled* Lift Every Voice and Sing *by artist Vivian Schuyler Key. Key won a cover contest with this piece, which features lyrics from the first verse of the song, a sensuous Lady Liberty with her hands up in supplication, and background scenes of black life in slavery and freedom. Used by permission of Crisis Publishing Co., Inc., the publisher of the magazine of the National Association for the Advancement of Colored People.*

stand against American racism and as advocates of the working poor. Given that large proportions of African Americans did agricultural labor, the leftists' image of them as America's peasantry wasn't far off the truth. However, this resulted in communists' often thinking of black people exclusively in conventional folk terms. It was true that the majority of African Americans still lived in a plantation economy and those in industrial centers were by and large pushed to the edges of the working classes. However, black culture was not simply what could be designated as "folk" according to European frames of reference. In fact, much of it, such as the anthem, was formal. Hence, when members of the Communist Party embraced "Lift Every Voice and Sing," it was usually set somewhat awkwardly alongside simple and rustic folk songs in songbooks and curricula.

At the Little Red School House, a left-wing day school in New York (the official name was the Elisabeth Irwin School), predominantly white children were taught to sing "Lift Every Voice" instead of one of the other patriotic anthems of the United States, in addition to traditional African American spirituals, labor songs, and rural European folk songs. Dina Hampton, in her book about activists educated at "Little Red," describes them as coming of age "in a counter-culture hothouse steeped in progressive pedagogy and radical politics. . . . At assemblies, everyone would stand to sing the Negro national Anthem ('Lift Ev'ry Voice') in place of 'The Star-Spangled Banner.' . . . Social studies, taught by 'a dyed-in-the-wool Marxist,'" formed the core of the curriculum, "with emphasis placed on the exploration of oppressed cultures."[58]

Although black formalism blended these forms as well, the effect was quite different. In black formalist settings the range of forms of expression, and the range in terms of substance, became a composition of identity of sorts, rich, nuanced, and vast in the range of accomplishment. In contrast, "Lift Every Voice and Sing" did not sound like the "proletariat" imagined by Marxists, even as it was the ballad of America's peasant class. This distinction paralleled the distinction between the mainstream Left and the black Left. While there was ethnic and geographic diversity in the mainstream white Left, the black Left in the early twentieth century operated within both a predominantly white leftist movement and a politically and philosophically wide-ranging group of black organizers, educators, and activists. In black communities of the 1920s, black leftists often worked alongside people who had quite different political philosophies from them. In this way, black communists and socialists anticipated the "Popular Front" turn of American leftist radicals toward working with the political mainstream by about ten years. The 1924 "Negro Sanhedrin," for example, was hosted by the politically moderate and capitalist Kelly Miller, a professor at Howard University and a member of the NAACP, and it was first conceived of by the radical William Monroe Trotter, who founded the National Equal Rights League and opposed the degree of control white NAACP members maintained over the organization as well as its more cautious political stances. In attendance at this "supreme council" of the race were black people from sixty-one organizations across the political spectrum, including the NAACP, the National Race Congress (a national organization focused primarily on suffrage rights), and the Communist Workers Party of America. Participants also included members of one of the most radical black organizations, the African Blood Brotherhood (ABB), a group formed to defend black people in the wake of the Red Summer of 1919. Their membership was largely comprised of West Indian communists and socialists. And although the ABB members were welcomed, some other delegates scoffed at them when they suggested that "The Internationale" be adopted as the song of black freedom. Again, black America already had its anthem, and it was embraced across the political spectrum.

A bigger frustration for ABB members participating in the Sanhedrin was Miller's refusal to seriously include a discussion of labor issues as central to black politics. Their frustration anticipated what would eventually lead founding member W. E. B. DuBois to also break with the group. There were many ruptures in black and between black organizations in the early twentieth century, based upon substantive political differences, although sometimes also on personality conflicts. However, the idea that it was necessary to gather and attempt to struggle across the differences, appears over and over again in gatherings like the Negro Sanhedrin of 1924. And this perhaps indicates something about why "Lift Every Voice" would be embraced by so many different organizations over a rather long period of time. A sense of linked fate, common identity, and shared purpose existed across borders of states, nation-states, and classes for black people under Jim Crow and colonialism. While the political ends might vary, the sense that their fate was shared went deep.

When we look to other works of art that served as companion pieces to "Lift Every Voice and Sing," particularly ones that emerge from the black Left, we see a pairing of a broad racial identification, with a race-based political ideology, often to powerful and provocative effect.

Claude McKay's poem "If We Must Die" was first published in 1919. Known as a manifesto of the spirit of the Harlem Renaissance, this poem by a member of the African Blood Brotherhood was a response to the racial violence that erupted throughout the United States in the Red Summer of 1919. During the 1920s it was frequently paired on black programs with "Lift Every Voice and Sing." The two pieces complimented each other. Both are heroic, though "If We Must Die" is much more militant, championing a willingness to give up one's life in the struggle for freedom: "If we must die, O let us nobly die, / So that our precious blood may not be shed / In vain; then even the monsters we defy / Shall be constrained to honor us though dead!"[59] "Lift Every Voice" is more contemplative, moving between endurance, striving, and transcendence. "If We Must Die" made "Lift Every Voice" feel more radical and bolder when placed alongside it. Together, they deepened the politics of black aesthetics.

In the 1920s and 1930s, there were also explicitly multiracial contexts in which the ideology of the radical Left was situated alongside the singing of, or reference to, "Lift Every Voice and Sing." At a 1929 protest in support of the unionization of black porters,[60] William Green, the president of the American Federation of Labor (AFL), spoke passionately in support of African American organized labor, after which the crowd stood and sang "Lift Every Voice." He invited them to sing the song, a marker of black collective identity, as an effort to make inroads with black workers after decades of hostility from white workers, and in the hope that the AFL branches that had a history of egregiously racist activity might be moved to change through the symbolism of this invitation. Ultimately, however, notwithstanding Green's worthy intentions, they were not enough to transform the AFL's poor treatment of black people. And so in retrospect, the singing resonates as a demand powerfully made, though unmet.

The relationship between the white Left and the masses of black people writ large in the United States dovetailed in some common causes: exploitation, domination, and the oppression of the peasantry and working classes. Therefore a symbol or signifier of blackness could readily be deployed for the Left's political messages, notwithstanding the uneasy alliances that frequently characterized the relationship between the white and black Lefts. This was evident in a humorous textual play on "Lift Every Voice" written by a black communist.

On November 12, 1932, the *Baltimore Afro-American* newspaper published lyrics to a parodic version of "Lift Every Voice and Sing" written by a man named Charles Gaines. The parody had also been published ten days earlier in the *Daily Worker*, a Communist Party newspaper in New York. However, its significance changed in those few days. In the week and a half between the *Daily Worker* publication and the *Afro-American* publication, the U.S. Supreme Court had decided *Powell v. Alabama*, reversing the state convictions of nine black youths from Scottsboro, Alabama,[61] who had been falsely accused of raping two white women on a train in 1931. Characteristic of Jim Crow justice, all but the twelve-year-old among them were rapidly convicted and sentenced to death. Their convictions had been appealed by the Lawyers Guild of the Communist Party, which took on cases that mainstream civil rights organizations, most notably the NAACP, shied away from as too dangerous. The Scottsboro trials garnered international attention as a sign of the depth of American racial injustice.

George B. Murphy, a slim, sharp-witted, pipe-smoking friend of DuBois, was a member of the family that owned the *Afro-American*, and served as the paper's Harlem correspondent. A leftist, Murphy mostly covered NAACP activities but was frustrated that the association had chosen a narrow approach to advocacy. He believed it was failing black America by not lodging massive protests in support of black defendants like the Scottsboro boys, and therefore leaving advocacy for black people who were unjustly convicted of crimes to others, in this instance the Communist Party. We can surmise that in publishing a communist-inflected parody of the NAACP's "official song" in one of the nation's most prominent black newspapers, Murphy was taking a subtle dig at the organization. The parody read as follows:

Lift every voice and sing
Til Communism rings
Rights with the true Soviet liberty;
Let our revolting rise
high as the listening skies
Let it resound loud as the rolling sea.
Sing a sing, full of the strife that the dark past has taught us,
Sing a song, full of the hope communism has brought us.
Facing a red, red sun, of a new day begun
Let us fight on til victory is won.

Stony the road we trod,
Bitter oppression's rod
Felt in the days when bourgeois bosses lied.

Yet with a steady beat,
will not our weary feet
Come to the placed for which our comrades tried . . .
We have come, over a way perseverance has watered
We have come treading our path through the blood of the slaughtered
Out of the gloomy past
til now our working class
Waves the red gleam of our red flag at last
Boss of our youthful years
Boss of our futile fears
You who have fought us all along our way;
You! Whose imperialist might
Forced us into the fight.
We shall forever struggle for workers rights.
So our feet stray from the places our boss where we met you
So our hearts drunk in our faith in Communism forget you
Shadowed beneath Red bands
Red ranks expand
True to man, true to Soviet Land.[62]

The parody was more than funny, it was a crude assertion of the black American condition as understood through the agenda of the Communist Party USA. This version did not catch on. There's no surprise there. It was a clever one-off, not a ballad or poem meant to be embraced or treated ceremonially. But the mere existence of this parody does further reveal how rooted the song was in black American culture, and how it might be referenced in an effort to insist that black politics become bolder.

The Great Depression devastated Americans and made the cause of leftists stronger. Black Americans who had already lived under Depression-like conditions faced even more adversity. Their migration to southern, midwestern, and northern cities temporarily largely ceased. But black Americans "moved" in another way. President Franklin Delano Roosevelt's New Deal policies would lead African Americans to overwhelmingly shift their political party allegiances away from the Republicans. They began to vote Democrat in order to vote for Roosevelt. Some New Deal policies significantly alleviated the suffering of the black poor, such as the Civilian Conservation

Corps, a public work relief program for unmarried and unemployed men, and the distribution of relief provisions, which provided basic subsistence when people were confronted with the possibility of literally starving to death. However, the entire New Deal enterprise was shot through with racial inequality.

That inequality of assistance during the Depression had economic consequences that African Americans feel to this day. A primary example is the National Housing Act of 1934, which established the Federal Housing Administration (FHA). The FHA was created to underwrite mortgages, thereby dramatically increasing the number of American homeowners through extended mortgage payback time frames (from five years to thirty) and a dramatically reduced required down payment (down from 50 percent to 10 percent). Under the administrative authority of the FHA, the Federal Home Loan Bank Board (FHLBB) contracted a survey of American cities in order to create "residential security maps." These maps nominally gave information on the level of risk for real estate investments. However, they defined neighborhoods with high percentages of African Americans and or high rates of racial integration as de facto high risk, regardless of other social or economic factors. As such, they named and made black neighborhoods ineligible for financing. At the same time, the prevalence of racially restrictive covenants in white neighborhoods, as well as white mob responses to black efforts to integrate predominantly black neighborhoods, made moving out of neighborhoods deemed high risk a virtual impossibility for black people in many cities. African Americans were not simply geographically constrained, they also were excluded from the federal program that would be the vehicle by which the majority of Americans would move into the middle classes and build wealth. At the same time, the jobs program of the National Recovery Authority under the New Deal gave white Americans preference in job placement and maintained a lower pay scale for African Americans. And the Social Security Act excluded the two most common forms of labor for African Americans—agricultural and domestic—from Social Security benefits. Furthermore, because the Agricultural Adjustment Administration incentivized landowners to reduce production, sharecroppers lost even that lowest-status work in dramatic numbers. In the midst of all this, the NAACP appealed to Roosevelt to support an antilynching bill, and even that he refused. The New Deal was, simply put, both separate and unequal.

The NAACP's second Amenia Conference was called by Joel Spingarn in 1933 in response to the Great Depression. The proceedings signaled a political shift of the NAACP more decidedly to the left. It was a widespread national shift, but in particular the NAACP had to respond to the challenges brought, and strides made, by the Communist Party, particularly in the South. For the first time as a group, the NAACP began to think about class as a central factor in the lives of black people, rather than framing the problems confronting black people overwhelmingly or solely in terms of race. New leaders emerged, including the young University of Chicago–trained sociologist E. Franklin Frazier and the Harvard-trained political scientist Ralph Bunche, both of whom situated their understanding of race in terms of economic conditions. Walter White, the executive director of the NAACP, however, was hesitant about taking a strong position regarding the economic agenda for black Americans, despite the shifting sensibilities of most of the membership and administration. In contrast, DuBois grew to identify as a socialist even more deeply in the 1930s, although he also maintained his belief that race was a central problem on its own, in terms of not merely the domestic color line but also the international one he had identified back in 1903.

An example of this emphasis can be found in a 1936 address given by W. E. B. DuBois at Symphony Hall in Boston. The program was sponsored by the Community Church of Boston, an experimental congregation with a free-form style of worship including regular lectures on contemporary social and political issues. It saw itself as fulfilling "the task of building a new social order out of the wreck left by the World War." DuBois's address was titled "The Italo-Ethiopian Situation: Its Relation to the Black People in Africa."[63] His lecture was preceded by an adagio by J. S. Bach, a selection by Claude Debussy, and, immediately before his talk, a symphonic performance of "Lift Every Voice." The Community Church of Boston was organized around a commitment to a "leveling out" of worship and a radically democratic liturgical practice. It preached openness in terms of authority and legitimacy in every arena, from sacred music to ecclesiastic roles. That the predominantly white and middle- to upper-class church brought the Negro National Anthem, "Lift Every Voice," and the cause of Ethiopian people against the colonial ambitions of Italy, to its congregation signaled the political searching and leftward impulses of the 1930s.

But much more significantly, with respect to growing leftist politics, "Lift Every Voice" served as the opening for the first conference of the National Negro Congress (NNC). In 1935 the Seventh World Congress of the Comintern announced that the Communist Party was going to create political coalitions and allegiances with other antifascist parties. This became known as the Popular Front. In the United States, rather than opposing Roosevelt and his New Deal policies, communists began to embrace them. They became more active in trade unions, in particular the Congress of Industrial Organizations (CIO), as well as in popular arts and music. The Popular Front also allowed for an even more facile merging between black culture and left politics than previous efforts.

The NNC grew out of discussions initiated by Communist delegates to the 1935 conference of the Joint Committee on National Recovery (JCNR) on the economic status of African Americans. Hoping to consolidate and unite various organizations working against racial discrimination, the JCNR created a committee of sixty organizers and activists to organize and host a conference in February 1936.

That month, 800 delegates from over 500 organizations gathered in Chicago. A. Philip Randolph, the founder of the Brotherhood of Sleeping Car Porters, who had once been a socialist but by 1936 had begun his drift to the right, was elected president of the organization. That Randolph wasn't on the far left didn't matter in the context of the Popular Front Communist Party politics of that era. The Front did not seek to proselytize but rather to participate and facilitate. By the conclusion of the conference, the delegates decided on an organizing strategy that included working on attaining fair employment and housing rights, ending police brutality, achieving membership in racially exclusive unions, and opposing fascism and imperialism.

Black Americans engaged in the political sphere and explored political ideologies in a plethora of ways in the 1930s. A good argument could be made that this was the time of the widest breadth of political imagination for Americans in general and for African Americans in particular. Certainly some organizations were relatively conservative, such as the Urban League, but others, such as the NAACP, the Communist Party, and the African Blood Brotherhood, stood somewhere between liberal and left. And the politics of many other local and national organizations varied depending upon the constituencies of their time and place.

Remarkably, then, sociologists in the 1930s painted these varying political imaginaries with one broad stroke: as nationalistic, and dangerously so. Prominent labor economist Walter Daykin described all black political and cultural development with skepticism and even derision. Of efforts to create a historical archive for African Americans, he wrote, "Certain elaborate techniques have been created by Negroes in order to develop their history and at the same time to spread this rapidly growing nationalism. Chief among these techniques is the Association for the Study of Negro Life and History, an organization which spreads facts about the race in order to keep Negro incidents in the range of the consciousness of the members of the group, particularly the younger generation. This organization is dominated by Carter G. Woodson."[64]

Though it was unquestionably a legitimate academic endeavor, Daykin treated black history as just shy of traitorous. In the face of lynching, restrictive covenants, and segregation, he called African Americans "hypersensitive" with respect to racism, saying, "Usually the members of an exploited group are abnormally subjective and as a result they are handicapped in an objective treatment of their own problems. So hypersensitive and suspicious do they become that they are likely to interpret almost any experience personally. Aggressiveness to overcome an inferior status often results."

For Daykin, even the efforts to establish and maintain black institutions, such as the black press, in the face of exclusion from those of the mainstream were a sign of alarming nationalist sentiment: "The dominating tone of the contemporary Negro literature is unrest which is a result of either real or imaginary neglect. Similarly the Negro press communicates a militant attitude. Furthermore Negroes are reacting negatively to specific white cultural traits, such as the white doll, and they are advocating the creation of their own traits such as Negro dolls and racial music. The Garvey movement emphasized a black Madonna, black Christ, and a black God. The Negroes are extremely sensitive as illustrated by their demands that they be called 'Mr.' and 'Mrs.'"

Daykin, unsurprisingly, saw "Lift Every Voice" as a sign of black infidelity to the nation-state, regardless of the song's content or the context in which it was sung:

A Negro national anthem has been written and is often sung at these celebrations. Negroes are urged to appeal to boards of education for the adoption of Negro history text books, or to induce libraries and schools to purchase Negro literature and pictures of notable men of the race. All Negroes are appealed to for knowledge of Negro family history or for any facts considered pertinent to Negro history. The above devices facilitate Negro ethno-centrism and assist in the formation of a body of Negro achievements to which the race can point with pride.

Negro historical writings are further characterized by racial biases, moralizations, and rationalization. Practically all the black historians are compiling data in order to interpret world history from a racial point of view. These historians are partisan, and often record data with the conscious purpose of gaining converts to the Negro's cause. Ethical judgments are passed upon events chronicled.[65]

Apparently, according to Daykin, any ambition that moved black people beyond the status of abject second-class citizenship was threatening. Likewise, any and all organizers and activists who pursued such goals were dangerous.

Scholar Thomas Gilbert Standing similarly offered a wary taxonomy:

Associated with the DuBois point of view is a group of somewhat less widely known individuals which with the exception of the Washington group includes most of those commonly recognized as race leaders. Of these James Weldon Johnson is perhaps nearest to DuBois in ability and spirit. Both have identified with the militant National Association for the Advancement of Colored People, DuBois as editor of its official organ, the *Crisis*, and Johnson is the author of what has come to be known as "The Negro National Anthem," "Lift Every Voice and Sing," which is frequently heard in Negro gatherings throughout the United States. Alain LeRoy Locke, professor of philosophy at Howard University, should be included in this group, as also should Walter White, assistant executive secretary for the NAACP. Kelly Miller, dean of Howard University, is one of the most competent and objectively minded of the DuBois school. There are other Negro writers, particularly among the younger poets, who might properly be classified in the group under discussion. Of these, Countee Cullen and Langston Hughes are among the more outstanding.[66]

Even Kelly Miller and Walter White, men who were unquestionably politically moderate, were classified as "of the DuBois school." They were all, according to Standing, black nationalists. The common thread of identity within the range of political ideologies that made black political life so rich and robust was grounds for condemnation by white sociologists. That Standing contrasted them to the "Washington school" in the 1930s was also something of an obfuscation. After Washington's death, the fault lines of black political life were no longer accommodation to segregation and industrial education, on the one side, and demands for political participation and liberal education, on the other. Rather, the political positions of black activists and thinkers ranged from an effort at inclusion along the terms of the current nation-state, to political and civil rights, to revolution (domestic and/or global). Rather than treat them as serious political thinkers, these white scholars imagined them as "artificial Negroes," as it were. Standing argued that the opposition of the members of the DuBois school to the conciliatory policies of Booker Washington, and their emphatic emphasis on the necessary leadership of the "Talented Tenth" was in large degree a rationalization of their own social position:

> Their general interests, tastes, and ambitions are such as would identify them with the most cultured society. But to full participation in the life of the inclusive society their color is an effectual barrier. It is an acute awareness of this fact that has tended to embitter them and has induced a somewhat reluctant identification with the socially inferior group. Naturally they are most concerned with the development of a cultured minority which will serve as a substitute for the larger society from which they are excluded. Yet, while the members of this group are working for the creation of an intelligent and distinctive Negro society, they are bitterly attacking the shortcomings of a democracy which makes such a course psychologically desirable. Their race conscious-ness and extreme sensitivity to the slightest suggestion of differential treatment on the basis of color, their demands for flat footed equality, imply the acceptance of universal rather than racial norms, yet they are constantly thinking and writing in terms of race.[67]

The depiction of middle-class African Americans as bitter, and as some-how misplaced in the context of the Great Depression, was analogous to the depiction of mixed-race African Americans as impotent and impossibly hy-bridized in the antebellum period. In both instances the characterization of "betwixt and between" black people as "damaged" justified the maintenance of the color line. And, further, it dismissed black aspiration and political imagination. Though the larger society recognized the "higher status" of a subcategory of black people, that status was also imagined as fundamentally deficient because it was incommensurable with the racial order. Undeniably, class conflict and elitism was present in black life, but the generalization of black elites as incommensurable with both the larger society and the black world due to their tastes and aspirations gave short shrift to the lifeworlds of the working-class, collective black cultural practices that marked common identity for members of all social classes, and the serious demands for equality being waged across the class spectrum.

An examination of characterizations offered by writers like Daykin and Standing also suggests that conventional assessments of the class cleavages in black life that were put forward in twentieth-century sociological literature might merit reconsideration, or at least serious interrogation. Perhaps the rift between the middle class and the working poor was not as deep as we've been led to believe. Perhaps it wasn't a rift at all but rather a product of the limitations of the white imagination when it came to black people. Moreover, the deep skepticism white thinkers felt toward black activism in that period, regardless of the political leanings of the actors, helps us understand the repeated efforts of black people at forging unity across ideological differences. There was no justice but rather "just us," as the saying went.

In March 1939, consistent with the sociologists' panic, the Associated Negro Press (ANP) reported that "Lift Every Voice" was under attack by people who thought it could be evidence of Communist Party influence. The ANP quoted an unnamed Glendale, California, publication: "Many people are puzzled about the Negro National Anthem. . . . Is the Negro national anthem a part of the theme of communists who have been telling the Negro that he will have a Negro Republic in the South as soon as the Soviet Regime is established in America? . . . Such propaganda flowing through the malls has found its way into the capital and into the hands of people who in the past gave little thought to such stories."[68] Although some communists embraced the anthem, this was a sign of their efforts to attach themselves to black people, and the influence was black culture on communists, rather than the other way around. The editorial foreshadows the McCarthy era, but it also gives deeper meaning to the concept of "linked fate." Black activists and organizers were under attack together, even when they couldn't stand each other or had vastly different political ideologies. It also helps explain the salience and appeal of some signs and symbols of consensus among black people, such as sharing "Lift Every Voice." All activism on behalf of black people, no matter where it sat on the ideological spectrum, meant putting one's neck on the line. Literally.

Chauncey Spencer, who came of age in Lynchburg, Virginia, during the 1930s as the son of Harlem Renaissance poet and race woman Anne Spencer, recalls, "Our home was always filled with distinguished guests who stopped for an overnight stay and sometimes even longer; W. E. B. DuBois, E. Franklin Frazier, Charles Spurgeon Johnson, and Howard Thurman. When our visitors were ready to depart, our family joined them on our front porch where we held hands and sang 'Lift Every Voice and Sing.' The song served as a prayer because we knew there was a strong possibility that some catastrophe like death could be waiting on the road for our departing friends as they headed south."[69] The leading black intellectuals DuBois and Frazier, along with Fisk University president Charles Spurgeon Johnson and one of the most celebrated black ministers in U.S. history, Howard Thurman, joined hands with Spencer and family and sang the anthem as a spiritual bulwark before going out into a society that was vicious to black people.

One arena of black life in the 1930s was unquestionably flourishing even in the midst of political and economic vulnerability. During the Depression, the federal government's WPA, in part fueled by competition with the writers groups and arts collectives of the Left, provided numerous venues for African American artists to work full-time on their art in far greater numbers than previously possible. It further institutionalized and funded the cultural production fostered by the Communist Party, and numerous black institutions at the beginning of the New Negro era, especially the NAACP and the Urban League, which both created space for black artistic production in their magazines: the *Crisis* and *Opportunity*.

The cultural policies of the New Deal, which included supporting writers clubs, art associations, and a range of opportunities to engage in creative expression, were critical for African Americans. So much so that they demonstrate that scholars can and should reperiodize the Harlem Renaissance. Arguably, the renaissance lasted well into the 1930s and existed in major cities other than New York, especially Chicago, Atlanta, and Washington, D.C. In the midst of this flourishing cultural life, "Lift Every Voice" served as both inspiration and trope for black artists who increasingly had time and space to create.

In Chicago, Alabama-born and Dillard College–educated writer Margaret Walker worked full-time for the Federal Writers Project. In that community she developed friendships with the celebrated writers Gwendolyn Brooks, Frank Yerby, and Richard Wright, as well as the groundbreaking modern dancer Katherine Dunham. In 1937 Walker published a poem titled "For My People" in *Poetry* magazine. It would become one of her most famous pieces and over the subsequent decades was often likened to and partnered with "Lift Every Voice and Sing," not unlike the way "If We Must Die" was in the prior decade. Several of the lines are as follows:

For my people everywhere singing their slave songs
repeatedly: their dirges and their ditties and their blues
and jubilees, praying their prayers nightly to an
unknown god, bending their knees humbly to an
unseen power;

For my people lending their strength to the years, to the
gone years and the now years and the maybe years,
washing ironing cooking scrubbing sewing mending
hoeing plowing digging planting pruning patching
dragging along never gaining never reaping never
knowing and never understanding.[70]

Like "Lift Every Voice," "For My People" is an ode to the historic journey and struggles of black Americans. But, appropriate for the times, it situates labor and the fleshiness of black living in "Afro-American modernist" aesthetics, as defined by Houston Baker in his discussion of Alain Locke's "The New Negro" as a "mastery of form and a deformation of mastery" that coalesced "mass and class . . . standard dialect and black vernacular, aesthetic and political concerns."[71] As I have suggested, this blend was already apparent in the theatricality of black formalism. But Baker notes the growing intimacy of the blend that appeared within the individual artistic productions produced by professional artists.

This "Afro-American modernism" appeared in the visual arts as well. Art historian Richard Powell describes artists of this period as embracing "a visually conservative but politically radical figurative art."[72] Indeed, the black figure or body, in art, at once transgressed the popular caricature of black form (such as Sambo and Mammy) and was situated in contexts rife with social meaning. One such work was produced by one of the most important black visual artists of the 1930s, who also found work in the New Deal and inspiration in "*Lift Every Voice.*"

Augusta Savage, who grew up near Jacksonville in Green Cove, Florida, was one of James Weldon Johnson's many protégés. As a child, she made figurines out of the red clay of her native region. Despite her father's censure (her small sculptures seemed to him to violate the Bible's prohibition against graven images), she continued to model clay as she matured. Eventually, Savage was selling her pieces at a Palm Beach County fair. Winning a fair prize encouraged Savage to apply to the distinguished Cooper Union School of Art in New York. She matriculated there and began her formal art training in 1921. Though her talent was well recognized, in 1923 she was rejected by a summer art program sponsored by the French government because of her race. Black newspapers and magazines, in particular the *Crisis*, decried the discrimination.

Like many other black women, Savage's day job through the 1920s was working as a laundress. She supported her nine-person extended family in a small Manhattan apartment, cleaning clothes and steadily creating art. Over the decade, she received commissions to do busts of both DuBois and Garvey. Later on, she sculpted Frederick Douglass, W. C. Handy, and Walter Gray. *After the Glory*, her antiwar sculpture, was placed in a park at Seventh Avenue and 155th Street in New York City. And, in a touching example of the collective impulse toward excellence, black New Yorkers and black women's groups in Florida raised money for her to continue her studies in Paris at the Académie de la Grande Chaumière. Savage also received a grant to support her study from the Julius Rosenwald Fund. After spending two years in Europe, from 1929 to 1931, Savage returned to New York and founded the Savage Studio of Arts and Crafts. This eventually became the Harlem Community Art Center, which was funded by the WPA. The Harlem Community Art Center was a vibrant, nurturing institution under Savage's guidance. She trained a host of future art luminaries there, including Jacob Lawrence, William Artis, Norman Lewis, and Gwendolyn Lawrence. Eleanor Roosevelt attended the opening ceremonies for the center on December 20, 1936, and the attention generated by that visit inspired the interest of Albert Einstein and Paul Robeson, among others. Savage proved to be a successful institution-builder in addition to a superior artist and teacher. Under Savage's directorship, the center "was heralded throughout the nation" as a model for WPA art centers.[73]

In 1937, Savage was offered a professional commission by the Board of Design of the New York World's Fair, to be held in 1939. She was one of only four women selected to present work at the fair, and one of only two black people (the other was composer William Grant Still). Savage was asked to create a sculpture based on the theme "The American Negro's Contribution to Music." She produced a work titled *Lift Every Voice and Sing*.[74] It was a sixteen-foot-tall plaster sculpture of a series of open-mouthed and round, fleshy-featured black people with bodies adjoined in the shape of a harp. In the front, a kneeling man held a plaque upon which the notes of "Lift Every Voice and Sing" were inscribed. Despite this clear tribute to the Negro National Anthem, the fair jury decided to change the title of the sculpture

Augusta Savage, a native of Green Cove, Florida, who would become a celebrated sculptor, was one of James Weldon Johnson's protégés. She was commissioned to create a piece for the 1939 World's Fair in New York City. Here she is pictured next to the sculpture that she titled Lift Every Voice. *In it, a group of African American singers are melded into the form of a harp, and the lyrics to the first verse of the Johnsons' anthem are inscribed on the bottom. Fair organizers, however, rejected the name Savage chose and called it* The Harp *instead. Courtesy of the Manuscripts and Archives Division, New York Public Library.* The New York Public Library Digital Collections, *1935–45, http://digitalcollections.nypl.org/items/5e66b3e8–80d0-d471-e040-e00a180654d7.*

to *The Harp*. Savage was greatly upset by this decision and wrote to James Weldon Johnson's widow, Grace Nail Johnson, about her frustration: "I resent the name as much as you do . . . and I am going tomorrow to see Mr. Rubin of the Fair to protest the use of [it]. . . . On the day that the design was accepted they even had me sing the 'The National Negro Anthem' for them; but they seem to feel that the title is too long and so they call it 'The Harp.'"[75] Rallies were organized in support of Savage's original title, and several newspapers issued objections in their pages. The Associated Negro Press reported that "admirers of the work last week were emphatic in declaring that 'The Harp' . . . falls far short of conveying the poetic response of the 'Lift Every Voice and Sing' theme responsible for Miss Savage's great work of art. They declared the shorter title inadequate for a work designed to express in material form the contributions of the Negro to the musical cultures of America."[76] But the fair organizers weren't swayed.

Savage's sculpture, however, was a great success. It was the most popular and most photographed work at the fair. Small metal souvenir copies and postcards depicting it were sold. Those are the only remnants of the sculpture remaining today. At the conclusion of the fair, because Savage had no funds with which to cast the sculpture, it was destroyed. To add insult to injury, because of the time she had taken off in order to create her landmark work, she was displaced as the director of the Harlem Community Arts Center, with the position turned over to fellow artist Gwendolyn Bennett.

Nevertheless, great collective pride was taken in Savage's display of black identity in art, and images of the sculpture circulated widely in the black press. Savage was heralded as an example of black excellence, and her use of the anthem stood as powerful evidence of its continued centrality in black cultural and artistic life. Moreover, the work of a black woman at the World's Fair was a display of black excellence to the "white world." While most black formalist practices took place within black communities, there were moments when it was on display for the larger society, taking the shape of political argument for inclusion in the body politic on the basis of such excellence. This dimension of the practice was closely related to Higginbotham's "politics of respectability," in which black people placed a "best foot forward" for the cause of racial equality. But this was not the heart of what black formalism entailed. Because the vast majority of black formalism existed in nearly exclusively black spheres, in church and schools and concerts and lectures, that zone must be recognized as its foundation. Hence, its externalization for the whole world to see was, for lack of a better word, unquestionably authentic, even as it was strategic. The argument presented for inclusion was on the basis of what black people truly were, not on what they were caricatured to be, or on what white people thought they should be.

At the end of the 1930s, a decade brimming with political and artistic activity, and yet also a time of sustained racial injustice, the American Society of Composers, Authors, and Publishers (ASCAP) entered its twenty-fifth year. James and Rosamond had both been founding members of the organization. James Weldon Johnson had died in a car accident in Maine a year prior, but Rosamond was on hand for the festivities celebrating the organization. ASCAP was the body that enabled American musicians to own the rights to their compositions. It was an important organ for black composers like the Johnson brothers, although it became a double-edged sword in the mid-twentieth century, as white composers often copyrighted and grew wealthy based upon their mimicry of black blues and folk musicians, who often died penniless.

For this anniversary, in 1939, ASCAP held a weeklong series of concerts, with each night devoted to a different aspect of American music. One of these was dedicated to African American musical achievement. Regardless of how much black people continued to be politically and economically excluded from the full benefits of American citizenship, their artistic achievement, through the vibrancy of renaissance, the entrepreneurship of recording artists and producers, and the many zones of contact across the color line, made it impossible to deny the enormity of black Americans' impact upon their nation's music. ASCAP's program paid tribute to this legacy. Rosamond, W. C. Handy, and Harry T. Burleigh planned the program for the night. They assembled a seventy-five-piece symphony orchestra and a chorus of 350 singers. William Grant Still (Savage's sole black colleague at the World's Fair) conducted his *Afro-American Symphony*. Spirituals, gospel, blues, ragtime, and jazz were also featured. The program opened when conductor Joe Jordan "lifted his baton and called forth from these forces a thunderous rendition of 'Lift Every Voice and Sing.'"[77] There was no more appropriate choice to initiate a celebration of the contribution of black people to American music. Theirs was not merely a worthy legacy, it was an inheritance of struggle, and a tradition forged in the midst of it. Whether the audience recognized it or not, like the attendees of the World's Fair who encountered Savage's larger-than-life sculpture, this audience heard the sounds and resonances of a nation within a nation, a people who could truly be described as one out of many.

CHAPTER THREE

School Bell Song

"Lift Every Voice and Sing" in the Lives of
Children in the Segregated South

. . . they sing 11 a.m. convocation
"Lift Every Voice and Sing"
1100 strong at the black school—
tears in everybody's eyes
I mean everybody!
—MICHAEL HARPER, "Prologue of an Arkansas Traveler"

I am always thrilled deeply when I hear it sung by Negro children.
—JAMES WELDON JOHNSON

Children, James Weldon Johnson stated, were the ones who first carried "Lift Every Voice and Sing" forward. But it was the deliberate cultivation of black children in formal educational and civic spaces that firmly institutionalized the song. That cultivation also shaped the youth of the black South who, in the mid-twentieth century, faced down white supremacy and transformed the nation and world.

In the early twentieth century, African American institutions prioritized the development and care of black youth. There were children's pages in black newspapers and youth branches of black political organizations. Most important, however, were the herculean efforts black Americans put forth to build schools. Schools would, along with churches and clubs, be integral to the rich and tightly networked associational life of black Americans. Schools were more than academic institutions. They were also places for the community to gather, for organizations to meet, for people to plan protests and plot ambitions. Ironically, school segregation greatly facilitated the frontal assault on a segregated society in the mid-twentieth century. In the early years of the century, a period of immense academic striving, "Lift Every Voice and Sing" became a signature feature of the curricula of black schools. It served multiple purposes: to educate, to inspire, to nurture collective identities, and to bolster a deep sense of worth in blackness. Schools were key institutions for the development of the generations of young people who would lead the civil rights revolution, and "Lift Every Voice and Sing" was a key part of black schooling. But let us begin close to the beginning.

As in chapter 2, in order to fully grasp the institutional significance of "Lift Every Voice and Sing," in this case in black schools, it is necessary to present a picture of what black education was and to what it aspired in the early twentieth century. By 1900, the year "Lift Every Voice and Sing" was written, all southern states required racial segregation in public schools.[1] At that point, 90 percent of black people in the United States still lived in the South.[2] The deliberate process of legal segregation is a lens through which to understand how the color line hardened at the turn of the century. For example, in 1901 North Carolina law stipulated that a child who was descended from any black person "to the third generation inclusive" was not allowed to attend white schools. This rule was amended in 1903 to apply to any child with any African ancestry, "however remote the strain."[3] Despite the fact that black people were the sector of southern society who lobbied most intensively during Reconstruction for the development of public education in the South,[4] the establishment of Jim Crow entailed not simply reduced expenditures for black schools but also funded fewer elementary schools for black students than the number provided for their white counterparts, and only minimal access to high school. This discriminatory state practice was upheld by the Supreme Court, in *Cumming v. Richmond County Board of Education*, 175 U.S. 528 (1899). The court affirmed the Georgia Supreme Court decision to allow Richmond County to close the only high school for black children under the pretense that it was too expensive to maintain, despite the fact that it kept high schools for white youth open. Precisely at the historical period that broadened access to public high school education for the masses of working-class white youth, including European immigrants who often had never before had access to high school, black communities, which fought so diligently for public education, were left out of this growing promise. Schooling was separate, and even more so, unequal.

In response to the particular challenges of educating black children in a pervasively and deeply unequal society, the National Association for Negro Teachers was founded in Nashville in 1904. Soon thereafter its name was changed to the National Association of Teachers in Colored Schools (NATCS) to include white teachers who taught black children, although the membership remained overwhelmingly black. J. R. E. Lee, the director of the academic department at Tuskegee, issued the call for the creation of the organization and served as its president for the first five years.

Prior to the development of the NATCS, most southern states already had local Negro teachers associations. Kentucky's Negro Education Association had been founded in 1877, and Alabama's in 1882 (by Booker T. Washington). Georgia's was created in 1878, Virginia's in 1888, Oklahoma's in 1893, and Florida's in 1891.[5]

These organizations, both local and national, focused their efforts on pursuing educational equality and excellence for black children. James Weldon Johnson, W. E. B. DuBois, Mary McLeod Bethune, and many other leading black intellectuals and activists held active memberships in the NATCS for many years and often lectured at NATCS events. James Weldon Johnson, for example, was elected president of the Florida Negro State Teachers Association in 1901.[6] The organizations collectively advocated for changes to the law and other funding sources that would allow for equalization of expenditures and resources. They also worked diligently to learn and share research on the best pedagogical and socialization practices for educators, school leaders, and parents to apply in the development of youth.

In an address delivered to the Alabama association in 1912, G. W. Trenholm, the president of Alabama State Teacher's College, argued that the association must work to collect and compile data on the state of schools for black children, build more and better schools, supplement the public school fund, lengthen the school term, establish more high school departments in grammar schools, and enrich the courses of study. He also encouraged teachers to stay in the school long enough to "do some real good as a teacher. . . . We must strive to win our boys and girls from ignorance as we are striving to win them from hell. We must build school houses for them as well as churches. We must support the teachers as well as the ministers, coworkers together in the same field. It is our divinely imposed duty to do both."[7] If, according to Trenholm, schools were as important as the church, in many communities they became comparably central to black public life and purpose.

Despite the well-known conflict between Washington and DuBois over industrial versus classical education for black children, they and the multitudes of other educators had a common investment in expanding educational access for black children. The existence of schools with adequate facilities couldn't be depended upon, notwithstanding how hard black people had struggled for public education in the South. As Theresa Perry observes, the conditions under which black students learned and teachers worked in the early twentieth century were dire: "The black schools were uniformly inferior, many of the rural school buildings being small, box-like structures with leaky roofs, broken windowpanes, few, more often no washing facilities, unplastered or unpainted walls, and cracked floors through which insects and rodents could enter at will."[8]

Nevertheless, the educators diligently pursued their self-proclaimed duty to provide excellent education for black children. But given the plantation economy, the resources at the disposal of the black community to build schools were limited. Philanthropy provided one solution. The John F. Slater Fund for the Education of Freedmen was established in 1882.[9] It substantially funded, among other institutions, Tuskegee University, Hampton University, Fisk University, Spelman College, and Claflin University. While their financial support was critical, the ideological constraints of Slater funds frustrated black people. Slater funds were supposed to be reserved for industrial education, to create good workers rather than independent thinkers. As in most instances, this pressure was circumvented by black educators, who always had more expansive imaginations for black children than their donors.

In 1895, Clinton Calloway, a native of Cleveland, Tennessee, joined the faculty of the Extension Department at Tuskegee. The Extension Department largely trained older rural students in rudimentary literacy and math skills as well as vocational education. Calloway noticed in his work that Alabama's black belt, in general, was in dire need of better elementary and high schools. He approached Booker T. Washington and suggested seeking funding for school development from Anna T. Jeanes and Julius Rosenwald. They were wealthy white Americans who had relatively liberal leanings on racial issues. Rosenwald ultimately agreed to invest in the development of schools for black children, first in Alabama in 1913 and 1914, under the condition that local people match the funds donated. Extension school students were key to this project. They contributed all they had—labor, wood, and time—to build schools for the black youth of rural Alabama.[10] The Rosenwald school program spread throughout the South in the 1920s. Local communities and the Rosenwald Fund together built almost 5,000 schools and 217 teachers homes in fifteen states from Maryland to Texas. Black communities in the agricultural South, still largely dependent on sharecropping, raised more than $4.7 million in this process.[11] Southern black schoolhouses transformed from dilapidated, one-room buildings to modest, well-made frame structures.

As historian James Anderson revealed in his groundbreaking work *The Education of Blacks in the South,* black Americans were engaged in a practice of double taxation as they built schools. DuBois described this process in 1911: "The Negroes are helping to pay for the education of the white children while the states are depriving the Negro children of their just share of school facilities." Black communities then taxed themselves again, either through fundraising or doing work in-kind to build Rosenwald schools or to support privately held schools. Dubois called these "heroic efforts to remedy these evils thru a wide-spread system of private self-supported schools and philanthropy . . . furnishing a helpful but incomplete system of industrial, normal and collegiate training for children of the black race."[12]

It is important to note that these efforts to build schools preceded Rosenwald's initiative. In 1911 the Negro Baptists of Texas reported more than $17,000 raised for their schools, and the secretary of education for the African Methodist Episcopal (AME) Church reported that black people had raised $32,600 for their schools.[13] Because the aspirations for schools preceded Rosenwald's input it is unsurprising that they also exceeded philanthropists' expectations of what the schools would be. As with the Slater Fund, the Rosenwald Fund was intended to support industrial education. But the efforts it helped finance became much more than that under the leadership of black educators.

The contributions of the Rosenwald Fund, combined with the labor and contributions of black communities, greatly increased the number of schools available to black children, though they failed to match the accessibility of public education that was available to white children. The buildings that were built, however, were designed with an understanding that black schools often served as community centers. Samuel L. Smith, formerly Tennessee's "Negro school agent," became the director of the Rosenwald Fund's Southern Office in Nashville in 1920. Following the lead set by architecture professors at Tuskegee, who had designed the first Rosenwald schools, Smith determined that "the best modern school is one which is designed to serve the entire community for twelve months in the year. . . . Whenever possible a good auditorium, large enough to seat the entire community, should be erected in connection with every community school. If there are not sufficient funds for an auditorium, two adjoining classrooms with movable partitions may be made to serve this purpose."[14] Furthermore, he recommended that buildings be built on at least a two-acre site and located near a corner of the property. That positioning would leave room for outhouses, a teacher's home, a play area, and some landscaping.

Other philanthropic supporters aided the committed labor of black community members seeking to build schools. William J. Edwards, founder of the Snow Hill Institute in Wilcox County, Alabama, and an alumnus of Tuskegee Institute, spoke at a meeting in Philadelphia at the behest of Booker T. Washington in the fall of 1902. While there, one of the Tuskegee trustees gave Edwards a letter of introduction to Anna Jeanes, a wealthy Quaker he thought might consider donating to the Snow Hill Institute. Edwards "described the condition of the public schools in the rural district. She gave keen interest to this part of the story."[15] Soon thereafter, Jeanes began giving Edwards money annually to support his school, in increments of $200 to $600. In 1906, when Booker T. Washington came to visit, she donated $11,000 to him and another $11,000 to Hollis Burke Frissell, president of Hampton Institute, Washington's alma mater. The following year, Jeanes established the Negro Rural School Fund and endowed it with a million dollars. The first Jeanes teacher was Virginia Estelle Randolph of Henrico County, Virginia.[16] She would serve the county for fifty-nine years as an educator, dramatically representing the commitment and significance of Jeanes teachers. By 1910 there were 129 Jeanes teachers working in 130 counties across thirteen southern states. By 1931 that number had nearly tripled.[17]

Jeanes teachers served rural communities. Oftentimes, these were places where black inhabitants lived at a subsistence level. Families were subject to demands of seasonal labor, which interrupted schooling for children born to sharecropping families. And Jim Crow was harshest. Jeanes teachers frequently taught all grades and ages in a single room, warmed by a single potbellied stove at the front of the room.[18] The age range was so great, in part, because even those who had missed most of their schooling due to work often tried to continue going to school past the age of eighteen, even if they were only skilled at a first- or second-grade level. In addition to academics, Jeanes teachers were often health and financial educators who worked on behalf of the entire community, their mantra being "doing the next needed thing."[19] They maintained a communication network across relative remote locations by means of the *National Jeanes Journal*. There, the educators reported on curricula, events, successes, and challenges in their local schools.[20] In Copiah County, Mississippi, Jeanes teachers held an annual "Achievement Day" that included exhibits from each school, literary contests, music programs, and a keynote address, as well as a basketball game, door prizes, and awards for academic achievement. The community also opened a Saturday school in an effort to make up for time the children lost working in the fields. Parents fundraised with cakewalk competitions, singing programs, and selling dinners. Out of the proceeds they paid the teachers to work on weekends.[21]

At the other end of the spectrum for black schools were superb institutions that provided a liberal elementary education, and others that offered a complete classical high school curriculum that could rival New England preparatory schools. They did so in well-resourced buildings with educators who had attended northern universities. Dunbar High School in Washington, D.C., was the most frequently cited example of a superior segregated school par excellence and the first black public high school in the nation.

Dunbar was originally named the M Street School, before being renamed in honor of Paul Laurence Dunbar, a gesture consistent with the early twentieth-century commonplace of naming black schools after accomplished and renowned black people. Dunbar became a feeder to elite northern colleges including Oberlin, Bates, Brown, Colby, Bowdoin, Amherst, and Harvard. Anna Julia Cooper, the fourth black American woman to receive a PhD (from the Sorbonne) and regarded by many as one of the first black women public intellectuals for her 1892 book *A Voice from the South*, began as a math and science teacher at Dunbar in 1887 and became its principal in 1902. Dunbar educated many of the most accomplished members of the black leadership class during segregation, including the celebrated poet Sterling Brown; leading educator and activist Nannie Helen Burroughs; attorney William H. Hastie; the first African American woman to earn a PhD, Sadie Mossell; and the dean of Howard Law School and architect of the *Brown v. Board of Education* litigation strategy, Charles Hamilton Houston, as well as a host of others. Its faculty at various points included Kelly Miller, Carter G. Woodson, and Mary Church Terrell. Research and curriculum development were key to Dunbar's success. For example, its History Teacher's Club in 1924 compiled a bibliography of black history. It had three working committees for this project: one focused on ancient history, one on medieval and modern history, and one on American history. At the end of the academic year, each committee reported to the group on its findings, thus expanding knowledge to the entire faculty and larger community.[22]

Singing "Lift Every Voice and Sing" was integral to the ethos of the illustrious school. Fannie Douglass, born in 1883, who married the grandson of

Frederick Douglass and whose older sister had attended Atlanta University with James and Rosamond, taught at Dunbar for many decades and brought "Lift Every Voice" to the school. She recalled that "when I went to Atlanta to attend the graduation services of my niece Jessie, they sang the Johnson brothers anthem 'Lift Every Voice and Sing.' When I began teaching in the schools—and I did shortly afterwards—I brought that composition, and I was the first one to introduce it in the Washington schools, and to all of Washington. Now everybody knows it, don't you see?"[23] Her friend Mary Europe, the sister of bandleader James Europe, was a fellow teacher at Dunbar for many years and "had the idea to give the children the very best in music." The curriculum at Dunbar, despite the vocational designation placed upon it by the school board, was in fact a liberal education rich in the visual arts, theater, and music as well as rigorous academic training.[24] The formalism embedded in the song matched the classical education the students at Dunbar received, and the complexity of the composition testified to the "very best" training in music and the arts.

Many historically black colleges also provided access to high school education, as did a number of boarding schools that were also established in the early part of the twentieth century. The tight connection between historically black colleges and universities (HBCUs) and K–12 education was both academic and cultural. HBCU faculty were involved at every stage of the school-building programs, as well as in developing curricula, and were active participants in the teachers associations. The socialization of black students into black formalism that occurred in the primary grades was extended into high schools and colleges.

The Lincoln Institute, a college preparatory high school that would send a significant portion of its graduates to historically black colleges and universities, was founded in Shelby County, Kentucky, in 1908, in response to the U.S. Supreme Court's upholding of the Kentucky Supreme Court's ruling that the integrated Berea College violated the state's segregation statute.[25] Berea educators and board members, as well as activist friends of the school, did not want to give up the mission of educating black people, and so Lincoln emerged in the aftermath of that devastating decision. Lincoln Institute was initially conceived of as both a high school and a junior college, but it eventually became solely a high school. Founders, however, were forced to make it a boarding school rather than a day school in large part because white landowners in Shelby County objected to the idea of a local high school that would potentially draw more black residents to the area.[26] Dunbar had certainly driven migration to Washington, D.C., and the Lincoln Institute might have done the same.[27]

But despite being kept from residing in large numbers in Shelby County, black Kentuckians nevertheless figured out how to run a superior black high school there. Lincoln Institute, like Dunbar, would train many students who went on to distinguished careers. Two of its alums, Whitney Young Jr. (whose father was the head of the school) and Horace Mann Bond (whose son Julian Bond would go on to become a leader in the civil rights movement), rose to public acclaim. Whitney Young Jr. became the executive director of the NAACP, and Bond served as president of both Fort Valley State University and Lincoln University, and as a member of the faculty at Fisk, Atlanta University, and Dillard. He also, notably, produced scholarship that sharply refuted the widespread mythology that African Americans possessed lower intelligence, work that undoubtedly was shaped by his formative experiences at excellent black institutions throughout the South.

In all of these varied types of schools in the segregated South, the students learned to sing "Lift Every Voice and Sing." Frequently it was a daily practice, but at some schools it was reserved for weekly assemblies. It was almost always a part of graduation. In North Carolina, for example, "at a typical Rosenwald elementary graduation . . . everyone sang 'Lift Every Voice and Sing.'"[28] The girls wore white dresses and the boys wore dark suits, each decorated with a carnation bouquet or boutonniere made of colored tissue paper. The programs would include a prayer and a scripture reading, as well as poetry and recitation. Both the valedictorian and salutatorian would deliver speeches to inspire their classmates in their future endeavors.

At the Beulah Rucker Oliver School in Gainesville, Georgia, founded in 1914, students started the day with devotions and "Lift Every Voice and Sing." The song was enmeshed in a curriculum that celebrated black culture and traditions. Students at the Oliver School studied African American history as a regular part of the curriculum, including lessons on Frederick Douglass, Nat Turner's Rebellion, and reading and reciting poetry by Langston Hughes and James Weldon Johnson.[29] The founder and principal, Beulah Oliver, wrote plays based on black history that her students would perform. Oliver, a pathbreaking educator, was the first African American woman in Georgia to receive a Rosenwald grant for her school, and the first woman of any race to establish a school in Gainesville. She had herself fought mightily for access to education. One of eight children born to a sharecropping family, she learned her letters by looking at the newspapers that plastered her family cabin's walls, a common method of insulation. Oliver worked her way through Knox Institute, an industrial school in Georgia, and upon completion of that program raised money to build her school by offering music lessons and making hats in addition to teaching. Reflecting on these efforts, she wrote, "I have had to sacrifice time, both day and night, to light a torch of instruction which I hope will cause the public to see the purpose of this much-needed institution for my race."[30]

While running the school, Oliver also pursued a bachelor's degree by correspondence from Savannah State, and finally completed it in 1944. Although her own education had been limited by the industrial education model, Oliver provided rigorous academic and religious training for her students in addition to a demanding schedule that included tending to livestock, pumping well water, maintaining property, and selling handmade rugs to raise funds for the school. While numerous black teachers went to northern universities to study in the early twentieth century, often paid for by their state governments according to the "separate but equal" rules of the *Plessy v. Ferguson* Supreme Court decision that the NAACP was steadily forcing states to comply with. But even someone like Rucker who didn't have access to the cutting-edge pedagogy that could much more readily be accessed up north, or to the elite black universities of the South, figured out how to provide an exceptional and culturally rich education to her students.

"Lift Every Voice and Sing" was a piece of this. It was a dimension of how black formalism existed within segregated schools of even the most bare and rugged sort. Noted twentieth-century blues and jazz critic Albert Murray, who grew up in coastal Alabama and matriculated at Tuskegee, eloquently captured this role of "Lift Every Voice," and the zeitgeist of black life that it represented, in his classic memoir *South to a Very Old Place* (1971):

> You remember how during your days at Mobile County Training
> School the rotogravure sepia images of DuBois in his satanic goatee,
> Booker T. Washington (close-cropped, beardless, full lipped and with-
> out mustache), Frederick Douglass (coin-perfect in his lion's mane),
> Harriet Tubman in her glorious bandanna . . . and all of the rest of them
> used to blend together in a sepia bronze panorama when the student
> body used to stand and sing "Lift Every Voice and Sing," . . . which
> everybody used to call the Negro National Anthem—but which for you
> was first of all the Brown American school bell anthem (the comb your
> hair, brush your teeth, shine your shoes, crease your trousers, tie your

tie, clean your nails rub a dub stand and sit and look straight make folks proud anthem). So far as you are concerned, not even Martin Luther King . . . could inspire his most eager followers to put as much aspiration and determination into "We Shall Overcome" as people always used to get into James Weldon and J. Rosamond Johnson's school bell song.[31]

In a paragraph, Murray encapsulates the formalism of grooming, attire, and comportment, as well as the aspiration and ritual attached to coming of age and being of school age in the segregated South.

Murray's alma mater had been established as the first county training school in Alabama in 1880. County training schools were rural institutions sponsored by the Slater and Jeanes Funds, which required a manual- and industrial-educational model. James D. Anderson describes how black teachers and community members efforts to evade the academic constraints of the county training school model were diligently policed by philanthropists, who sought only to train black people to be workers, not intellectuals or full participants in the political and social world of the nation.[32] Murray's recollection reveals, however, that teachers nevertheless found ways to give students a broader sense of themselves and their potential through curricula and through ritual singing of the Negro National Anthem.

The distinguished jazz trumpeter Dizzy Gillespie also fondly recalled the role of the anthem in his education. Dizzy, whom Murray described as "an irrepressible showman and prankster, belong[ing] in the triumvirate of trumpet definitive style setters with Armstrong and Miles Davis,"[33] was born and raised in rural Cheraw, South Carolina, just south of the North Carolina border and 150 miles inland. Cotton fields, in Gillespie's day, covered more than 75 percent of the landscape and the vast majority of the 1,300 black residents, Dizzy included, picked cotton for a living. Teachers were the only black public employees. Firefighting, police, and road maintenance were "whites only" jobs. A mere ten teachers worked at the one school that served black children. The town spent ten dollars a year on educating each black child and forty dollars on each white one.[34] Dizzy fondly remembered his school, named Robert Smalls, after an enslaved man who commandeered a Confederate ship during the Civil War, delivering seventeen of his fellow enslaved people to freedom and later serving five terms as a member of Congress as well as a persistent advocate for black citizenship. Gillespie described the humble building named after this heroic figure as "a quaintly pretty little school [with] one little wooden building on the side of Front Street that housed the primer grades and a larger brick building that housed the first through ninth grades. This little wooden building on the side had only one story. After you stepped off the sidewalk onto the school grounds, you'd go up those little brick stairs and right there in front, every morning, we'd have our assembly. We'd have to stand at attention and sing 'Lift Every Voice and Sing, til earth and heaven ring.'"[35]

This daily habit was obviously influential to the future musician, as he recalled it so tenderly in his memoir. But it is also worth noting that musicianship generally was a part of school practice in the segregated South. Surveying early curricula, it becomes clear that sight reading of music and music theory were common courses in black schools. Additionally, music education outside of school was a frequent expenditure. This necessarily meant it was highly valued given how strapped most black communities were economically. Dizzy's childhood friend from Cheraw, John Motley, recalled, "We couldn't vote, we couldn't use the library. And they drummed into us that menial labor was our lot. All we had was school, the church and music. And our black public school didn't really meet our needs because it ended in the ninth grade; the white schools went on through the twelfth. So it was church and music."[36]

The educator and native Mississippian Mildred Hudson similarly learned "Lift Every Voice" in the context of the rural segregated southern community and ascribed deep spiritual meaning to the school bell song.

We sang it in our small wooden church and at the beginning of each school day. Surrounded by thick willows, pecan trees, oaks and pines, we crawled under our one-room schoolhouse and sang the song during recess. At home, my mother, Willie Ester Wright Hudson, born in 1912, would sing "Lift Every Voice" as she went about her daily chores. She would lift her proud brown chin and strike the perfect note as she reinforced what had by then become our family's dream: "Let us march on til victory is won." We desperately needed that song. I grew up in a segregated black world of rich soil, pungent gospel flavor and swinging in the rhythm of the blues. But it was also a world where the KKK ruled and black men often found themselves facing death with a noose around their necks.

The contrast between "a generous and loving black community but also a world teeming with white supremacists, white sheets, and red-faced white men with rancor dripping from their hearts"in Johnson's life was in fact captured in the words to the song,[37] which spoke of endurance, striving, and ascent notwithstanding the devastation of a racist society. Recollecting the horror of Emmett Till's murder Hudson added, "As a child, of course, I did not have many ways to analyze national issues or ask the right questions, but singing the right songs helped."[38]

Guided group singing of "Lift Every Voice and Sing" was a means of socializing black children. It gave them a way of understanding the world and finding self-worth despite its meanness. It also could provide a pathway toward forging identity. Evelio Grillo, who migrated to Florida in the 1920s from Cuba, described his experience at Booker T. Washington High School:

> The faculty at Booker T. Washington High fully confirmed our identity as black youth. . . . One vehicle that our teachers used to inculcate a sense of history and a determination to make things better was the "Devotions" period held every day at 15 minutes before noon. One teacher or the other would give an inspirational talk or read a great passage urging us to strive to do our best. Sometimes the program would open with the singing of a spiritual or of a patriotic song like "America the Beautiful." Always we closed with a rousing rendition of "Lift Every Voice and Sing." The characters and personalities of our great committed teachers led us to develop comfort with our identity as black Americans. They placed the mission ever before us: nothing less than freedom and equality. In our daily contacts with them they made us feel as co-conspirators in the struggle to bring the walls of racial injustice and discrimination down.[39]

The immanence of daily singing developed into an intimately held knowledge. Not simply of history, but also resilience and resistance. It, along with a host of complementary ritual practices, created young people who were able to recast and ultimately transform this nation and world.

While Evelio learned to become a black American through these ritual practices, black American children also learned to see themselves as part of a global community like their parents. In the 1920s children's branches of the NAACP learned African songs, performed plays about historic figures such as Crispus Attucks and the Haitian independence leader Toussaint-Louverture, created scrapbooks of black achievement with clippings from newspapers, and learned to sing "Lift Every Voice and Sing." The September 1921 edition of the *Crisis* includes a discussion of the Dyer Antilynching

Bill that was being introduced in Congress (it passed the House but failed in the Senate in 1924), an argument for Pan-Africanism, and a report that "one hundred leaders of the Student Young Men's Christian Association, at their annual summer conference at Gibsland, Ia, announced that they will introduce into their schools and colleges 'Lift Every Voice and Sing,' the national Negro hymn." This context was appropriate, as the hymn was always embedded in a sense of a larger black world. The educational function of the song extended out of formal classrooms to the educational mission of churches and other civic institutions to instruct children about the vast world to which they belonged.

And for some, their communities themselves were international in composition. When Nannie Helen Burroughs Training School for Women in Washington, D.C., held its fifteenth commencement in 1925, it featured student orations and spirituals, and in the standard ritual of black formalism the students and audience sang "Lift Every Voice and Sing" together at the beginning of the program. Distinguished black minister Vernon Johns delivered the commencement address, and prizes were granted to the most accomplished students: The first honor prize, a gold watch, was delivered to Miss Eleathea Stubblefield of Liberia, West Africa. The student orations, also reserved for exceptional students, were titled "We Can Win" by Clara Leticia Walker, also of Liberia, "Domestic Science in Terms of Health and Happiness" by Willa Lee Green of Porter, Oklahoma, and "The World Is Looking for Rowana" by Edna Mae Cook, a local student.[40] This ceremonial program provides an important reminder that black American life throughout the twentieth century included the broader black world, particularly in its educational institutions, which drew students from the Caribbean and Africa, as well as from various parts of the United States. Under the banner of a single song, the imagined community of the black world striving to escape the thumb of colonialism, Jim Crow, and racism, could band together.

The domestic world black Americans inhabited was itself networked and complex. Teachers were fundamental participants in this matrix. Recently, education historians have increasingly argued that the role of black teachers in the road to civil rights has been underestimated. For example, Vanessa Siddle Walker shows, in detailed analyses of records of local chapters of teachers organizations and the NAACP, that educators and the NAACP waged parallel, interdependent, and overlapping struggles for educational equity, with black educators often important figures in political organizing.[41] Moreover, as Theresa Perry notes, the role prominent black thinkers and organizers such as W. E. B. DuBois and James Weldon Johnson played in the development of black children in the early twentieth century has been neglected. Teaching was understood as not just a job but also a calling. It was also one of the few professions available to college-educated black people, and as a result many of them built careers serving black youth. They pursued their work not simply as training but also as a social justice movement. In addition to the active connections between the local and national teachers organization, women's clubs, as well as the national Congress of Colored Parents and Teachers (i.e., the national black PTA), worked closely with teachers (quite unlike the mainstream national PTA, which was often in conflict with educators).[42] These were collective and communitarian labors.

The proceedings of the Kentucky Negro Educational Association's annual meetings offer a glimpse into how communities were forged to do this collective work. In 1926, for example, the association assembled at Quinn Chapel in Louisville for its fiftieth annual session.[43] In attendance there were teachers, school librarians, and members of the state parent teacher association. As part of the first evening's program, sociologist E. Franklin Frazier gave a lecture titled "Contribution of Social Service Work to the Education of the Negro in the South," and Charlotte Hawkins Brown delivered an address titled "What to Teach Negro Americans." As with most annual meetings, it included presentations from educators and leaders from rural as well as urban schools, from both the elite and the underfunded. Evening activities included a storytelling competition and a *Pageant of Progress* about the history of black education in Kentucky that was attended by over 5,000 people. Later conventions often overlapped with those of the Youth Council of the Kentucky Negro Educational Association, creating a truly multigenerational gathering.

The 1936 edition of the *Kentucky Negro Educational Association Bulletin* featured a recommended "School Improvement Day" program. The model "improvement day" consisted of group singing of "America the Beautiful" and "The Battle Hymn of the Republic," along with prayers and presentations offered by children and adults on school beautification, the state of black schools, historical figures, and poetry. The conclusion of the day was singing "Lift Every Voice and Sing." In each instance, when the Negro National Anthem was partnered with patriotic songs and often spirituals, children learned a form of what DuBois would term "double consciousness" that they were both American and black. They were taught to lay claim to American identity notwithstanding segregation and also to cultivate racial pride and a sense of their membership "behind the veil," as something meaningful and worthy of celebration. The children were also being taught responsibility to their community.

This sense of responsibility and interdependence was part of the purposes of the school beautification program which the journal delineated, stating that the goal was: "To bring the people of the community together at the school house for the purpose of getting better acquainted with each other and to get better acquainted with the school and its needs. . . . To review some of the things being done in the field of Negro Education in Kentucky. . . . To pay homage to the men and women who have given their lives and means that all children might have an elementary education—rural, village and city children alike."[44] And to this end, the article stated, particular appreciation was due Booker T. Washington, and his work with the Jeanes and Rosenwald Funds.

In addition to regular meetings the *Kentucky Negro Educational Association Bulletin* was published every four months and included educational news and notes. When they gathered, these educators, parents, librarians, and youth sang "Lift Every Voice and Sing." The ritual was palimpsestic. Their sense of being bound together across the diversity of black experiences in the nation is apparent. They thought of themselves in sophisticated terms and went back to their communities and shared that sensibility with their pupils. They also enlisted children in the practice of building community. Everyone worked to deliberate around the challenges of all types of education. That they sang "Lift Every Voice" at these meetings further deepened the connections. Their singing was a mirror to the charge they undertook not merely to teach the song to children, but to vest it with deep meaning. The ritual singing of "Lift Every Voice" was a training in the development of black formal, civic, and associational culture, a form of teacher training and a form of training the teachers provided their pupils.

For schoolchildren the song stood as an invocation, setting the terms as to how one ought to approach the school day. At graduations and at the conclusion of meetings of professional organizations it also could serve as a benediction. That black formal culture often took on a liturgical structure makes sense given how central church was to black life. But it also indicates that there was a ritual devotion to the art of discipline and achievement in the face of Jim Crow. Mattye Tollette Bond, an educator born in 1895, recalled learning the words to "Lift Every Voice and Sing" at eleven years old. Upon entering Lane College in Tennessee to complete high school, it became a regular ritual in her life: "At our assemblies we all sang 'Lift Every Voice and Sing' and I was proud to show that I knew every word. We continued to sing 'Lift Every Voice and Sing' through normal school and college. I married, became a teacher, and taught the words of 'Lift Every Voice and Sing' to my students. They also proudly sang the Johnsons' song in our assemblies."[45]

One benefit of segregation was that it removed black teachers from the direct oversight of white elites. This enabled students to sing an alternative anthem that was explicitly black. Educators in both public and private schools had greater leeway to develop curricula that spoke directly to the experiences and identities of their students. Teachers sometimes hid pedagogical materials when white philanthropists or school board members came to visit, but during regular school days most children had access to more schooling than the vocational education that the powers-that-be believed was appropriate for them, and to schooling that spoke to their identities as well. Moreover, teachers could instruct the children in ways that deliberately resisted the racial caste system of the society. William Gray, past president of the United Negro College Fund, remembers "Lift Every Voice" as part of this resistance: "One of the few benefits of growing up in the South was that each day in school, we slowly and majestically sang this melodious anthem that was created by one of our poets—a song that promises us that if we keep struggling, we will see the light of freedom because of our faith."[46]

While "Lift Every Voice" does sometimes appear in northern and midwestern school programs in the early twentieth century, it was far more common in the South. Martha Smith, who grew up in Willard, Ohio, recalled that "I never heard the song until, as a college student in the 1950s, I journeyed to Talladega College in Alabama. Southern-born blacks probably heard this song from babyhood."[47] And a 1940s migrant from Jackson, Mississippi, to Kansas further captured the particularly southern practice associated with this song: "My mother attended all-black schools—black students, teachers, administrators. Every morning, after pledging allegiance to the flag . . . teachers and students sang the black national anthem 'Lift Every Voice and Sing.'" Years later, when she attended a Martin Luther King rally at which the audience was invited to sing it, she was "surprised and embarrassed to find that few northern blacks knew the song."[48]

Likewise, activist-scholar Herb Boyd remembered a boy who migrated from Georgia to his Detroit neighborhood in 1951. The Detroit kids made fun of the migrant's drawl and gold tooth: "He was the butt of our jokes, until one day he told us stories about Booker T. Washington and George Washington Carver. We thought we were pretty smart but none of us had ever heard of these great men. . . . But Willie wasn't through. We were sitting around one afternoon, reciting poetry, mostly playing the dozens, when Willie stunned us with a recitation of 'Lift Every Voice and Sing.' Again he had our attention, and even more so when he sang it. Without knowing it, Willie had given me my first lesson in black studies."[49] Boyd shows that black southern teachers were giving kids "black studies" long before that designation was embraced. And the anthem was an encapsulation of all those lessons. Boyd's recollection also speaks to the manner in which the complete immersion within community that southern segregation created allowed for "a world within a world" (fragile though it was in the face of racial violence and domination). In this world, a people the nation reviled could cherish themselves and share bodies of knowledge. Although northern cities were often de facto segregated, the absence of a structure in which two distinct systems of social organization existed made such a "world within a world" more elusive and perhaps even seemingly less desirable for residents. The possibility of accessing the larger society held a powerful appeal. And yet northern black Americans, mostly though not entirely migrants from the South, sustained "Lift Every Voice and Sing" in their own ways.

Without segregated black schools—and their entire infrastructure from principals to superintendents, athletic directors, and teachers associations— northern black children's access to both "Lift Every Voice and Sing" and the broader cultural practice of black formalism was different. It was less likely to be a daily or weekly routine, and more often associated with "bigger" ritual occasions like Emancipation Day services, Negro History Week programs, or the gatherings of civic associations. For those who had access to higher education, attending historically black colleges was another space in which they would experience singing "Lift Every Voice and Sing" ritually. While certainly cherished in the North, in some ways the relatively modest world of the song there in the early to mid-twentieth century portended its future diminishment all over the nation in the late twentieth and early twenty-first century.

However, in the early to mid-twentieth-century northern cities, church became the place where northern black youth were most likely to learn the song. Novelist Charles Johnson recalls that he was eight years old in Evanston, Illinois, when he was first introduced to it: "I asked my mother what this particular song was about. 'Just listen,' she said gently elbowing me into silence as the choir sang. . . . 'This,' she informed me, 'is the Negro National Anthem.' This, her tone said, is important. . . . My mother was saying that it was necessary for me to understand this poem if I wanted to grasp something essential about her, my father—and myself."[50] In any instance it was a song of community, of black formalism, and of dignity in identity.

Though he spent the bulk of his twentieth-century career as a full-time musician and composer, Rosamond returned to his early work as an educator when he served as the director of the New York Music School Settlement for Colored Children from 1914 to 1919. Settlement schools were common in the North, but they usually excluded black children. In the North, like the South, even when schools weren't segregated black adults often had to organize alternative sites in order to provide opportunities for their children that were otherwise denied. And black intellectuals and artists of all sorts were enlisted in these efforts, irrespective of how distinguished they were. The attention to the development of black children was embraced across the board, and though Rosamond spent less time as an educator than James, teaching was an essential part of his legacy. Rosamond and James together published work that was used by educators and civic associations to teach black history and culture. *The Book of American Negro Spirituals* (1925) and *The Second Book of Negro Spirituals* (1926) were compiled by the brothers together. Rosamond independently edited *Shoutsongs* (1936) and the folk-song anthology *Rolling Along in Song* (1937) and James edited *The Book of American Negro Poetry* (1938).

One dimension of black associational life was the development of out-of-school learning communities organized by groups of civic-minded adults. The development of a learned print culture for a black public aided these educators, who did their instruction outside of schools as well. The Anna T. Strickland Art Club in Fort Smith, Arkansas, for example, frequently held programs in the late 1920s and early 1930s that combined recitation, speeches, readings, and collective singing of the anthem. Colored Elks Clubs, a network of fraternal mutual aid societies that cropped up across the nation in the early years of the twentieth century, offered college scholarships and held oratorical contests for high school students. Formalism even infused gatherings that were mostly just occasions to have fun. The Baptist Sunday School of Falls Church, Virginia, held its annual picnic at Western View Farm in August 1921. The majority of the pupils motored up in a truck, while others went with their parents and in hay wagons. An illustrated lecture on "Keeping Fit" was given to the boys in the afternoon. Games were indulged in and plenty of ice cream was served free. As a closing feature, all the children gathered in the large outbuilding where a piano was situated and sang the Negro National Anthem, "Lift Every Voice and Sing."[51]

Hence, when Carter G. Woodson, founder of the Association for the Study of Negro Life and History (ASNLH), created Negro History Week in 1926, he institutionalized practices that black educators and intellectuals had engaged in for at least two decades. Teachers and community educators who had culled newspapers and searched for books by black authors and on black experience (and even those who had written them) found in Woodson a person who would streamline instruction in black history and expand the production of literature for black children. DuBois, in retrospect, asserted that Woodson's establishment of Negro History Week was perhaps the single greatest accomplishment of the 1920s renaissance.[52] Woodson's work was influenced by Marcus Garvey's vociferous celebration of all things black, and it extended the work of the black press, especially that of the *Crisis* and *Opportunity*, as well as the work of educators of previous decades. With his initiative, the pattern of naming black schools after black historical figures like Frederick Douglass, Paul Laurence Dunbar, and Toussaint-Louverture was scaffolded by the creation of documents that filled in their stories. As was the case in preceding intellectual and educational work, Black History Week programs articulated identities that were both American and much larger. By "1929 the association was offering for sale reproductions of 160 photos of significant blacks. . . . [Woodson] also produced specialized pamphlets that included bibliographies on various aspects of Negro history and prepared a table of 152 important events and dates in Negro History which sold for 50 cents by the early 1930s."[53] Negro History Week programs included parades with participants dressed as historically significant figures. Negro History Week breakfasts and banquets featured lectures on black history and the recitation of black poetry. Black civic institutions also hosted special exhibitions and presentations during that special week each February.[54]

While Negro History Week was a special time, Woodson's *Negro History Bulletin* served as a resource for daily pedagogical endeavors and general intellectual interest in black life all year round. According to Pero Gaglo Dagbovie, "The *Bulletin* . . . had many functions. Written in a simple language to help black teachers who had little or no knowledge about black history it supplemented "whitestream" American history textbooks of the time and was the vehicle by which schoolteachers and other concerned citizens helped Woodson take black history into the homes of the black masses. . . . It also served as a platform for blacks, from elementary schoolchildren to community activists to schoolteachers to professional scholars, to openly discuss and even publish their thoughts about black history."[55] The *Bulletin* was the more accessible and livelier companion to Woodson's more scholarly publication, the *Journal of Negro History*. Nevertheless, it was serious and well-researched.

In addition to the *Bulletin,* the ASNLH produced Negro History Week kits that were available by mail order and published juvenile and adult literature to facilitate instruction in black history. One example of a children's book Woodson wrote and published was *African Heroes and Heroines*. He dedicated the book to his Uncle George "who in captivity in America manifested the African spirit of resistance to slavery and died fighting the institution." The book includes chapters on the Ashanti and Dahomey, the conflict in South Africa, East Africa, and one on "the evils against which Africans fight," a reference to colonialism, along with other essays on African history and culture.

Woodson was not alone in his endeavors to give children access to a complex black world. For example, in 1932 Langston Hughes and Arna Bontemps collaborated on the children's book *Popo and Fifina*, about two Haitian children who moved from the countryside to a home by the sea. And in 1934 Bontemps published *You Can't Pet a Possum*, about a boy in rural Alabama. Woodson was also not the only scholar working to develop a black historical archive. Arturo Schomburg, a Cruzan-German, Puerto Rican–born immigrant, and Marylander John Edward Bruce together founded the Negro Society for Historical Research in 1911. It became the largest archive of African diasporic holdings in the country and is held at what is now called the Schomburg Center for Research in Black Culture. Woodson, however, distinguished his work with his efforts to institutionalize knowledge, and as such he is often considered the founder or at least the foundation of black studies. Literary scholar Houston Baker revised this common formulation by arguing that Woodson *alongside* the work that classroom teachers did in segregated schools created black studies. Further, teachers made black studies an exercise that was meaningful both politically and intellectually:

> Academically, black studies may be seen as an empiricist outgrowth of the Negro History movement. I mean this only in the sense that

the word "study" marks a particular public space in Negro schooling. Whether most of us knew his name or not, Carter G. Woodson was the man we were honoring in those meagerly resourced but nevertheless committed Negro History weeks of our youths. In Louisville—at Virginia Avenue Elementary School—we saw the blackboard décor from last year come out again, and we recited the mantra of Negro contributions to America: from George Washington Carver's peanuts to Ralph Bunche's Nobel Prize. Ms. Carter, an aristocratic avatar of nineteenth century Negro Club Women, handled her pitch pipe as though it were the lyre of Orpheus. She led us through the Negro National Anthem, transporting us from the dark blight of what she assumed were our home lives to the light of proud Negro achievement. "Children," she would intone, "you must never be ashamed of being Negroes!" She instructed us that "Dr. Woodson wants us to be proud of our history."[56]

In Baker's estimation the song, under the direction of teachers, served not only to teach history but also to develop racial pride in students, a pride that contradicted a world that would diminish them.

For the 1929 celebration of Negro History Week at the Haines Normal and Industrial Institute in Augusta, Georgia, the seniors decorated the chapel with pennants of black colleges: Atlanta University, Lincoln, Howard, Paine College, Morehouse College, and Walker Baptist. Haines was a private day school founded in 1883, and by 1929 it served over 900 students. The Monday program featured the first-year class presenting on black pioneers, with particular focus on the black sailors who accompanied Christopher Columbus and on black explorer Matthew Henson. On Tuesday, the second-year class spoke about the "Negro in Business," with a focus on black-owned insurance companies. On Wednesday, the juniors delivered a program on literature and art in which they discussed Rosamond Johnson, Henry Ossawa Tanner, Meta Warrick, and Samuel Coleridge Taylor. The Thursday program on black education was presented by the seniors and focused on their founder, Lucy Laney, as well as Charlotte Hawkins Brown and Mary McLeod Bethune.[57] The Haines Institute was a cultural center of sorts and therefore this event was likely enjoyed by the entire community and not just the pupils. Concerts, public lectures by nationally renowned speakers, and a variety of social events were held there. Lucy Laney, its founder, was a member of the active and well-connected black intelligentsia of the early twentieth century.

She was also a founding member of the local chapter of the NAACP and was active in both the NACW and the YMCA and YWCA. Laney had founded both the first black kindergarten in Augusta and the first nursing program for black women in Augusta, in addition to building her own school.

The seniors who focused their Negro History Week program on education chose not simply three prominent black women but women who were deeply connected to each other through the networks of black politics, civic culture, and education. Mary McLeod Bethune had taught at Haines Institute before starting her own school. She had learned under the tutelage of Lucy Laney and adopted Laney's philosophy about the importance of educating girls for the betterment of the entire community. She recalled that she "was so impressed with [Laney's] fearlessness, her amazing touch in every respect, an energy that seemed inexhaustible and her mighty power to command respect and admiration from her students and all who knew her. She handled her domain with the art of a master." Bethune, who rose to great heights as the first female president of the NATCS, the president and founder of the National Council of Negro Women, and one of the only black advisers to the Roosevelt administration, ventured out from under the wing of Laney to build her own school in 1904. She rented a house for eleven dollars a month. The student benches and desks were fashioned from discarded crates. Teachers and parents raised funds for the school by selling fried fish plates, sweet potato pies, and ice cream. Theologian and political leader Howard Thurman described the pride the entire black community of Daytona took in Bethune's school:

> As a boy growing up in Daytona, I was of course familiar with how Mary McLeod Bethune started her school and I knew the mission she was fulfilling. . . . In that first decade of the century, Mrs. Bethune provided a unique leadership, involved in all the problems of Negro life in town, and at times she was the spokesperson on behalf of the entire Negro community. We attended commencement services at the school whenever Mamma would take us. They inspired me, even though it was a girls school . . . the very presence of the school, and the inner strength and authority of Mrs. Bethune gave boys like me a view of possibilities to be realized in some distance future.[58]

Charlotte Hawkins Brown was also a mentee of Laney's. Born in Henderson, North Carolina, she was reared in Cambridge, Massachusetts, where she met Alice Freeman Palmer, the second president of Wellesley College, who became a benefactor and assisted Brown in her pursuit of higher education. Brown recalled "the face of the black woman, Lucy Laney, thrown upon the canvas one night in a Cambridge church and a white man's description of her achievement in spite of her color determined my career as an educator and builder."[59] Brown, like Bethune, studied Laney's methods for a year. In 1905, when Brown opened her school, she named it after Palmer but built it in the tradition of Laney. The Palmer Memorial Institute became a distinguished college preparatory school program learned from her mentor. "Lift Every Voice and Sing" was its official school song, a mark of excellence and unapologetic blackness.

These three educators, connected to each other as members of the NACW's southern branch, as members of the NATCS, and as people who had worked together and who shared educational missions, reveal the layered richness and mutual as well as community and institutional benefits of black associational life. Their examples also signify something that has probably already occurred to readers. Although the composers were men, the leaders and educators who imparted the anthem, and the formal culture in which it sat, were mostly women. This point is particularly important given how, as future chapters will explore, black formalism provided the foundation for the freedom movement of the mid-twentieth century. It was the foundation of the struggle. The seniors at Haines Normal Institute understood the foundation their growth relied upon, forged by three distinguished black women educators, and in turn celebrated it with their community, references to their history, and by repeatedly singing the Negro National Anthem over the course of Negro History Week in 1929. Indeed, the song almost functioned as a foundation out of which stories of individual greatness, woven together in the fabric of community, might emerge as both distinct and part of the whole in which everyone could take pride.

There are a plethora of such stories of intertwined missions and legacies, and of excellent segregated black schools. Atlanta University, long considered the premier black institution of classical education in Georgia, ran a laboratory school in the 1930s and early 1940s. Other black colleges ran laboratory schools in this period as well, including Virginia State University, Alabama State University, and Tuskegee Institute and Talladega College, also both in Alabama. Among the pupils of the Atlanta Laboratory School were Martin Luther King Jr. and his sister Christine. Consistent with the principles of the laboratory school movement founded by John Dewey at the University of Chicago, "the curricula consisted of a unified and social problems core (with, seemingly, no preplanned structure core in the upper levels). No grades were assigned as the staff incorporated narrative assessments. With a staff of 11 teachers for a 200-student enrollment in grades 7–12, the Lab School was a true experimental school site."[60]

Elizabeth Garlington, who also attended the Atlanta Laboratory School, recalls that in the 1920s, "before this magnificent song, we sang songs like 'John Brown's Body' or "The Battle Hymn of the Republic.' These were abolitionist songs. But "Lift Every Voice and Sing' was by a black person. It was written out of the experiences and hardships of black people and it's a beautiful song because it raises our hopes and dreams."[61]

Ironically, the author of the poetic rendering of "John Brown's Body" (as opposed to the popular nineteenth-century song), Stephen Vincent Benét, called for a "black-skinned epic" to coexist with his ode, feeling that he hadn't captured the spirit of black people adequately in his own work. Apparently he wasn't aware that one already existed as part of a fabric of community. This isn't altogether surprising, since black civic life was out of view for the vast majority of white Americans.

But that civic life was vibrant. Negro History Week was not simply for students and their families. It provided an opportunity for the entire community to be educated and celebrate. Nettie Asberry, chair of the History Department of the State Federation of Women in Washington, reported in 1930 that in Washington state "Negro History Week was generally observed throughout the state. . . . In Tacoma perhaps the biggest demonstration was made." At the AME church, organized by members of the booklovers club, they began with "Lifting as We Climb," then heard papers on Frederick Douglass, "the Negro in Literature," and "the Negro in History." Interspersed between these papers were spirituals and songs from black composers Harry Burleigh and Samuel Coleridge Taylor. The event concluded with "Lift Every Voice and Sing."[62]

The resources advertised and shared in the *Negro History Bulletin* could be put to direct use in such programs. The October 1, 1938, issue of the *Negro History Bulletin* includes a book review of *The Family* by Evangeline E. Harris, a teacher in the Lincoln School of Terre Haute, Indiana, with illustrations by M. Mikel Williams. Harris's book includes fictional stories and accounts of the lives of Booker T. Washington and Paul Laurence Dunbar, and it concludes with "Lift Every Voice and Sing." The review is partially critical, observing that the book should be larger and more detailed, but it recognizes that *The Family* is nevertheless "skillful."[63]

The May 1941 issue of the *Bulletin* features a pantomime written by Ruth White Willis, secretary and member of the National Housewives League in Baltimore. She titled her work "Let Our Rejoicings Rise," after a phrase in the anthem. Her pantomime tells the history of the Negro from the dawn of time to the present, much like earlier pageants, but Willis's is written specifically to be performed by schoolchildren. It begins with a character referred to as "Mr. Ages" softly humming "Lift Every Voice and Sing." The first child comments: "How beautiful you sing our new song." The second child says, "But when did you learn our new song? We just learned it today in school for Negro History Week." Mr. Ages responds, "'Tis a new song indeed. But the thought is old, as old as the dawn of civilization." Willis puts in the words of Mr. Ages a statement about the universal aspirations present in the Negro anthem. He refers to it as "our new song" and at the same time acknowledges that it is a timeless work specifically born of black experience.

The pantomime continues:

THIRD CHILD: How can that be? It is the "Negro National Anthem," it has been written only since the freedom of the Negro in the United States.

FOURTH CHILD: How can the thought of the "Negro National Anthem" be as old as civilization or history, when the Negro has no history except that which deals with the period of slavery in the United States?

Mr. Ages disabuses the children of this misconception. He opens the "book of Negro history" in his hands and begins with the story of Ikhnaton (Akhenaton), the founder of monotheism, and asserts that "Egypt is in Africa." After his presentation the second child says, "Think of it. The Negroes a great people—Pharaoh's ruling a vast territory—capturing and enslaving weaker races and giving to the world its first civilization." Then Mr. Ages turns to Ethiopia, Nubia, and Meroe, before discussing Africans landing at Jamestown in 1619, and the black people who served on Spanish expeditions to the New World. He describes great black thinkers of Europe: Alexandre Dumas, Angelo Solimon, and Samuel Coleridge Taylor, before asking the children to reflect on "current Negro people of Achievement": Roland Hayes, Paul Robeson, Marian Anderson, Dorothy Manor, Countee Cullen, Langston Hughes, Richard Wright, George Washington Carver, "and many others who make us 'Lift Every Voice and Sing.'" They conclude the pantomime by singing "Lift Every Voice and Sing."[64]

The task of ensuring that black children understood that slavery was not the sum total of their ancestry was not only an effort at historical accuracy but an attempt to explicitly countervail conceptions of inferiority that threatened to fester in a society in which black people were subjugated at every turn. Harvard professor Martin Kilson recalled that in his segregated Pennsylvania elementary school "there were two black teachers, Mrs. Helen Perry Moore and Mrs. Evelyn Brown Wright. Mrs. Moore, who ran the Penllyn Elementary School, preached a get-up-and-go ethos to black children and used our freedom anthem 'Lift Every Voice and Sing' to communicate this ethos at the school-year opening ceremony, on Armistice Day, on Lincoln's birthday and during Negro History Week."[65] Kilson also remembered singing "Lift Every Voice" at the conclusion of segregated Boy Scout meetings in his community. It was both an in-school and out-of-school educational practice, one that inculcated high self-regard and collective pride as well as a sense of history.

In the November 1, 1948, issue of the *Negro History Bulletin*, the lyrics to "Lift Every Voice" were published with a description of how the anthem ought to be used pedagogically, written by Muriel Wellington, a resident of Boston.

1. Purpose: To acquaint all schoolchildren with the knowledge of the Anthem; and to give Negro children a sense of race pride. To make the hymn a song that all children recognize and know how to sing.
2. Motivation:
   1. Tell the story of James Weldon Johnson
   2. Tell appropriate slave stories in conjunction with stories about contemporary Negro heroes that all children know about.
      Ex. a. Harriet Tubman b. Lena Horne
   3. Play the music for appreciation of rhythm and tune
   4. Show pictures of
      a. Slaves
      b. The Working Negro
      c. The Negro in church
      d. The Negro in business
      e. The Negro on the farm
      f. The Negro at home.[66]

Wellington goes on to suggest that teachers have students study the words and their meanings (e.g., "harmonies" and "rejoicing") in addition to contemplating the repetition of phrases and providing explanation of their meaning. She recommends that pupils dramatize elements of the song, as well as draw and sculpt (out of clay) aspects of its story. At the conclusion of the article she states that by the end of these exercises students should know the song, and moreover that we *all* should know the words clearly: "The Negro Anthem should have a place on all planned programs because of its beauty and because it is representative of our children." Wellington's lesson was what today would be referred to as a thematic curriculum. Through the theme of the song, children would learn about music, social and economic history, and culture.

Longtime clubwoman and civil rights activist Dorothy Height described the pedagogical lesson that was central to how she learned the anthem as a member of the Harlem Christian Youth Council. For Height it was an occasion for meditation and political awakening. "We read it aloud together, then shared our sense of its meaning. Once we sang it, it became our own. We sang the third stanza prayerfully, feeling one another's sense of struggle and hope. To this day, I find it hard to sing just one stanza. The words and melody linger on."[67]

James Weldon Johnson died in a 1938 car accident in Maine after an illustrious career. For the final eight years of his life, he served as the Spence Chair of Creative Literature at Fisk University in Nashville. This endowed chair was created specifically for Johnson, in recognition of his extraordinary accomplishments. In the middle of his tenure there, he taught for a year at New York University, thus serving as its first black professor. As a professor he taught literature, American law, and music. By the time of his death, he had already joined the ranks of black heroic figures students learned about during Negro History Week. After his demise, Augusta Savage immediately set about sculpting a bust of him.

Johnson's widow, Grace, a notoriously persnickety woman, was not pleased with Savage's work. So she purchased it and kept it from public display for decades. James's niece, Rosamond's daughter, Mildred Johnson Edwards, would honor his legacy otherwise, however. She had already followed in her father's and uncle's footsteps as an educator, founding the Modern School in Harlem in 1934 and Summer Camp Dunroven in Pine Bush, New York, in 1933, both intended to primarily serve African American young people. Education was a family tradition, as was the Negro National Anthem.

Mildred recalled, "At the time when I was born, 'Lift Every Voice and Sing' was well into its 'early adolescence.' In our home the song was a living entity—you could say that it was, for me, an older sibling. My parents' friends and colleagues would seldom allow an evening of social activities or en salon to end without my father J. Rosamond Johnson, playing the piano and letting them show off their harmonizing on 'Lift Every Voice and Sing.'"[68]

The Modern School blended the formalism of the black institutional culture of the South (Mildred was born in Jacksonville) with the pedagogical lessons she learned in the teacher training program of the elite, predominantly white Fieldston School in New York. She wrote, "I founded the Modern School, a progressive experiment in secular elementary school education for local youngsters. 'Lift Every Voice and Sing' was used for all official school functions and assembly. It was apparent that the song would be of great help as we strove to foster a sense of heritage and pride for the primarily African American pupils who relied on us for development and support."[69] What the Modern School accomplished in New York, or the Dunbar School in Washington, D.C., or the Haines, Lincoln, and Palmer Institutes down south—that is, provide a superior education rivaling the best in the nation—reflected a widely held aspiration for black families and their children.

Despite the noble efforts to build schools, and the extraordinary achievement in some of them, it was clear by the 1940s that there still simply weren't enough schools for black children. But the momentum for education meant that even when there wasn't enough for black children (food, resources, access, schools), they nevertheless participated in an educationally aspirational community. Congresswoman Maxine Waters recalls how at the James Weldon Johnson Elementary School she attended in St. Louis, "I sang the Negro National Anthem when I was hungry—I sang the Negro National Anthem when my tooth was hurting because of an exposed cavity—I sang the Negro National Anthem when I did not know there was a future for a little black girl with twelve sisters and brothers."[70]

In the 1930s and 1940s, New Deal educational programs and employers' increased interest in hiring high school graduates, combined with a decrease in the number of jobs available to teenagers, led to an ever-increasing number of black youth trying to enroll in high school. However, across the South access to public high school education for black youth was woefully inadequate. Creativity was a requisite for black educators and intellectuals to do their work, and creativity was not limited to traditional education. Many black educators, primarily women of letters, were not teachers but nevertheless spent lives committed to fulfilling the ideals of progressive democratic education promulgated by John Dewey. In 1952, for example, the black community in Durham, North Carolina, celebrated ten years of bookmobile service. The bookmobile service had circulated over 5,000 books and provided service to 1,830 borrowers in fourteen communities in its first ten years. Over the course of its service, two black women librarians, Serena Warren Williams and Ray Nichols Moore, not only provided access to literature but expanded the collection, created annexes, and developed new branch libraries. They also featured art exhibits by black visual artists, established a book review forum, and delivered books to the Negro hospital. Their tenth anniversary program included a presentation by Evelyn Day Mullen, a field librarian, titled "The Library beyond the Walls" and began with a singing of "Lift Every Voice."[71] As evidenced so many other circumstances, the anthem marked the celebration of black achievement of all sorts.

The out-of-school institutions that existed for black children, in particular in the Jim Crow era, are too little known. This is a shame because they were enormously important. They socialized black children into associational life and provided opportunities to learn beyond the formal classroom. This was especially meaningful for children whose parents often worked long hours and had few individual resources to supplement their education. Gertrude Parthenia McBrown, who served as theater director at the Dunbar School in Washington, D.C. in the 1930s, as well as director of the Southeast Children's Theater group, was one of many black women who educated children beyond the school walls. In 1936 she published a beautiful picture poetry book for black children, covering history and ethics and decorated with block print illustrations by the celebrated visual artist Lois Mailou Jones.

By the 1950s McBrown had moved to New York, where she worked as a librarian for the Carter G. Woodson Collection of books on black history for the Queens Central Library and visited New York public schools to lecture about black history. On February 1, 1958, the Negro History Bulletin published one of her plays. Her career serving black children spanned three decades, and in this final published play the reader can see her deep commitment to giving black children a strong identity through both study and play. The first scene is described as taking place in a classroom with books on tables and shelves, and the walls covered with images of historic black figures as well as those of white people who helped racial progress. Each child holds a black history scrapbook.

The children begin by singing "America," then they recite the pledge of allegiance. Next they talk about having clipped newspaper articles and searched for books all year, because their school textbooks don't include black history. They name important books that have been written about black history and important figures like Revolutionary War hero Crispus Attucks, pioneering pharmaceutical chemist Percy Julian, famous dramaturge Ira Aldridge, and white abolitionist Wendell Phillips. They conclude with the observation that no history of America could be complete without the mention of the first poets of the land that James Weldon Johnson honored in his ode "Black and Unknown Bards," poets "who gave us the songs of faith, sorrow, love and hope: the Negro Spirituals." Then they sing several spirituals and conclude with "Lift Every Voice and Sing."[72]

The play is explicitly about both self-activity and self-advocacy. It depicts, for children, the process of creating one's own history, and yet it is also a critique of the social order that kept black people at the margins, both literally and figuratively. Not too subtly it reminds adults to be mindful about the stories and history their children may not be getting access to. The anthem positioned at the conclusion is a benediction that suggests these efforts at discovery are only a beginning. In depicting the children pursuing knowledge of black history and culture, and in refuting their invisibility in the public sphere, McBrown implicitly advocates for black children to develop the kind of critical consciousness that foments activism. She and her colleagues were nurturing race girls and boys who would become race women and men. The critical consciousness they fostered, over decades, bore fruit. And the youth were being prepared as the adults made gains in the struggle for equity and justice.

Through the 1920s, 1930s, and 1940s, the NAACP pursued court cases throughout southern states to equalize teacher salaries, get states to provide school buses for black children, and ensure black access to public graduate and law schools. Finally, it shifted gears to take on segregation as a legal regime inconsistent with the promise of equal protection. The team that Charles Hamilton Houston, a Dunbar and Harvard graduate, assembled to bring a series of cases that climaxed in *Brown v. Board of Education* (1954) had come of age in the thickly networked world of black schools and associational life. Future Supreme Court justice Thurgood Marshall, the NAACP's chief counsel when the case was decided, was a native of Baltimore. He had attended Frederick Douglass High School and completed his undergraduate and law degrees at historically black institutions: Lincoln University and Howard Law School. Future federal court judge Robert Carter, also on the team, attended Lincoln and Howard Law, in addition to earning a master of laws from Columbia University. Even New Haven native and future federal judge Constance Baker Motley, whose parents had migrated from Nevis, attended Fisk for a time before finishing her BA at NYU and graduating from Columbia Law School. Her mother, Rachel Baker, was the founder of the New Haven branch of the NAACP. I mention these details of their lives to indicate how important black associational and institutional life was to cultivating people who would dedicate their lives to the cause of racial equality. Ironically, however, their legal victories threatened to unravel the world that made them. They sought to end the racial caste system in the United States, and the separate and unequal worlds that it created.

The *Brown v. Board of Education* decision, published on May 17, 1954, declared legal segregation in U.S. public schools to be unconstitutional. On November 11 of that year, Rosamond Johnson died. The New Negro generation was crossing over, and the civil rights generation was emerging.

Some black thinkers had long-standing reservations about the goal of school desegregation. Both Zora Neale Hurston and W. E. B. DuBois expressed these reservations publicly. DuBois, who fundamentally distrusted white educators, wrote in an article in Howard University's *Journal of Negro Education* that "race prejudice in the United States today is such that most Negroes cannot receive proper education in white institutions. If the public schools in Atlanta, Nashville, New Orleans and Jacksonville were thrown open to all races tomorrow, the education that colored children would get in them would be worse than pitiable. It would not be education. And in the same way there are many public school systems in the North where Negroes are admitted and tolerated but they are not educated, they are crucified."[73]

The Kansas attorney in the *Brown* litigation even quoted DuBois in his defense of segregation as saying, "It is difficult to think of anything more important for the development of a people than proper training for their children; and yet I have repeatedly seen wise and loving colored parents take infinite pains to force their little children into schools where the white children, white teachers, and white parents despised and resented the dark child, make mock of it, neglected or bullied it, and literally rendered its life a living hell. Such parents want their children to 'fight' this thing out—but, dear God, at what a cost!"[74] Hurston simply wondered "how much satisfaction can I get from a court order for somebody to associate with me who does not wish me to be near them."[75] Both Hurston and DuBois earned the ire of the NAACP with their comments. But even if it was deemed necessary by African Americans in general (and the NAACP in particular) to dismantle legal segregation, there was little ease or comfort to be taken in the prospect of integration with a population that had deemed you inferior since the founding of the nation.

The named plaintiff in *Brown v. Board*, Linda Brown, hailed from Topeka, Kansas. For the first four years of her schooling she attended the segregated Monroe School, where she undoubtedly sang the Negro National Anthem on a regular basis. It was everywhere in Topeka: school programs, churches, civic association meetings, and the like. At another segregated Topeka elementary school, named for Booker T. Washington, the students sang the anthem every morning. They learned black history and the school leadership and teachers cultivated high self- and collective regard among the students.[76] The teachers understood their role, in part, as preparing students for an integrated future, not just in high schools (which were already integrated in Topeka before the *Brown* decision) but also in the coming desegregated society. And yet, even after desegregation was implemented with relatively minimal uproar in Topeka, there were some black parents who decided to keep their children in the black schools because they knew they would receive better treatment and greater encouragement from teachers of their own race.[77]

In the Deep South, however, the Supreme Court decision didn't make much difference at the outset. Southern state governments, agents of the state, as well as the general white public, simply refused to desegregate. In 1955, the second *Brown* decision asserted that states had to comply but allowed them to find locally appropriate approaches to desegregation. Massive resistance ensued.

Today, young people in the United States learn about the drama of such resistance through the story of the desegregation of Central High School in Little Rock, Arkansas. In places such as Little Rock, small handfuls of black students who integrated formerly white schools were met with hostility, intimidation, and even violence. In others, the entire public school system was shut down to avoid desegregation. In some places, white parents opened private academies to serve their children and largely abandoned public education. All manner of refusal was pursued. This is the part of the story we generally know, but what is much less frequently contemplated are the larger costs of efforts to desegregate to black communities. In both Topeka, where Linda Brown was raised, and Little Rock, and many places in between, in both the North and the South, a well-developed, nurturing educational praxis and effective systems and structures to socialize and teach black children were present and thriving during Jim Crow. Teachers were revered members of those communities. They participated fully in associational life, and they were frequently organizers and activists. Historian Scott Baker describes these educators "as tenacious institution builders who rallied African American communities behind the improvement of schools that became the institutional base for the movement. . . . Local activists in Alabama and Mississippi remember that exemplary teachers were advocates who taught students to analyze things, instilling in young people the belief that change was up to us. . . . Teachers across the South were crucial to the cause through the encouragement and support they provided to students who boycotted schools, registered voters and organized direct action."[78]

Yet in pushing desegregation efforts, these teachers put their profession at risk in order to work toward opening up the society. In the years following desegregation, 90 percent of black principals lost their jobs, primarily in the South.[79] In 1954, there were 82,000 black teachers; during the eleven years after the court ruling, nearly half of them lost their jobs. In all but rare instances, desegregation meant that black students would integrate into white spaces and not the other way around. Additionally, black athletic and band directors, theater directors, and dance instructors found themselves out of cherished roles. Because the massive white resistance to desegregation led to white flight, black people lost both their educational institutions and a set of professional jobs and still never gained school integration. American schools to this day remain nearly as racially segregated as neighborhoods. But the change wrought by formal, if not *actual* desegregation, this process of transformation, loss, and retrenchment, was a slow one.

Because of the massive white resistance to integration, in some places black schooling continued undisturbed. This is evidenced by even a cursory look at what was happening in black schools in the year following *Brown v. Board of Education*. In the January 1, 1955, issue of the *Negro History Bulletin*, for example, there is an elaborate description of suggestions about how to treat Negro History Week using "Negro History Kits" by Nerissa Long Middleton. The guidelines reserved Monday for music, Tuesday for art, Wednesday for sports, Thursday for literature, and Friday for a salute to youth. At the conclusion of it all the group was to sing "Lift Every Voice and Sing." This ritual program assumed a black school, with black formalist traditions and black instructors.

In 1955, there was a program in honor of Silas Floyd in his hometown of Augusta, Georgia. Floyd was a graduate of Ware High School, the public high school for blacks founded in 1880. By 1902 he had become a celebrated author, minister, and educator. The American Baptist Publication Society of Philadelphia had published his book *The Gospel of Service and Other Sermons* (the first book of sermons by an African American it had ever published) and the National Baptist Publishing Board of Nashville had published his work *The Life of Reverend Charles T. Walker DD*, a biography of one of his ministerial colleagues. Floyd's poetry and essays appeared in national magazines as well, and he was named a member of the American Academy of Political and Social Sciences in 1902, only the fourth black person to hold that honor after Booker T. Washington, Major Richard R. Wright, and W. E. B. DuBois. Calling Floyd the "Paul Laurence Dunbar of the South," the *Augusta Chronicle* wrote, "It is a matter of pardonable pride that an Augusta colored man is able to find himself quoted almost every month in literary magazines."[80] Silas Floyd also wrote children's books, including the landmark *Floyd's Flowers, or Duty and Beauty for Colored Children* (1905), one of the earliest books written specifically for black children.

Floyd was a teacher and principal in Augusta schools for many years and also wrote a weekly column for the *Chronicle*, a local newspaper, titled "Notes among the Colored People." At the culmination of this 1955 National Negro History Week in his honor, teachers sang "Lift Every Voice" and offered silent prayer in memory of Silas Floyd. His niece Camille Saxon read his piece "My Little Georgia Home," and a youth group called the Floydettes sang the spirituals "Nobody Knows the Trouble I See" and "I Couldn't Hear Nobody Pray."

A year after *Brown v. Board of Education*, black people of Augusta held a program that was a layered celebration of their history and culture. Silas Floyd's daughter, Nora, was married to Rosamond Johnson and was the mother of Mildred Johnson, who by that time was heading the Modern School and Camp Dunroven. The multigenerational commitment to the development of black children created such criss-crossings of family and history quite frequently. Renowned black intellectuals of every sort served as educators and participated in a plethora of political, social, and professional educational organizations together.

But soon these institutions and the tight fabric of connection they created would begin to fray. They became a bittersweet memory in light of what was to come after the revolutionary 1960s. And as the world changed, a yearning for the feeling of the black past was palpable. Romanticism aside, it was undeniable that extraordinary communities were created by black Americans on "the margins of society." Economic deprivation, physical violence, and a social order organized around the idea of black inferiority hadn't kept black people from building themselves a world.

Maya Angelou, perhaps the most famous African American woman writer of the twentieth century, published her first book in 1969, in the midst of the midcentury upheavals. It was a memoir titled *I Know Why the Caged Bird Sings*. The book is an unflinching look at the love and heartache of growing up in rural Stamp, Arkansas, as a poor black child in the 1930s and 1940s. In the book she uses her experience to paint a picture of traditional black southern life. It tells how it was and invites speculation as to where it might have gone.

The elementary school Angelou attended, which she describes as the place where she developed her love of learning, was a Rosenwald school named the Lafayette County Training School. Before the Rosenwald funds came, the colored school in Stamps met in local Colored Methodist Episcopal and African Methodist Episcopal churches. Then, in 1907, with funds from the Slater Foundation and the community, they built a two-story schoolhouse. In 1929 a replacement was built with Rosenwald funds. The new Lafayette County Training School was built facing southward in order to let east-west sunlight shine into the classrooms without the more intense glare of southern sunlight. It was built on a large plot in order to facilitate school activities and other social and civic gatherings. Notwithstanding the improvements to prior facilities and care in planning, Angelou noted that the school was inferior to its white counterpart:

Unlike the white high school, Lafayette County Training School distinguished itself by having neither lawn nor hedges nor tennis court nor climbing ivy. Its two buildings (main classrooms, the grade school and home economics) were set on a dirt hill with no fence to limit either its boundaries or those of bordering farms. There was a large expanse to the left of the school that was used alternately as a baseball diamond or a basketball court. Rusty hoops on the swaying poles represented the permanent recreational equipment, although bats and balls could be borrowed from the P.E. teacher if the borrower was qualified and if the diamond wasn't occupied.[81]

Despite the wide gap between the promise and the prospect, at Lafayette Angelou learned and grew. As she approached her eighth grade graduation, Angelou and her classmates were gleeful about their accomplishment. The entire community celebrated with them: "Parents who could afford it had ordered new shoes and ready-made clothes for themselves from Sears and Roebuck or Montgomery Ward. They also engaged the best seamstresses to make the floating graduating dresses and to cut down secondhand pants which would be pressed to a military slickness for the important event."

The formalism of the graduation extended to the smallest of details in preparation. "My class was wearing butter-yellow piqué dresses, and Momma launched out on mine. She smocked the yoke into tiny crisscrossing puckers, then shirred the rest of the bodice. Her dark fingers ducked in and out of the lemony cloth as she embroidered raised daisies around the hem."[82]

However, in the midst of their graduation festivities an unexpected white guest arrived and disrupted the ceremony. Mr. Donleavy, a white politician, reminded them from the podium of their lowly status in the society and knocked the wind out of the moment. Angelou responded, "Constrained by hard-learned manners I couldn't look behind me, but to my left and right the proud graduating class of 1940 had dropped their heads. . . . We were maids and farmers, handymen and washerwomen, and anything higher that we aspired to was farcical and presumptuous. . . . The man's dead words fell like bricks around the auditorium and too many settled in my belly."

Mr. Donleavy left abruptly, as soon as his remarks were complete. Angelou marveled that their class valedictorian, Henry Reed, "a small, very black boy with hooded eyes, a long, broad nose and an oddly shaped head," was nevertheless able to deliver his months-practiced valedictory address without a hitch:

> Henry had been a good student in elocution. His voice rose on tides of promise and fell on waves of warnings. The English teacher had helped him to create a sermon winging through Hamlet's soliloquy. To be a man, a doer, a builder, a leader, or to be a tool, an unfunny joke, a crusher of funky toadstools. I marveled that Henry could go through

with the speech as if we had a choice. I had been listening and silently rebutting each sentence with my eyes closed; then there was a hush, which in an audience warns that something unplanned is happening. I looked up and saw Henry Reed, the conservative, the proper, the A student, turn his back to the audience and turn to us (the proud graduating class of 1940) and sing, nearly speaking,

Lift ev'ry voice and sing
Till earth and heaven ring
Ring with the harmonies of Liberty . . .

It was the poem written by James Weldon Johnson. It was the music composed by J. Rosamond Johnson. It was the Negro national anthem. Out of habit we were singing it.

Our mothers and fathers stood in the dark hall and joined the hymn of encouragement.

And with that, Henry, the graduates, and their community, restored the beauty of the moment from the assault of white supremacy. "We were on top again. As always, again. We survived. The depths had been icy and dark, but now a bright sun spoke to our souls. I was no longer simply a member of the proud graduating class of 1940; I was a proud member of the wonderful, beautiful Negro race."[83]

The Negro National Anthem was a tool of transcendence. It was a tool for community-building. It was remembered by Angelou as reflecting the very spirit of black resilience. But in the coming decade the anthem would change. It would twist and turn, its meanings would be transformed with the shifting energies of black political life in the midst of the Second World War and the rise of racial liberalism and McCarthyism.

CHAPTER FOUR

The Bell Tolls for Thee
War, Americana, and the Anthem

Mine eyes have seen the glory of the coming of the Lord;
He is trampling out the vintage where the grapes of wrath are stored.
—JULIA HOWE, "The Battle Hymn of the Republic"

Let a new earth rise. Let another world be born. Let a bloody peace
be written in the sky. Let a second generation full of courage issue
forth; let a people loving freedom come to growth. Let a beauty
full of healing and a strength of final clenching be the pulsing in
our spirits and our blood. Let the martial songs be written, let the
dirges disappear. Let a race of men now rise and take control.
—MARGARET WALKER, "For My People"

Martin Luther King Jr.'s first public speech was delivered on April 17, 1944, at the state convention of the Colored Elks Clubs held at the First African Baptist Church in Dublin, Georgia. Each local chapter of the Colored Elks sponsored a high school student for the convention's oratory contest. Young King, representing his father's chapter, was the winner in 1944. Such contests were a commonplace in the segregated South. They were occasions to revel in the much-celebrated southern oratorical tradition, and for the community to gather to nurture youth. And such contests were also a dimension of black formalism, one of the ritual practices that entailed certain expectations of grace, dignity, elegant execution and appearance, and an audience that was attentive and appropriate. That fall the gifted fifteen-year-old would matriculate at Morehouse College in Atlanta, another one of the many sites of his life in which black formalism would be both expected and nurtured.

King's speech topic was "The Negro and the Constitution." It was both patriotic and critical. He asserted that if black Americans were given the vote, "they will be vigilant and defend, even with their arms, the ark of federal liberty from treason and destruction by her enemies." And yet, he was also damning of America's refusal to recognize the earned citizenship of black people, saying, "Yes, America you have stripped me of my garments, you have robbed me of my precious endowment."

In the midst of the speech there is a subtle reference to "Lift Every Voice": "On January 1, 1863 the proclamation emancipating the slaves which had been decreed by President Lincoln in September took effect—millions of Negroes faced *a rising sun of a new day begun.*" King had likely attended many Emancipation Day ceremonies, assemblies, and services in his young life where the community sang "Lift Every Voice," and he had joined with schoolmates and other community members in its collective meditation on the promise of freedom, and its persistent denial. It would become evident over his career that it was one of the foundational "texts" to which he would return repeatedly in his sermons. In this regard the anthem for Martin Luther King Jr. was like Bible verses or "The Battle Hymn of the Republic." It was part of his sermonic archive and used to add texture and emphasis. Here it signified the glorious promise of emancipation. Next he turned to the deferral of true liberty: "America gave its full pledge of freedom seventy-five years ago. Slavery has been a strange paradox in a nation founded on the principles that all men are created free and equal. Finally after tumult and war, the nation in 1865 took a new stand—freedom for all people. The new order was backed by amendments to the national constitution making it the fundamental law that thenceforth there should be no discrimination anywhere in the 'land of the free' on account of race, color or previous condition of servitude. . . . Black America still wears chains."

King spoke as the United States was fighting a war against Nazi Germany and the rise of fascism. African Americans, in the midst of the war effort, often reminded their countrypeople that their loyalty to the nation yet and still far exceeded the nation's to them: "So as we gird ourselves to defend democracy from foreign attack, let us see to it that increasingly at home we give fair play and free opportunity for all people."

African Americans overwhelmingly supported the wartime effort, notwithstanding the hypocrisy of the United States fighting fascism abroad while Jim Crow flourished at home. Fascism was familiar to a people who had been enslaved, Jim Crowed, and murdered with impunity. Antifascism was an obvious position for them to hold. And yet they also were in a position, in the midst of World War II, to insist that the U.S. government address domestic fascism against African Americans and Japanese Americans, as well as the foreign policy that supported colonial domination of the black world.

In the mainstream of American politics, a new vision of American racial liberalism emerged in response to fascism abroad, one that supported racial equality as a formal matter but resisted criticisms of imperialism or economic exploitation. King's adolescent blending of the Negro National Anthem, an antifascist sentiment, and an argument for the actualization of the promises of Reconstruction encapsulated how many black Americans engaged with the idea of racial liberalism. Eventually, in order to build an interest convergence between the federal government and black aspirations for full citizenship, some members of the black leadership class abandoned international alliances with anticolonialists in Asian, Africa, and the Caribbean. But in the 1930s and early 1940s we see a more inchoate blend of patriotism and racial advocacy from a varying range of black artists, political figures, and regular folks. And we also see a dynamic relationship between this argument for inclusion, and the American government's growing racial liberalism, which had as an undercurrent strong anticommunist politics and real anxieties about the appeal of radical leftist politics to some sectors of the black American population.

Inklings of this dynamic began in the late 1930s. In particular, the mass media became a vehicle for the promotion of racial liberalism. Public radio broadcasts of that era reveal the shift toward racial liberalism, with a number of features focused upon black history and culture. Historian Barbara Savage attributes much of these to Ambrose Caliver, a Virginia native with degrees from Knoxville College, the University of Wisconsin, and Columbia University who had served as a high school teacher and as a dean at Fisk University before being appointed to the position of "senior specialist in Education of Negroes" in the Federal Office of Education.[1] Later, during FDR's first term, Caliver became a member of FDR's famous "Black Cabinet." In addition to Caliver's extensive documentation of educational disparities and challenges for African American people, he used radio broadcasts to advocate for educational equity. This included an annual "national radio broadcast on African American education during American Education week" through the 1930s and the broadcast of Eleanor Roosevelt's keynote address at the National Conference on Fundamental Problems in the Education of the Negro in 1934.[2]

To place issues facing black youth in the mass media was a significant transition. But the depictions weren't always as racially progressive as they were likely intended to be. In 1938 a segment on "The Negro" was prepared as part of the CBS series *Americans All*. Belatedly, W. E. B. DuBois and

Alain Locke were invited to comment on the script, and they found a show filled with offensive plantation stereotypes. After their vociferous objections, the script was revised to include a history of the Fisk Jubilee Singers and a performance of "Lift Every Voice" in order to restore some dignity in representation.

That "Lift Every Voice and Sing" became part of the "representation" politics of mass culture indicates how invested black Americans, in the midst of World War II, were in presenting black formalism as the public "face" of the black community. Those rituals and codes became part of the argument against the racial stereotypes featured on film and radio, and part of how the rise of racial liberalism enabled black participation in the representation of black people.

"Lift Every Voice and Sing" became part of the politics of representation in local broadcasts as well as national ones. In Washington, D.C., in the spring of 1940, a local station, WMAL, featured a series of educational programs performed by the pupils of the Garnet-Patterson School with the cooperation of NBC. For the March 7 program, they presented a creative mix of classical traditions. The broadcast began with the students paying an imaginary visit to Henry Wadsworth Longfellow, followed by a recitation of Joyce Kilmer's poem "Trees" against the backdrop of music by Oscar Rasbach. Another group recited Mark Antony's oration over the body of Caesar. Finally, the children discussed the lives of celebrated black writers: Paul Laurence Dunbar, Langston Hughes, and James Weldon Johnson. The Garnet-Patterson School Glee Club finished the program by singing "Lift Every Voice and Sing."[3] This was yet another public display of the traditions of black formalism, intended for mainstream consumption. And for the white public, this broadcast also integrated black people into representations of literature and art with which whites were widely familiar, representations that were deemed "worthy" and classical. This was something new for the American mainstream. There were, of course, long-standing white audiences for black art, but this display of the cosmopolitanism of black school culture was distinct and it portended a broader integration of black people into the American popular media and imagination.

Then in 1941 and 1942, with the war around the corner, Ambrose Caliver produced a nine-part radio documentary titled *Freedom's People* that featured black achievement in science, history, music, and athletics. "A stellar display and a stealthy deployment of black culture itself," Savage writes,

"*Freedom's People* made a compelling political argument for equal opportunity and racial justice on a medium that had appropriated and exploited that culture and on a show that was sponsored by a primary target of black protests: the federal government."[4] The opening medley for the series included bits of "My Country 'Tis of Thee," "Lift Every Voice and Sing," and "Go Down, Moses." Over the course of the series, performances by Count Basie, Paul Robeson, and the choirs of Tuskegee, Howard, and Fisk Universities were used to tell the story of African Americans. The final episode explicitly appealed for an end to segregation.[5]

The blending of Americana and the Black National Anthem was an indication of the argument for racial inclusion being made by African Americans. And at the same time, American patriotism was central to building support for the war effort. Racial representation became a means for claiming fidelity to and membership in the United States at once.

Local broadcasts also revealed the analogy that was increasingly being drawn by black activists between antifascism abroad and antiracism at home. In a 1944 Washington, D.C., radio broadcast sponsored by the Negro Publishers Association, "the Negro Press threw out a challenge to America to the effect that it was all out to save democracy, but that it wanted it definitely understood that the Negro Press would not be content until every citizen of America was given the rights to which the term democracy applies." The program was broadcast in the cherished month of February (when Negro History Week and the birthdays of Lincoln and Douglass were all celebrated). Thurman L. Dodson offered a tribute to the black press and asserted that they had been demanding on issues of racial justice while remaining patriotic. As part of this broadcast, the chorus of the Juvenile Police Project sang a song titled "We Are Americans, Too," a wartime anthem written by Eubie Blake and Andy Razaf and published by W. C. Handy.

"We Are Americans, Too" is about black participation in the Revolutionary War, the Civil War, the Spanish American War, and World War I, although like "Lift Every Voice" it never explicitly mentions race. The refrain is nevertheless a demand for full citizenship:

Somewhere out there in the parade
Loudly, proudly and undismayed
We'll be singing this song many millions strong
We are Americans, loyal Americans
We are Americans, too.

This was followed by a coloratura soprano, Madame Lillian Evanti, singing the melancholy "Birdsongs at Eventide."[6] The program concluded with "Lift Every Voice and Sing." The black press celebrated in this program was essential to black political life, and the *Pittsburgh Courier*, arguably the most nationally significant Negro newspaper of the time, had mounted one of the most significant wartime initiatives in support of racial equality. It was called the Double V campaign, standing for Victory against fascism abroad and Victory against racism in the United States. The campaign was inspired by a letter to the editor from James Thompson, a Wichita, Kansas, reader, that said in part,

> I suggest that while we keep defense and victory in the forefront that we don't lose sight of our fight for true democracy at home. The "V for Victory" sign is being displayed prominently in all so-called democratic countries which are fighting for victory over aggression, slavery and tyranny. If this V sign means that to those now engaged in this great conflict then let colored Americans adopt the double VV for a double victory. The first V for victory over our enemies from without, the second V for victory over our enemies within. For surely those who perpetrate these ugly prejudices here are seeing to destroy our democratic form of government just as surely as the Axis forces.[7]

The black press, while supporting the war effort, also reported on segregation and racial inequality across the nation and in the armed forces. As a result, the U.S. military banned black newspapers from its libraries or confiscated and burned them when soldiers got ahold of them. The federal government might have been pursuing a public commitment to racial liberalism, but it wanted to keep a tight hold on troop loyalty. However, the prohibition against black newspapers didn't prevent black soldiers from covertly circulating them, and the double V campaign significantly boosted the domestic circulation of black newspapers.

The doubleness of purpose that characterized black wartime politics shaped black ceremonial and ritual practices associated with black formalism as well. Graduation ceremonies of black schools in the early 1940s consistently placed patriotic anthems such as "My Country 'Tis of Thee" or "The Star-Spangled Banner" alongside "Lift Every Voice and Sing." And in 1943, the March on Washington Movement (MOWM), a civil rights advocacy group, named its conference after the song "We Are Americans, Too," which captured the Double V sentiment.

The March on Washington Movement was the brainchild of A. Philip Randolph, president of the Brotherhood of Sleeping Car Porters, and Bayard Rustin, a pacifist organizer who worked with the Congress of Racial Equality (CORE) and the Fellowship of Reconciliation, an international network of nonviolent social justice organizers. They planned a massive black-led "March on Washington" to protest segregation in the armed forces and wartime industries. The group had begun organizing in 1941. Their march was initially scheduled for July 1 of that year. However, a week before the planned date, President Roosevelt issued executive order 8802 establishing the Federal Employment Practices Committee (FEPC), and the organizers, out of respect for the president's integrationist effort, canceled the march.

Roosevelt's FEPC directed federal agents to accept black people in job training programs in defense plants and forbade discrimination by defense contractors. Although the March on Washington Movement's national protest was canceled, similar protests were nevertheless held by local organizations in various cities. For example, in March 1941 somewhere between 3,500 and 5,000 people attended a mass protest in Kansas City, Kansas, against racial discrimination in the defense industry. After that event, both houses of the Kansas legislature passed a resolution banning discrimination in labor unions.[8] Black political influence was growing and being exercised through the efforts of active members of black associations.

In 1943, the MOWM was still pushing the federal government to adopt racial equality. The movement's conference in Chicago that year culminated with an interracial banquet honoring A. Philip Randolph. Randolph was strongly patriotic, but he continuously pressured the government to secure racial equality for African Americans. The MOWM called the banquet a rally for victory over Hitler, Hirohito, and Mussolini by "enforcing the Constitution and abolishing Jim Crow." The political action of African Americans was the wind to their sails. Earlier that year in Detroit, the NAACP, other black associations, and the United Auto Workers supported a demonstration against racism in Detroit that 10,000 attended. This was promising for the MOWM organization, which was planning its own march against racism in Washington.

Attendees sang "The Star-Spangled Banner," "God Bless America," "Lift Every Voice and Sing," and a song that would become much more famous in the 1960s, "We Shall Not Be Moved." The Brotherhood of Sleeping Car Porters had been singing "Lift Every Voice and Sing" at their gatherings for years, and it was even published in their newspaper the *Messenger*, but now in the midst of the war, the song was literally and figuratively encased in Americana and the new patriotic form of militant integrationism.

World War II was a watershed in American race relations. One million black men were drafted, and a half a million were stationed abroad.[9] Another million African Americans at home worked in wartime industries.[10] White workers panicked at this infusion of blackness into the labors of citizenship and militarism. And in many places they responded violently, with attacks on black soldiers and defense industry workers. But this backlash didn't sway African Americans from wartime effort; they were fighting for the ideals of the nation: democracy, equality, and liberty, both at home and abroad.

Black schools were part of these efforts as well. In 1944, the Fort Valley State University student paper in Texas published a selection of poems from black college students fighting in the armed forces. They were printed under the heading "Lift Every Voice and Sing Said the Poet: Poems from Our Men in the Armed Forces."

The first poem, "Jungle Paradise," by Roy L. Rumph, tells of the discomforts of "New Guinea," where Allied forces were stationed. New Guinea was colonized by the Dutch. The Japanese attacked it in 1941 and 1942 with the hope of making their way past it and advancing all the way to Australia. American forces were stationed in New Guinea and charged with halting Japan's incursion. It was a particularly uncomfortable place for American soldiers, and many suffered from malaria and dysentery.

Rumph's first stanza reads:

Out here in the jungles of New Guinea
It rains most every day
And the big mosquitos encountered here
Can carry a bunk away!

The poem concludes with:

So take me back to the U.S.A.
Let me hear the trolley bell
For this Godforsaken country
Is a substitute for hell!

There is no hint, in this poem at least, of identification with the colonized people of New Guinea, whose native land was being fought over by colonists and fascists. As such, it is a quite distinct articulation of black identity from what emerged in 1930s black leftist communities, although both used the anthem as a form of representation. This playful poem was not, like many others, an expression of global blackness. Instead it reads as simply, and humorously, American.

Following that poem there were two by Corporal Harrison E. Lee. The first is a love poem to a girlfriend left behind in the States, the other is called "The Forthcoming Day" and repeats "over the road to hell, we wished for the victory bell" a refrain finally altered to "over the road to hell, we can hear the victory bell."[11] That the road to victory, in war and in America, was "hell" was a much bolder testimony to black suffering than Johnson's stony road and bitter rod. But the double V sentiment in this particular poem is submerged. Again, it is rather straightforward Americana.

"Lift Every Voice and Sing" was not in and of itself, however, an ode to the United States, even if it was placed in the midst of patriotic assertions. And it especially was not a war anthem. Johnson noted that his and Rosamond's song was not bloodthirsty in the manner of other American anthems. That is true. But during World War II "Lift Every Voice and Sing" was caught up in the spirit of war. And this was yet another example of how black communities used the song distinctly from the authors' intended purposes. It was the Johnson brothers' song, but it was black America's anthem.

In 1942 the Southern Sons recorded "Lift Every Voice and Sing," with "Praise the Lord and Pass the Ammunition" as the B side. "Praise the Lord and Pass the Ammunition" was based upon contemporary folklore about a chaplain who was said to have uttered after the attack on Pearl Harbor, "Praise the Lord and pass the ammunition," suggesting that the bombing made even the meek and mild ready for war. The review of the Southern Sons record in the *Dallas Morning News* describes it as follows: "'Praise the Lord' . . . emerges as a real spiritual which is probably something like what composer Frank Loesser had in mind before the dance bands appropriated it and stylized it for dancing. Another good wartime spiritual, 'Lift Every Voice and Sing,' is sung by the quintet on the reverse side."[12]

Even the editors at *Time* interpreted "Lift Every Voice" as a feature of wartime Americana. In the September 14, 1942, issue, an article reads,

A thousand Negroes stood last week in a public park in Dallas singing to an orchestra's accompaniment. On the program was a number entitled "Lift Every Voice and Sing." Called out Director A. H. Jackson: "How many of you know the song?" Almost every hand shot up.

Wherever Negroes gather in the U.S., hands rise just as quickly to such a question. To them "Lift Every Voice and Sing" is the No. 2 song to the national anthem. While white people bemoan the lack of suitable patriotic songs, even find fault with "The Star-Spangled Banner"'s annoying octave-and-a-half range, colored people have quietly adopted a rousing anthem of their own. . . . . Timelier today than its author could have realized is its first chorus:

Sing a song full of the faith that the dark past has taught us;
Sing a song full of the hope that the present has brought us;
Facing the rising sun of our new day begun,
Let us march on till victory is won.[13]

While the implication in the *Time* piece was that the victory being sought was abroad, African Americans were explicitly seeking victory both here and there. However, some black commentators believed that singing the anthem was a threat to this goal. In response to such detractors, Peter Dana of Atlanta's *Daily World* wrote, "James and Rosamond Johnson's beautiful and moving song 'Lift Every Voice and Sing,' sometimes called the 'National Negro Hymn' and sometimes the 'National Negro Anthem'—both erroneously—has been taking quite a beating in certain portions of the colored press, but on talking, singing, thinking and feeling national unity this reporter sees no reason why that fine and stirring song which would sing a song full of the faith that the dark past has taught us, sing a song full of the hope that the present has brought us, should appear to be a counter-force to unity or common national aspirations."[14]

But even when "Lift Every Voice" was deployed in the most patriotic fashion possible, for African Americans it usually served the spirit of the Double V campaign. And that was difficult work. The contradiction between America's self-conception as free and the reality of the unfreedom of its black citizenry was made manifest in the war, and extended in its aftermath. This was not a peculiarly southern problem. In the North, violent responses to efforts at residential integration were quite common. For example, in 1945, when a black family moved into the second floor of an old unpainted house on Throop Street in a Polish and Italian section of Chicago, five of their windows were immediately shattered, and "neighbors" threatened to burn their house down. This was simply one instance of many in which mob violence was the response to residential desegregation across the Midwest and Northeast. It was also consistent among white workers, who often struck to protest the hiring of black workers alongside them. Whiteness and its benefits were usually jealously guarded, notwithstanding the nation's fight against Nazism.

Time reported on a Chicago white minister who responded uniquely and courageously to this violent incident:

> Last week the Rev. Douglas Cedarleaf, 31, decided to take a stand. First, he preached a sermon, "Vandalism in Throop Street," to his Erie Chapel Presbyterian Church [white] congregation [which included the Strongs]. Then he taught them the great Negro anthem, "Lift Every Voice and Sing." And then he asked them to escort the Strongs home. Some 135 of the congregation's 175 did. Throop Street heard them coming: they were all singing the anthem. At the Strongs' doorstep they formed a circle. Curious neighbors leaning out of their windows saw the minister give the Strongs a Bible, heard him preach another sermon on tolerance.[15]

That *Time* published this story was a sign of the ascension of racial liberalism. Notably, this new racial liberalism entailed a rejection of Marxist or socialist critique, and even the social democratic impulses of the New Deal, and limited its progressivism to a stand against explicit racial discrimination. That is to say, it is worthy of note that the story did not include a discussion of the economic exploitation of black tenants, or the suppression of their wages relative to white people. The problems of black Chicagoans were compounded by residential segregation but by no means limited to it. And even the problems of residential segregation were as much economic problems as anything else. White residents saw accumulation in the value of their homes the whiter their neighborhoods remained. And excluding black families from them, as well as the crowding and ghettoization in black communities, made it extremely difficult for black families to accumulate wealth. So while racial liberalism was in some ways a dramatic step forward in the expression of American values, it fundamentally ignored the fact that class and economic power were not simply important but fundamental to how black people had been kept at the bottom of the social order. They were usually the last hired and the first fired. They were the most exploited and occupied the least respected jobs and neighborhoods.

However, African Americans could see some tangible gains in the era of racial liberalism. The United Negro College Fund was established in 1943, and through the collaboration of a number of historically black colleges and donors it kept the doors open to many institutions that had fallen into financial crisis during the Depression. Adam Clayton Powell Jr. was elected to Congress in 1944. And black union membership rose from 150,000 to 1.25 million between 1935 and the end of the war.

Victory at home nevertheless remained a difficult task. And black associational life was filled with discussions about how to achieve it. The Georgia 1945 NAACP convention, attended by Martin Luther King Sr., who was both an NAACP member and a member of the Colored Elks Club, was titled "Achieving Democracy in a Post-war Georgia." Conference attendees sang "America" and "The Battle Hymn of the Republic" on the first day of the gathering. They began with "Lift Every Voice and Sing" on both the second and third day. On the third and final day, Martin Luther King Sr. provided the invocation, and NAACP lawyer Thurgood Marshall, who was then in the midst of executing Charles Hamilton Houston's plan to equalize and desegregate the South, delivered the keynote address about legal paths to integration. Everyone present knew arduous work confronted them. The country would not embrace them easily, notwithstanding the noble service of African American servicemen and women during the war.

A 1961 short story by Herbert L. Shore published in *Phylon* (a journal founded by DuBois at Atlanta University) retrospectively rendered the doubleness of blackness that made postwar celebrations of victory over fascism abroad something of a fool's errand for black Americans. It is told from the perspective of Ben, a white lieutenant and second-generation immigrant who is haunted by the death of one of his fellow navy men, a black man from his hometown referred to as "Lijah." Ben goes to Lijah's family to offer his condolences. In the midst of his visit, other visitors arrive and tell the family that a police officer has just killed a black boy for stealing a little bit of coal. They describe a procession from the morgue to the city hall in protest, and Ben saw it, too, in his mind's eye:

They were tramping on the pavement, and the blue-coated men stood still and silent. Ahead was the city hall, white and clean in the sunshine. The cars stopped at street corners, while the crowd passed. Then they began to slow down, barely moving, forming a huge throng before the city hall. The coffin was passed hand over hand above the heads of the crowd until it came to rest on the steps of the city hall and suddenly the crowd was bareheaded. A Voice began, "Lift every voice and sing, /

Let earth and heaven ring . . ." And others joined, swelling the sound to a hymn of defiance.

This domestic death in the midst of a story of wartime death frees Ben to tell Lijah's parents how Lijah died but also how he lived under the U.S. flag, segregated on a warship, where he was routinely insulted and debased in the midst of the fight against fascism.[16] In this story, the anthem is not situated in the midst of Americana. Instead it is a "hymn of defiance" toward American racism and hypocrisy. Ben is forced to painfully confront this hypocrisy. Lijah's parents already know it all too well. It is the story of their lives as black Americans.

Strategic conflict in black activist circles over how to pursue civil rights grew tense in the postwar period. DuBois's difficulties became symbolic of that conflict. In the early 1930s he opened the pages of the *Crisis* to wide-ranging discussions of the utility of Marxist thought, racially based economic cooperatives, and other leftist institutions participating in the fight against race prejudice. This led to increased antagonism between him and his colleagues at the NAACP, especially the moderate executive director who succeeded Johnson in 1930, Walter White. DuBois first resigned in 1934, attributing his departure to a protest over the NAACP's lack of a coherent economic policy for black folks during the Depression. He accepted an appointment as chair of the Sociology Department at Atlanta University, where he had already been teaching as a visiting professor during the winter of 1934. At Atlanta he founded and edited *Phylon* from 1940 to 1944. There, too, he published his most important historical work, *Black Reconstruction*.

In 1944, at seventy-six years old, DuBois accepted an invitation to return to the NAACP to serve in the newly created post of director of special research. Although the organization was still under Walter White's leadership, the NAACP was addressing the labor issues that DuBois considered paramount as well as legal discrimination. Even the court strategy of its legal branch focused increasingly on the economic consequences of segregation. In rehiring DuBois, the board seemed to recognize that his economic, labor, and global political concerns mirrored those of the black community writ large. Clearly, DuBois thought that his return meant that the organization would both study and bring pressure to bear on the U.S. government regarding the coming postwar settlement and how it would affect black peoples in Africa and the diaspora. When the United Nations held its founding conference in San Francisco, DuBois represented the NAACP there and served as a consultant to the U.S. delegation. During this period, he also wrote two more books that spoke directly to these concerns: *Color and Democracy: Colonies and Peace* (1945) and *The World and Africa: An Inquiry into the Part Which Africa Has Played in World History* (1947). Both criticized European nations and the United States for their colonial and neocolonial ravaging of Africa and Asia.

Because of the crises caused by the Depression and World War II, there weren't any Pan-African congresses for the eighteen years between 1927 and 1945. But in 1945, George Padmore, an Antiguan Trinidadian Marxist, reignited the tradition and organized a Pan-African Congress in Manchester, England. The participants, recognizing DuBois's central role in the development of the Pan-African Movement, declared him the president of the congress in 1945. However, this congress differed from previous ones. There were more African representatives than in the past, and this time they didn't come as individuals but as representatives of political parties. The same was true of the participants from the West Indies. Delegates at this gathering, in general, were more radical in their assertions than delegates of the past congresses. They wanted an end to colonialism and the exploitation of African resources by European countries, and they discussed tactics for the destruction of colonialism and resource exploitation, including strikes and boycotts. Trade unionists, students, and socialists in attendance pushed the congress to be more outspoken as a collective body. Delegates from the Caribbean and Africa asserted the right to elect their own governments, arguing (as DuBois had fifty years earlier) that political power was essential to ending racial domination.

Many of the participants became future national leaders in their respective countries, including Kwame Nkrumah of Ghana, Nnamdi Azikiwe of Nigeria, and Jomo Kenyatta of Kenya. All three had important political and ideological connections to black Americans and West Indians prior to the Congress. Nkrumah had attended Lincoln University, a historically black college in Pennsylvania. Azikiwe had attended Howard University and was mentored by William Leo Hansberry (the uncle of playwright Lorraine Hansberry), who was a specialist in African history and a speaker at the 1927 Pan-African Congress. And Jomo Kenyatta had participated in a black intellectual community in London in the 1930s that included Ralph Bunche, Amy Ashwood Garvey (Marcus Garvey's widow), Paul Robeson, George Padmore, and C. L. R. James. The congress of 1945 merely served to formalize the transnational network of black resistance. Its final declaration called for unity among the colonized and subjugated, and for collective and coordinated resistance. African American activists and politicians were deeply inspired by this, and the black press touted it. Among those who publicly expressed their common cause with African liberation were Adam Clayton Powell, Paul Robeson, and, of course, DuBois. Importantly, however, this transnational black political unity lay in tension with the vision of racial liberalism being promoted by the federal government.

As ever, in the 1940s DuBois learned from and was responsive to the events and developments of his time. Conflicts with the U.S. delegation to the United Nations (which included Eleanor Roosevelt, who was also a member of the NAACP board) and disillusionment with the evolving role of America as a postwar world power reinforced his growing radicalism and his refusal to be confined to a safe domestic agenda. He was not a liberal, he was a member of the Far Left.

DuBois became a supporter of the leftist youth organization the Southern Negro Youth Congress (SNYC) at a time of rising hysteria about communism and the onset of the Cold War. SNYC was first established in 1937 at a gathering of over 500 delegates in Richmond, Virginia. Their organization was set against the backdrop of two national crises: (1) the Scottsboro case and (2) a white mob attack that had taken the lives of seventy African Americans in Birmingham, Alabama. The mob violence began when a tubercular youth was sentenced to life imprisonment for allegedly shooting three white women despite the fact that it was established at trial that he was in his hospital bed at the time of the shooting. In 1935, many future SNYC students had attended the meeting that led to the National Negro Congress, and they responded by creating their own organization, which included participants from virtually all of the historically black colleges as well as high school students and young adults who were out of school.

SNYC activism ranged from studying the inflated prices of commercial goods sold in black communities to tobacco workers' fight for better wages and labor conditions. They organized local farmers, sharecroppers, and domestic worker unions and encouraged black workers to join the Congress of Industrial Organizations. They also performed educational functions. They were teachers of reading and writing. They explained the democratic process to those who had been excluded from it. Like the *Crisis* and *Opportunity* magazine, they also held art and poetry prizes through their newsletter *The Cavalcade*. In local communities, SNYC organized arts programs and lectures for young people. Its members assisted in the development of libraries and clubs, and—as a precursor to the mid-1960s work of another student group, the Student Nonviolent Coordinating Committee (SNCC)—they encouraged black southerners to register to vote. They did so with an innovative performance project, the Caravan Puppeteers, which staged puppet shows about voting rights. From 1937 to 1948, SNYC formed chapters in ten southern states, with a total membership of 11,000 at its peak.

Although a radical organization, SNYC also worked "within the system." It sought to enlist the support of Eleanor Roosevelt for several of its initiatives and participated in fact-finding work for the Fair Employment Practices Committee that Roosevelt created in response to the demands of the March on Washington Movement.

In 1946, the ninth annual convention of the Southern Negro Youth Congress took place in Columbia, South Carolina. Diane McWhorter described that year's gathering:

> The celebrity lineup included Harlem congressman Adam Clayton Powell; Howard Fast, the white communist whose Reconstruction novel *Freedom Road* had become a youth congress bible; and again Paul Robeson, who led the audience in a round of James Weldon Johnson's "Lift Ev'ry Voice and Sing," known as the "Negro national Anthem." The guest of honor, W. E. B. DuBois, gave his speech in a chapel so crowded that loudspeakers were set up on the lawn. Its premise was memorable for its improbability, "The future of American Negroes is in the South," and declared over and over that the revolution for black freedom worldwide would take root in that cradle of segregation. He urged the audience to stay there and fight.[17]

The anthem was invoked in a way distinct from the commonplace of the early 1940s. This was not as a signal of black integration into the "American ethos" and patriotism. Here it was part of a reemergent black radical tradition, following in the footsteps of black socialists, communists, and nationalists of a generation prior. Although there was, as with the National Negro Congress, a political range in attendees, at heart the SNYC was a far left organization.

A deep political rift was coming in black America, notwithstanding the success of the Pan-African Congress and the SNYC conferences to bring black people of various political ideologies and identities together. Events in the NAACP were a bellwether. In 1947 an informal poll of the staff in the NAACP national office showed that 70 percent of them supported Vice

President Henry Wallace in his bid for the presidency. Executive Director Walter White warned everyone on staff to *not* campaign for Wallace. White was a strong supporter of Truman, even though it was clear Wallace had a much stronger position on civil rights and also showed greater support for working-class people. DuBois was one of the many staff supporters of Wallace. This put him at odds with Walter White yet again. The board was thereafter courted strongly by Harry Truman, who was an aggressive opponent of any left-wing or socialist organizations or policies. Truman's suspicion of the Left included the SNYC, which was tracked by the FBI under his administration. Particular alarm was raised when the SNYC publicly supported Henry Wallace. In fact, the worry over black support for Wallace was national. He'd garnered public support from Paul Robeson and inspired the young (and not-yet-famous) playwright Lorraine Hansberry to campaign for him (in the process she also joined the staff of Robeson's newspaper, *Freedom*). In addition to his support of civil rights, Wallace was very critical of the Marshall Plan, and he invited both communists and socialists to participate in his campaign, although he identified as a progressive.

Wallace's running mate, U.S. Representative Glen Taylor of Idaho, was invited to give the keynote address at the 1948 SNYC spring convention in Birmingham. Police Chief Bull Connor responded with predictable brutality, threatening to arrest any black person seen talking to a white one during the conference. Bomb threats were directed at the Sixteenth Street Baptist Church, where the conference was supposed to be held (a harrowing anticipation of events to come), and as a result the pastor decided not to let the SNYC use the church. The conference opened instead at the smaller Alliance Gospel Tabernacle Church. Few people attended, the result of the red-baiting in the local press combined with the threat of a violent attack. Bull Connor stuck a makeshift wooden segregation sign in the yard of Alliance Gospel Tabernacle. When Glen Taylor stepped outside of the church, Connor placed him under arrest.

Racist intimidation was also often political intimidation in the 1930s and 1940s. The widespread assertion that Wallace was a "red," a charge repeated by not just segregationists but also the executive director of the NAACP, was a sign of the McCarthyism that was coming to sweep the nation. But more than that, it signaled the coercive power of postwar liberalism. Liberalism framed the outer limits of the kind of calls for justice black people were "supposed" to make. And this was understood and adopted by more than a few influential black people. At times, this meant going further than encasing "Lift Every Voice and Sing" in Americana; it meant rejecting the very idea of a black anthem. For example, in honor of Flag Day in 1948, a black newspaper in Atlanta, the *Daily World*, proclaimed, "We have no other anthem; for we are Americans, citizens of the great Republic of the United States," as a means of showing their patriotism and deflecting the anticommunist discourse that attended every effort to pursue black social and political efforts and inclusion. Professing 100 percent loyalty, however, implicitly meant minimizing connections to Africa and the struggles of working people around the globe.[18]

The Southern Negro Youth Congress would only continue for one more year. In 1948 it rapidly lost the support of many formerly eager participants, including HBCU presidents and members of the Urban League and the NAACP. Many of these people moved toward the mainstream of racial liberalism, or at least away from the Far Left. For the 1948 campaign, despite the political leanings of the majority of its staff, the NAACP officially supported Harry Truman. And as the Cold War sedimented, the shift to the center by these organizations, as well as by mainstream political institutions, had a devastating impact on black political activity. Soon any and all aggressive efforts to address racial inequality could be labeled "red." Unions were pressured by the federal government to purge both communists and members who were simply antiracist. The NAACP's support of Truman was a deal of sorts: the organization disengaged from anticolonialism and affiliation with labor organizers, Marxists, socialists, and other leftists, and in return it got a modest and ultimately superficial commitment to civil rights. Truman did indeed call for new civil rights legislation. He revitalized the FEPC and signed an executive order to desegregate the military. However, at the 1948 Democratic Party convention Truman was silent on civil rights, despite his knowledge that black voters would be a decisive force in the presidential election that year. Truman's support only went so far. He didn't want to rock the boat with southern white Democrats, whom he considered an essential constituency.

Hubert Humphrey, however, then the mayor of Minneapolis and a Senate candidate, was a much stronger supporter of racial equality. Humphrey delivered a speech at the Democratic convention that called for racial equality and challenged the thinly veiled bigotry behind the slogan "states' rights." Incensed, the Mississippi delegation marched out of the auditorium and immediately created the Dixiecrat Party. In short, Dixiecrats were Democrats who passionately believed in maintaining legal segregation and white supremacy. In the end, Truman couldn't hold his party together, even though he maintained the NAACP's fidelity to it with minor promises.

Although it took time for the arrangement to take root in the many local chapters of the NAACP, this alliance between it and the Democratic Party was a key force in shifting the center of gravity for black politics for the next twenty years. In the 1940s a growing number of black political figures, including some NAACP members, were primarily aligned with bastions of power, not unlike Booker T. Washington once was. They could sustain support by tapping into some of the organic patriotism born in black folks generally in light of World War II, as well as some glimmers of hope that black people felt with the rise of racial liberalism. The fight against fascism was not, for black Americans, a mere abstraction but was hard fought abroad and now to be fought at home. The Double V campaign they embraced during the war was carried into the next phase of black politics. But ultimately notwithstanding these organizations negotiations with the powers that be, they couldn't deliver on the goal of strong federal government support for black Americans.

And while the shift in mainstream black politics, led by the NAACP and the Urban League, was toward an exclusively domestic civil rights framework, this did not destroy the black radical imagination and black socialism, nor did it eradicate all black organizations that pursued an international black freedom movement, but it did complicate and diminish their work and send them into the shadows.

DuBois delivered a talk titled "Behold the Land" at the closing session of the final conference of the SNYC in 1946. Echoing Frederick Douglass's appeal to the Exodusters,[19] as well as his own lectures from years past, DuBois urged the young people once again not to flee southern racism by going north, but to stay and fight. In the speech, he identifies the South as part of what we now term "the global South":

Here in this South is the gateway to the colored millions of the West Indies, Central and South America. Here is the straight path to Africa, the Indies, China and the South Seas. Here is the path to the greater, freer, truer world. It would be a shame and cowardice to surrender this glorious land and its opportunities for civilization and humanity to the thugs and lynchers, the mobs and profiteers, the monopolists and the gamblers who today choke its soul and steal its resources. The oil and sulphur, the coal and iron; the cotton and corn; the lumber and cattle belong to you the workers, black and white, and not to the thieves who hold them and use them to enslave you. They can be rescued and restored to the people if you have the guts to strive for the real right to vote, the right to real education, the right to happiness and health and the total abolition of the father of these scourges of mankind, poverty.

Such internationalist politics would remain a gentle undercurrent in black political life, but its most public proponents would suffer mightily.

That year, in an interview conducted in Paris, Paul Robeson was quoted as likening U.S. policies toward Africa to those of Hitler and Goebbels toward Jewish people. In the United States, this statement was met with widespread public outrage. And in August 1950 the U.S. government revoked Robeson's passport for eight years. Protesters who supported Robeson circulated flyers in response that read "Lift Every Voice for Paul Robeson."

In 1950 DuBois ran for U.S. Senate in New York on the Progressive American Labor Party ticket and received an impressive 206,000 votes. Soon thereafter, he was targeted for investigation by the FBI. In February 1951, DuBois was indicted for "serving as an agent of a foreign principal" because of his antiwar work with the Peace Information Center in New York. He was eighty-two years old. The National Committee to Defend Dr. W. E. B. DuBois, established in response, urged supporters to "'Lift Every Voice' in a mighty chorus of protest!" In November, DuBois was released after a federal judge, finding no evidence that he was an agent of the Communist Party, dismissed the charges against him. However the State Department illegally withheld his passport for seven more years. As he fought against this punishment, DuBois received no support from the NAACP, which he had worked to build for so many years, or from his fraternity, Alpha Phi Alpha, and only minimal support from black newspapers. Many didn't mention him at all. His books were removed from public libraries in the ultimate sign that had become a persona non grata in his own country.

The use of "Lift Every Voice" by activists who supported both Robeson and DuBois echoed its earlier use by Claudia Jones, the Trinidadian Communist Party leader who published a popular pamphlet called *Lift Every Voice for Victory* in 1942. Her pamphlet used the story of Joe Louis to mobilize antifascist sentiment among African Americans and encouraged them to advocate for the United States to enter World War II as a commitment to rejecting all forms of fascism and racism.

Other small pockets of leftists continued to reference "Lift Every Voice and Sing" after the Robeson and DuBois defense campaigns. The group People's Songs was founded in New York in 1945 by three white leftists: the folklorist Alan Lomax, folk singer Pete Seeger, and Lee Hays. The trio believed music could serve as a means of pushing progressive social change. They had published a quarterly newsletter beginning 1946, which included some folk music, but they were ultimately bankrupted after putting all their resources behind Henry Wallace's campaign. When they returned to publishing in 1953, they titled their collection of folk music *Lift Every Voice: The Second People's Songbook*. This was likely both in honor of Paul Robeson and a reflection of the ongoing identification of some segments of the white Left with the cause of black freedom. This songbook would provide the foundation for the folk music revival of the 1960s, a hallmark of 1960s counterculture. It also featured a good deal of Robeson's songs.

Something particular was being invoked in the associations made between the Negro National Anthem and DuBois and Robeson. It was as though leftists were imploring masses to remember the many-decades-long commitment these activist artist intellectuals had shown for black people. It was an appeal for public support when Robeson and DuBois were at their most vulnerable. The invocation of the anthem was more than a clever effort to capitalize upon its gravitas and the sentimental associations it would elicit. It was also a reminder about who had fought for black Americans, and an assertion that those who had fought for them must be fought for in kind.

But a younger man would figure more prominently than these older leaders as a symbol of racial uplift and the politics of racial liberalism. Jackie Robinson, the first black man to play in Major League Baseball, was handily deployed as a symbol for civil rights and a cold warrior. The pages of a black historian's memoir of his schoolboy years in New Jersey capture the pride Robinson brought to black Americans.

Unlike other special assemblies, no one, not even the teachers, knew the subject of this special assembly. Our school, New Jersey Avenue School, was an enviable physical plant "for a black school" I had heard adults say. New Jersey's auditorium could seat about 400 people on its main floor about half that number in its balcony. . . . Mr. Gregory said that something had happened yesterday that was a first, and a great day in Negro History (both were always capitalized by his generation even in their speeches). He wondered if any of us knew what this momentous event was. . . . Almost without thinking I raised my hand. As I remember it, I also raised my entire body out of my chair and waved wildly. No other hand in the auditorium was raised. "That little boy in the back. If you think you know, come on up here." . . . He said, "Tell the school what you know." I fairly blurted out, "Branch Rickey signed Jackie Robinson to a contract to play baseball for Montreal, the Brooklyn Dodgers' farm team!" Through that whole shouted sentence I maintained my grin and my leaning pose. . . . With that, Mr. Gregory started clapping and of course everybody joined in and almost immediately we were singing 'Lift Every Voice and Sing,' the Negro National Anthem."[20]

The anthem baptizes the moment; it signifies the enormous symbolic importance of Jackie Robinson's breaking the color barrier. There was a reason to hope, his achievement suggested, that the walls were ever so slowly coming down.

Two years after Jackie Robinson joined the major leagues, he was summoned to testify before the House Un-American Activities Committee. The subject was "Communist infiltration of minority groups," and Paul Robeson was of particular interest. Specifically, they wanted Robinson to tell them whether Robeson's statement that African Americans would be reluctant to fight for the United States against the U.S.S.R. was true. The event was staged for Robinson to rebut Robeson. But in the midst of that task, Robinson made a powerful statement about both African Americans' desire for civil rights and implicitly criticized the HUAC pattern of seeing all social protest as conspiratorial subversion.

The white public should start toward real understanding by appreciating that every single Negro who is worth his salt is going to resent any kind of slurs and discrimination because of his race, and he is going to use every bit of intelligence such as he has to stop it. This has got absolutely nothing to do with what Communists may or may not be trying to do. And white people must realize that the more a Negro hates communism because it opposes democracy, the more he is going to hate any other influence that kills off democracy in this country— and that goes for racial discrimination in the Army, and segregation on trains and buses, and job discrimination because of religious beliefs or color or place of birth.

And one other thing the American public ought to understand, if we are to make progress in this matter: The fact that it is a Communist who denounces injustice in the courts, police brutality, and lynching when it happens doesn't change the truth of his charges. Just because Communists kick up a big fuss over racial discrimination when it suits their purposes, a lot of people try to pretend that the whole issue is a creation of Communist imagination.

But they are not fooling anyone with this kind of pretense, and talk about "Communists stirring up Negroes to protest" only makes present misunderstanding worse than ever. Negroes were stirred up long before there was a Communist Party, and they'll stay stirred up long after the party has disappeared—unless Jim Crow has disappeared by then as well.[21]

In an act of equivocation, however, Robinson also insulted Paul Robeson, saying that Robeson "has a right to his personal views, and if he wants to sound silly when he expresses them in public, that is his business and not mine. . . . He's still a famous ex-athlete and a great singer and actor."[22] The media jumped on the criticism, which at once diminished Robeson's work as an activist and intellectual and condescendingly dismissed him. Eleanor Roosevelt interpreted it for the public as she saw fit: "Mr. Robeson does his people great harm in trying to line them up on the Communist side of [the] political picture. Jackie Robinson helped them greatly by his forthright statement."[23]

Robinson would later regret his jab at Robeson. Paul Robeson had played an important part in bringing black baseball players, and specifically Jackie Robinson, into the major leagues. Robeson, and a delegation he'd gathered, met with the baseball commissioner, Kennesaw Mountain Landis, and major league owners in 1943. Robeson was, back then, highly regarded by Commissioner Landis for being an outstanding athlete, artist, and humanitarian. During his speech to the major league owners, he declared that "the time has come when you must change your attitude toward Negroes. . . . Because baseball is a national game, it is up to baseball to see that discrimination does not become an American pattern. And it should do this this year."[24] After the meeting, the commissioners and owners decided to remove the color bar. But it wasn't until 1945 they selected Jackie Robinson. He was not the best player in the Negro leagues, but he was the one they considered the best representative of the Negro race. He was clean cut, polished, and "All-American." Robinson played for two years on a Dodger farm team before integrating Major League Baseball.[25]

The idealization of Robinson in contrast to the denigration of Robeson, obscuring the fact that there would be no Robinson without Robeson, anticipated a politics of distinction rooted in racial liberalism that would haunt the coming civil rights movement. The idealization of a single "patriotic" black leader in contrast to others who were deemed troublemakers, militants, or communists became a practice embraced by both powerful politicians and the popular media. It often led to not just a misrepresentation of those who were demonized but also misrepresentations of what the idealized black public figures and organizers were actually fighting for, as would be the case with Martin Luther King Jr. The idealization and depiction of "chosen" black leaders within the narrow frames of racial liberalism could also influence and delimit the future trajectory of organizers and activists. Many who emerged in the 1940s and 1950s, like Ralph Bunche and Whitney Young, slowly veered to the political right and turned away from militancy as they become more established. And while they maintained a commitment to racial justice, their activism became domestic and rights-based rather than economically, internationally, and protest-oriented.

And yet a political Left not only was quietly sustained but also remained essential in the development of the freedom movement protests and organizing that we tend to call, too narrowly, the civil rights movement. Recently, scholars have been extending the chronology of the black freedom movement of the 1960s backward to include the industrial unionism, communism and socialism, New Deal activism, and anticolonialism of the 1930s and 1940s, and to argue that the organizations devoted to those politics set the stage for antiracist protests during the 1950s and 1960s. Scholars are also noting how, like educators and other civic leaders, leftists and labor organizers stayed in the thick of the movement through the 1960s. Notwithstanding the Cold War, there were activists in the 1950s and 1960s who maintained Marxist and Popular Front philosophies and who had been members of the Council on African Affairs (CAA), the National Negro Congress (NNC), the Civil Rights Congress (CRC), and the Southern Negro Youth Congress (SNYC). As historians Martha Biondi[26] and Penny Von Eschen[27] have both asserted, the National Negro Labor Council (NNLC) and the CAA operated in New York until the mid-1950s. In various ways, radical leftists continued to play a role in organizing around American racism despite living under a government that scapegoated them.

Historic leftist magazines, such as *New Masses* and *Masses and Mainstream*, are a useful resource for exploring this political community. *Masses and Mainstream* was edited by Herb Aptheker, a Marxist historian and principal political theorist for the American Communist Party who also is credited with developing the concept of the "ideology of white supremacy." Its February 1950 issues offer an extended political and artistic meditation on black history. Aptheker had been a strong advocate of Negro History Week for years. An example is found in a February 11, 1947, article in *New Masses,* another Communist Party–affiliated publication for which he often wrote, titled "Negro History—Arsenal for Liberation." In it Aptheker describes Negro History Week as not just a celebration but also a meaningful and radical political act.

From 1951 on, the February issues of *Masses and Mainstream* would regularly and explicitly be dedicated to Negro History Week. The February 1950 issue, of interest here, isn't described as such, but its content amounts to just that. Its first essay, "Words and White Chauvinism," was written by Lloyd Brown. Brown was a labor organizer, a member of the Communist Party, a journalist, a novelist, and also a friend and editorial companion of Paul Robeson's. He later would write Robeson's biography. Born Lloyd Dight, Brown chose his surname to honor the militant abolitionist John Brown, a reflection of his own radical politics. In this article, Brown explores the symbolism of color and argues that black people shouldn't worry too much about the positive associations in English attached to "light" or "white" and the negative ones associated with "darkness" or "black." Although he acknowledges that white people use white skin as a metaphor and sign for greater value, Brown writes that generally speaking the language of light and dark doesn't necessarily assert white superiority. According to Brown, the question of context is important:

> Consider this fact: there is a song "Lift Every Voice and Sing" which is popularly known as the Negro national anthem. It is generally sung at conventions, commencements, and formal occasions concerned with Negro life and struggle. It contains this line: "Sing a song, full of the faith that the dark past has taught us. . . ." And not only is the oppres-

sive past of slavery "dark," but the future of liberation is "Where the white gleam, of our bright star is cast." If this conception was inherently or even inferentially white chauvinist, we would have the anomaly of a militant people adopting an anthem which vilifies itself! But obviously, here, the Negro people are merely using the traditional color symbols for their general meaning.

Brown's essay reveals how deeply intellectuals pursued their confrontation with the problem of white supremacy. They were concerned not only with political formations and economic relations but also with language and its implicit associations. It is also interesting, however, that Brown deems the singing of "Lift Every Voice" to be militant. This is a provocative counterpoint to the conception popularized less than a decade prior that the song was a feature of American patriotism, as well as a shift away from militancy in mainstream black political life. Although the song is unquestionably patriotic, it isn't obvious to which nation or to whom that patriotism is due. Some listeners and singers interpreted the song as celebrating loyalty to the United States. Others interpreted that loyalty as to a black nation that superseded any government, especially one so consistently oppressive in its treatment of black people at home and abroad.

The second piece in the issue was written by Atlanta-born and Brooklyn-reared Alphaeus Hunton, the executive director of the Council on African Affairs and husband of the late Addie Hunton. Alphaeus Hunton is described by Penny Von Eschen as "one of the most neglected African American intellectuals"[28] of the 1940s and 1950s. Hunton worked as an English professor at Howard University and as an editor of the CAA's *New Africa* magazine before he moved to West Africa with his second wife, Dorothy, in 1960. Working for the CAA, he criticized postwar liberalism for its silence on and support of colonialism. He advocated a Pan-Africanist political vision and systematically analyzed the structural and historic relationships between Africa, the Caribbean, and the United States. He maintained an active engagement with African independence leaders such as Kwame Nkrumah and Nnamdi Azikiwe. Hunton was, moreover, an applied intellectual. For example, he spearheaded campaigns in support of Nigerian trade unionists and the Africa National Congress in South Africa.

Hunton's article in this issue is titled "Upsurge in Africa." The essay begins with a challenge to the idea behind the term "Darkest Africa." Hunton turns from a critique of dominant representations of Africa to a challenge to the political actions associated with imperialist ideas. He rejects the then widely held Western belief that colonialism in Africa would save the British Empire from expiration.

> The present and would-be exploiters of Africa have left just one thing out of their precise calculations and pat blueprints—the people of Africa. The 180 millions of them are rising, organizing, and fighting with increasing strength to break their chains, and this spells the nemesis of colonial exploitation in the last continent left to the imperialist gang. How long can they hold Africa? With the help of guns from the United States, arsenal of world imperialism, the government agents of European and American monopoly are engaged in a brutal war of repression against the African people in a desperate effort to postpone their V-A Day as long as possible. Since World War II, national revolts and widespread strikes have swept every area of Africa.

Hunton's radicalism was thoroughgoing and deviated from both the sexist and anti-intellectual tenor of much of American political discourse. He describes anticolonialist organizing in Ghana, Nigeria, and Somalia, emphasizing the importance of both intellectuals and women in the development of African liberation movements: "In Africa as in Negro America, black women have been in the vanguard of the fight for freedom. They have gone on strike against the vicious pass system in South Africa and against the head tax in Nigeria. They have been jailed and beaten and killed along with their husbands and brothers." He concludes with a global critique of domination, fascism, and capitalism:

> Here in America, too, the Negro people's struggle for full equality and democracy is at the core of the fight against American fascism. The fight of black Americans for their rights is the Achilles heel of American reaction. . . . Thus are the struggles of the 180 million Africans and the 15 million black Americans closely linked. To allow these front lines of the war against imperialism to be breached and broken is unthinkable, to strengthen them is to guarantee the successful building of a new world order of peace, friendship and equality among all people.

In 1951, a year after this issue of *Masses and Mainstream* was published, Hunton was imprisoned for six months as a result of the Department of Justice charge that the CAA was in violation of the McCarran Internal Security Act of 1950. The CAA was subsequently disbanded. Racial liberalism was not simply an argument, it was a piece of a coercive juridical regime that punished those who ventured far outside of its confines.

The February 1950 issue of *Masses and Mainstream* follows Hunton's essay with a series of drawings by Charles White, a distinguished African American visual artist who for two decades had been associated with the political Left. The series of images is titled "LIFT EVERY VOICE . . ." The ellipsis after the words suggests that the images will guide our interpretation of what assessment or action ought to follow our viewing.

The first drawing, "Toward Liberation," depicts a man moving past an unlocked gate, his finger pointed upward. A tree stands behind him, perhaps a lynching tree, perhaps a figure of an agricultural past. The viewer is led to imagine that the subject (and, implicitly, the viewer) will take steps toward freedom.

The second drawing, "Ingram Case," shows Rosa Ingram and her two sons in jail, clutching the cell bars. Ingram and her sons were convicted, and sentenced to death, in 1948 for murdering a white landowner in rural Georgia. The landowner had attempted to rape Ingram, and her sons had come to her defense. The case was widely covered in the black and leftist press, and it elicited a strong response from leftists and civil rights organizers across the nation. Mary Church Terrell, leader of the Women's Committee for Equal Justice committee of the Civil Rights Congress, a leftist organization in the tradition of the National Negro Congress, mobilized the public campaign in support of the Ingrams, while the NAACP provided legal support. A central figure in black politics for decades, Terrell had been a founding member of the NAACP and the Delta Sigma Theta Sorority, as well as an active member of black women's clubs, a suffragette, and an advocate of integration, work that included helping to lead a successful campaign for the integration of the American Association of University Women. Terrell's stature allowed her to serve as a bridge between organizations with deep political differences. But the bridge itself showed that the ties between the mainstream and radical black activists weren't entirely destroyed.

With this image of the Ingrams, Charles White rendered black liberation struggles as ones requiring that black people address the problems of both sexual violence and incarceration, as well as the economic domination that gave planters the power to rape and jail with impunity in the rural South. He rendered the "stony road" and "chastening rod" of "Lift Every Voice" in a contemporary outrage, implicitly encouraging action.

The third drawing, which is untitled, shows a woman with her head covered standing before a group of men, ministering to them. She could be Sojourner Truth, or Harriet Tubman, or any of the countless other women who had served on the front lines of freedom movements. Like Hunton's earlier essay, the centrality of black women and their issues in racial justice organizing was asserted in White's work.

The fourth and final drawing is called "The Living Douglass." Frederick Douglass stands in the upper right corner, leading the way. Around him men are pulling back barbed wire. One in the front holds a scroll, another in the back left corner, a book. Literacy, reading and writing, is yet again imagined as part of the path to freedom. And just as "Lift Every Voice" had been written in the tradition of Douglass, here the song's words are used to reinvigorate the spirit of Douglass, in word and deed.

In an article published in *Masses and Mainstream* several years after this issue, Charles White wrote that "my major concern is to get my work before the common, ordinary people, for me to be accepted as a spokesman for my people, for my work to portray them better, and to be rich and meaningful to them. A work of art was meant to belong to people, not to be a single person's private possession. Art should take its place as one of the necessities of life, like food, clothing and shelter."[29] In the tradition of Vivian Schuyler Key and Augusta Savage, White made visual art that sought to articulate the collective spirit of black America as it struggled for liberation. And like them, White participated in the porous, varied, richly textured, and interconnected web of black associational life, and his art reflected that. DuBois had famously stated in his 1926 essay, "Criteria of Negro Art," that "all art is propaganda." This was as much argument as assertion. As assertion it was something of an overstatement. But the argument reflected the sense of common purpose embedded in black associational life. And black art in the early twentieth century was created in the midst of a set of cultural and political concerns, and an active community, such that communal concerns and practices often fueled the work, and in turn inspired the communities that witnessed it. For White, like his predecessors in their respective moments, this was a powerful instance in which the "people" were represented in his work under the banner of their cherished anthem.

The dominant pop culture story we tell and hear of the civil rights movement tends to follow the standard narrative applied by postwar liberalism. This is to our great detriment. It emphasizes men over women, lawyers over teachers, the NAACP over all other organizations, the Southern Christian Leadership Conference (SCLC) over SNCC, the robust antifascism of the war over the chilling anticommunism of the postwar period, and so on and so forth. In the process of disciplining our recollection of history, the complex political configurations involved in waging the civil rights struggle are often erased. But contemplating the role of "Lift Every Voice and Sing" in the 1940s and 1950s enables us to undertake an abbreviated but nonetheless quite rich exploration of the black political landscape. Unions, nationalisms, communism, socialism, as well as liberalism infused the movement for decades before the *Brown v. Board of Education* decision. And the appearance of "Lift Every Voice and Sing" here and there throughout these struggles at once shows how deeply rooted the anthem was in black life, and also how it could provide an inspiration or rallying cry for people of divergent perspectives.

In his 1956 recording of "The House I Live In," from the album *Sonny Boy*, the renowned saxophonist Sonny Rollins concludes the song with a brief quotation of the first line of "Lift Every Voice and Sing." This was a few months before Rollins recorded his landmark social movement album, *Freedom Suite*. Rollins's quotation holds particular significance because "The House I Live In" had been composed by Earl Robinson, who, at the time of the Rollins recording, had been blacklisted as a communist. The lyrics to "The House I Live In" were written by another prominent white leftist, Abel Meeropol, the man who adopted Julius and Ethel Rosenberg's children after their execution for being convicted of being communist spies. Meeropol was also author of the haunting classic about lynching, most famously recorded by Billie Holiday, "Strange Fruit."

Rollins said he was moved to record "The House I Live In" because "Earl Robinson had written 'Ballad for Americans' for Paul Robeson, which meant a lot to me when I was growing up," and he wanted to put in his own political commentary by quoting the Negro National Anthem. Placing "Lift Every Voice and Sing" within "The House I Live In" suggested a house within a house, the contained unfree amid the "land of the free" out of which the black American freedom struggle emerged. But it also paid homage to the interwoven nature of the radical left tradition, the black formalist and associationalist one, and the black creative imagination as twisting, turning, and sometimes overlapping threads in the black freedom struggle. But another event, one that broke the dam and led America into its social revolution, was surely on Rollins's mind when he teased his listeners with a strain of the Negro National Anthem: the Montgomery Bus Boycott.

CHAPTER FIVE

Shall We Overcome?

Music and the Movement

Ain't gonna let nobody turn me around,
Turn me around, turn me around.
Ain't gonna let nobody turn me around.
I'm gonna keep on walkin', keep on talkin',
Marchin' down to freedom land.

—Freedom song

The Montgomery Bus Boycott was precipitated by the act of Rosa Parks, a longtime activist and well-respected member of the black Montgomery community. Parks refused to yield her seat on a city bus to a white man. She was arrested and fined. The networked associations of Montgomery, long committed to organizing against segregation, responded with a call to boycott the segregation of the city's public buses.

The complex orchestration and fortitude that were necessary for black Montgomery to wage a boycott lasting over a year were extraordinary. Montgomery residents inspired protests and organizing that would follow, throughout the South. Dorothy Posey Jones, the organist of First Baptist Church on Ripley Street in Montgomery, remembered how important it was for the Montgomery community to sustain the spirit and resilience of the boycott through their long campaign. She recalled the particular importance of singing "Lift Every Voice" at the mass meetings that were held during the boycott (which began on December 5, 1955, and ended December 20, 1956). Regular First Baptist meetings served to renew the community's sense of purpose and faith. "They sang 'Lift Every Voice and Sing' at a regular tempo, and the third (stanza) was the prayer section, so we slowed it down. . . . Every seat was filled, the balcony, every place was filled."[1] The organ reverberated throughout the church and microphones piped the sound into the overflow basement room.

The unisonance, the fellow feeling, the hope for the realization of that imagined community as well as the actual community buoyed the boycotters. And they prevailed. On November 13, 1956, in *Browder v. Gayle* (352

U.S. 903), the U.S. Supreme Court ordered Montgomery to integrate its bus system. It was during the Montgomery Bus Boycott that Martin Luther King Jr. first shone as a movement leader. He was anointed by an older generation of Montgomery activists that included trade unionists and people who had belonged to the Brotherhood of Sleeping Car Porters, like E. D. Nixon; club women and teachers, like Joanne Robinson (a professor at Alabama State University); and NAACP activists, like Rosa Parks; along with many other local residents.

Ten days after the boycott ended victoriously, King delivered an address at an Emancipation Day program in Atlanta. It was, however, less a commemoration than a rally. Times were changing and there was reason for excitement. King's speech was an extended riff on "My Country 'Tis of Thee," resounding with the repeated "Let freedom ring." That first day of 1957, in the intimate black Atlanta world, he also anticipated his most famous March on Washington speech, which would be delivered on a world stage in 1963.

My country 'tis of thee,
Sweet land of liberty,
Of thee I sing.
Land where my fathers died,
Land of the Pilgrim's pride,
From every mountain side,
Let freedom ring.

At this point in King's speech, however, the pianist began to play "Lift Every Voice and Sing" in the background. It continued until the end of his speech:

As I heard a great orator say some time ago, that must become literally true. Freedom must ring from every mountain side. Yes, go out determined this afternoon, that it will ring from the snow-capped Rockies of Colorado. Let it ring from the prodigious hill tops of New Hampshire. Let it ring from the mighty Alleghenies of Pennsylvania. Let it ring from the curvaceous slopes of California. But not only that. From every mountain side, (Yeah) let freedom ring. Yes, let it ring from every mountain and hill of Alabama. Let it ring from every mole hill in Mississippi. Let it ring from Lookout Mountain of Tennessee. Let it ring from Stone Mountain of Georgia. From every mountain side, let freedom ring.

"Lift Every Voice" was the backdrop to an early version of the sermon that would come to define the movement. But eventually it would cease to be the sound of the movement.

In the late 1950s, however, the variety of ways we see "Lift Every Voice and Sing" appear in black political life suggests both the continued influence of the song, and how the cultural practices associated with the Deep South, shaped civil rights movement organizing. In 1957, during the months leading up to the struggle to integrate Little Rock's Central High, the city's Phyllis Wheatley YWCA held a book review program. It opened with a singing of "Lift Every Voice and Sing." Then the attendees heard Mildred Henderson review a book written by Charlie May Simon, *All Men Are Brothers,* a pictorial biography of Albert Schweitzer. The author, a white Arkansan woman, was present and spoke as well. The book included a substantial discussion of Schweitzer's work as a medical missionary in Africa. The author took this work to be Schweitzer's response to Jesus's call to become "fishers of men." However, in the process of proselytizing, Schweitzer developed a strong criticism of European colonialism of Africa. Although he did not fully commit himself to the cause of African liberation, this black organization's celebration of Schweitzer in 1957 was symbolic of the slowly shifting American sensibility regarding racial justice that had been fostered by racial liberalism, and the persistent though muted tie to the African continent and diaspora that African Americans felt and their allies sometimes recognized. Schweitzer intoned a responsibility for whites to undo the harm done to indigenous and enslaved people the world over, writing, "I will not enumerate all the crimes that have been committed under the pretext of justice. People robbed native inhabitants of their land, made slaves of them, let loose the scum of mankind upon them. Think of the atrocities that were perpetrated upon people made subservient to us, how systematically we have ruined them with our alcoholic 'gifts,' and everything else we have done. . . . We decimate them, and then, by the stroke of a pen, we take their land so they have nothing left at all."[2] That charge resonated with those who had also been subject to domination on these shores.

Although Pan-Africanism waned during the 1950s and early 1960s, largely because of McCarthyism and the deals struck between the U.S. State Department and the civil rights establishment, threads of connection remained, albeit greatly muted in comparison to the earlier part of the twentieth century. And "Lift Every Voice and Sing" was a consistent motif in moments of pan-African solidarity. The *Chicago Defender,* for example, reported frequently on Ghanaian independence, which was won in 1957. Martin Luther King Jr., along with many other organizers, looked to Ghanaian independence as a source of inspiration in their domestic movement. And Kwame Nkrumah, Ghana's first president, had deeply felt decades of connection with black American intellectuals and activists. In a 1957 article for the *Chicago Defender*, George F. McCray, a black American labor organizer who worked in Africa, reported, "Several weeks ago Nkrumah's Convention People's Party held a gigantic rally at the Sports Stadium. They sang 'Lift Every Voice and Sing' better than do American Negroes then poured a libation calling upon our ancestors."[3] The *Defender*, at that point black America's most popular national newspaper, also reported that at the All African People's Conference of 1959, held in Ghana, "Lift Every Voice and Sing" was sung by Robert A. Lee, an African American physician and expatriate to Ghana. Several of the conference speakers paid tribute to African America for the seeds of Pan-Africanism, and for educating African leaders like Nkrumah. Expatriate reporter McCray was there again as well. He'd traveled for the occasion to Ghana from East Africa, where he was heading a trade union leadership school. And while no Americans were official delegates to that All African People's Conference, a number of black Americans were present, including scholar St. Clair Drake, educator Horace Mann Bond, and Charles Diggs, a black member of Congress from Michigan. Greetings were announced from A. Philip Randolph and the NAACP, as well as other black civil rights organizations.[4]

"Lift Every Voice" was presented in some other quarters as a symbol of black Americans' efforts to push against the door, then slightly ajar, to full citizenship. In 1957, the first radio variety program in the Midwest featuring black talent was broadcast from Youngstown, Ohio, every Sunday afternoon from 2:00 to 2:30 and hosted by LaFrances Chapman Johnson. The program was titled *Lift Every Voice*[5] and used the song as its theme music, rendered by the A. C. Bilbrew Choir of Los Angeles. "Each Sunday a guest speaker presented by Mrs. Johnson discusses some project or subject of general interest to the community." Additionally, talent shows, music, and comedians were featured on the program. In 1957 in Chicago another series of radio broadcasts titled *Lift Every Voice* featured church choirs and their pastors from the South and West Sides of Chicago on Saturdays from noon to 12:30.[6]

Black radio programs in the 1950s tended to focus on news and public affairs relevant to black people, as well as on church and social events, and, of course, music. They became forums for charismatic deejays to become local celebrities. These deejays shared their thoughts and entertained their listeners. But even shows without such personalities were successful. *Listen Chicago*, the first news discussion program aimed at African Americans, debuted in 1946 and ran until 1952. A 1948 newspaper discussion of this program described it as follows:

> To this forum are brought leaders of progressive thought, men and women who have something to say to Chicago. National Credit takes only a sponsor identifying line at the opening and close of the presentation. The entire program is devoted to discussion of subjects like "Democracy and Education," "Civil Rights—and Wrongs," and "Erasing the Color Line."
>
> Most commercial broadcasters in the Windy City were certain that the program was doomed to failure. It was a "heavy" show. It was on the air at the wrong time of day. It displays very little conventional showmanship.
>
> They were wrong. The program is catching on. The National Credit Clothing Company can trace definite business to its sponsorship. The station is receiving real fan mail on the program. Once again it is being proved that community service can be commercial.[7]

Even if the audience for black radio was primarily black, the growing presence of black subject matter on the airwaves indicated that black people were moving further into the mass media sphere on their own terms and not simply as the butt of jokes. And the mainstream radio presentations of black culture and history were also a sign of growing liberalism around the idea of race, and a slow warming to the idea that black Americans were fully American; simply one type of American among other Americans, as though they were just another ethnic group. Yet these hints of liberalism coexisted with entrenched segregation and economic inequality in the North, and a passionate commitment to legal racial stratification as well in the South.

For liberals in the political establishment, the limits of racial justice continued to be rigorously guarded. Paul Robeson's passport still had not been returned when he performed in Oakland, California, in August 1958. He began his concert with "Lift Every Voice" and two and a half hours later ended with a selection from *Othello*. In between he sang Franz Schubert's "Sleep My Little One" as well as Chinese, Yiddish, and Russian folksongs.[8] In a few months his passport would be restored, as the McCarthy era ended. It was as though the U.S. government no longer felt threatened by a radical

Left that had been so diminished. But even the more modest political vision entailed by what came to be known as civil rights would provide a bold challenge to America, one that transformed the nation and owed a debt to Robeson and his comrades.

Ralph Bunche, a Nobel Prize–winning negotiator, diplomat, and political scientist who was one of the black leaders most connected to the White House and political power in the 1950s, spoke in Birmingham at the Sixteenth Street Baptist Church in 1959. He came at the invitation of the Periclean Club. One of many active black associations in Birmingham, the Periclean Club regularly brought distinguished leaders to the city to give lectures on their areas of expertise. The club was also one of many associations in Birmingham that held meetings at the Sixteenth Street Baptist Church. Others included the Semper Fidelis Club, the Imperial Club, and the Alabama State Teachers Association.[9] Bunche had once been a socialist but by the late 1940s was unquestionably a liberal Democrat. In 1959, he spoke to the Pericleans about racial incidents from his youth and urged his listeners to never run away from a fight for principles. Although Bunche was awarded a key to the city by the mayor of Birmingham, he was denied a hotel room in the city. The "Magic City" would not respect even the most distinguished and assimilated black person.

The Periclean Club program, as these things often did, implicitly and explicitly rejected the ideology of white supremacy with its black formalism. It began with an organ prelude by Mrs. Bonna MacPerine Samuel. Then the audience sang "The Star-Spangled Banner." Mrs. A. G. Gaston, the wife of the wealthiest African American man in Birmingham and a cofounder of Mary McLeod Bethune's National Council of Negro Women, introduced Bunche. After he delivered his address, the Dunbar Chorus, named after Paul Laurence Dunbar, sang the Negro spiritual "Let My People Go." The final song was "Lift Every Voice and Sing," followed by a benediction. The three songs on the program signaled the participants' common lot as Americans, as descendants of the people who sang the sorrow songs in slavery, and as members of black social, civic, and political organizations. Regular folks in the room stood alongside wealth and distinction. Without exception, they all lived on the disfavored side of the color line.[10]

The freedom movement through the 1950s was planned largely by local institutions like this. People used civic associations, schools, and churches, as well as unions and political organizations—left, liberal, and moderate—as the structures through which they planned protests, boycotts, and court

cases. Though perhaps not as politically varied as the 1930s, the 1950s movement was well-organized and depended on the deep structure of networked
black life for its execution. Just as the 1954 *Brown v. Board* school desegregation decision rested upon the work not only of the NAACP but also of the
teachers and local community organizations that supported the plaintiffs,
the organizing that multiplied after *Brown* included many different types
of organizations.

When the young people who integrated Central High in Little Rock in
1957 traveled to lecture about their experiences, they were supported by a
tradition and a set of community practices they'd learned from birth. They
were reminded, even after having left segregated schools rich with black
formalism, that that community remained and that they could be nurtured
by it when they returned from the viciousness of the segregationist white
masses. For example, when Melba Patillo and her mother, Lois Patillo, spoke
at First Baptist in Little Rock, it was at the behest of the Youth Fellowship,
which organized and nurtured the identity and the mission of black young
people in that city. Together they sang "Lift Every Voice and Sing."[11] The
spirit of unisonance that day, we can imagine, was one of hope that Melba
would understand that when she ventured out of black institutions to integrate a white school, she carried an entire community's support and dreams
with her.

This was how it was. Black associations, with black formalist expressions,
led by black adults, pursued the goal of racial justice in organized and strategic fashion. But in 1960 things changed. In Greensboro, four North Carolina
A&T students acted spontaneously. They'd been cut and sewn in the black
associational life of schools and churches and civic organizations, Negro
History Week, and the "stand up straight" grace of black formalism. But they
did something unprecedented and beyond the standard ways and means.

On February 1 these four students sat down at a lunch counter. On February 2 they were thirty. On February 3 they were fifty. Sit-ins, as a form of
protest, were not new. But the time, place, and number in Greensboro were.
And their spontaneous energy signaled that the student movement to come
would have a different, more insurgent and more improvisational, structure.
The youth would lead, and they would foster new songs and new tactics and
develop new styles of leadership. By the end of February—that month during which these young people had been raised to honor their ancestors and
freedom fighters, their culture and traditions, the month that included Negro

History Week and Douglass's and Lincoln's birthdays—50,000 students had conducted sit-ins and protests all over the South.

After the spontaneity, it was time for them to organize themselves. On April 15, 1960, 200 students gathered at Shaw University in Raleigh.[12] They were the youth wing of King's SCLC, but they had decided to create their own independent organization in the tradition of the SNYC. It was to be called the Student Nonviolent Coordinating Committee (SNCC, pronounced "Snick"). The conference had been called by Ella Baker, then the secretary of the SCLC. Baker, who was politically committed to the nonhierarchical and democratic participation of everyone in the movement, from the youth to the elders, taught, challenged, and encouraged the young activists as they met. During the conference, Guy Carawan, a white leftist who had been invited, began teaching the students songs. Carawan, who had been trained at the Highlander Folk School, was a member of the People's Songs collective and an active participant in the folk revival movement.[13] Two weeks earlier, at the Highlander Folk School's Annual College Workshop, he had taught the eighty-three students present his reinterpretation of some traditional spirituals and hymns, and he was invited to do the same in Raleigh. These songs were in some sense a return gift. In them, Carawan reworked traditional black music to speak to the movement and the moment. The most significant of these, which he ended the first night of the conference with, was "We Shall Overcome." Years later he described the roots of his reworked composition in this fashion: "The old words were . . . 'I'll Overcome someday, I'll be all right / I'll wear the cross, I'll Wear the Crown / I'll be like him, I'll Sing My Song Someday.'"[14]

"I'll Overcome Someday" was a song written by the Reverend Charles Albert Tindley, a popular black Methodist minister who led a multiracial congregation in Philadelphia. "I'll Overcome Someday" appeared with seven other songs in a hymnal published in 1901. The hymn took its content from Galatians 6:9, "Ye shall overcome if ye faint not. . . . And let us not be weary in doing good, for in due season we shall reap, if we faint not." These words resonated with the arduous struggle black Americans saw before them, and had confronted in the past when Tindley first penned them.

And although "We Shall Overcome" textually came from the Tindley hymn, it was sung to the melody of a different song: black gospel composer Louise Shropshire's hymn "If My Jesus Wills." Shropshire was a close associate of both King and of Birmingham's leading activist, Fred Shuttlesworth.

She was also part of the Highlander Folk School community, as well as the nationally networked Baptist and Church of God in Christ black religious communities.

Carawan's remix of Tindley's words and Shropshire's melody caught on quickly. It was easy to learn and its structure accommodated improvisation. Its slow pace left room for call and response, as well as individual variation in collective song. It was not formalist, but it was spiritual and could be rendered beautifully in black vernacular styles. It was also easily accessed by any and all voices.

Back in New York, however, the not-yet-famous black writer and performer from Stamps, Arkansas, Maya Angelou, was still singing "Lift Every Voice and Sing." In 1960 she and Godfrey Cambridge hosted the "Cabaret for Freedom" at the Village Gate to raise funds for Martin Luther King Jr.'s SCLC. Angelou and Cambridge were inspired to do so by a speech delivered by King in New York. Angelou described the power of that encounter:

> He began to speak in a rich sonorous voice. He brought greetings from our brothers and sisters in Atlanta and in Montgomery, in Charlotte and Raleigh, Jackson and Jacksonville. A lot of you, he reminded us, are from the South and still have ties to the land. Somewhere there was an old grandmother holding on, a few uncles, some cousins and friends. He said the South we might remember is gone. There was a new South. A more violent and ugly South, a country where our white brothers and sisters were terrified of change, inevitable change. They would rather scratch up the land with bloody fingers and take their most precious document, the Declaration of Independence, and throw it in the deepest ocean, bury it under the highest mountain, or burn it in the most flagrant blaze, than admit justice into a seat at the welcome table, and fair-play room in a vacant inn.

For their "Cabaret for Freedom" Angelou and Cambridge gathered an impressive roster of performers, but the audience was perhaps even more impressive, including the writer John Killens and his wife, Grace; Lorraine Hansberry's widower, Bob Nemiroff; Ossie Davis and Ruby Dee; and Sidney and Juanita Poitier. Every seat at the Village Gate was taken. Angelou described the evening in her second memoir, *The Heart of a Woman*: "The show began and the performers, illuminated with the spirit, hit the stage and blazed. Comfortable with the material of their own routines, comedians made the audience howl with pleasure and singers delighted the listeners with familiar romantic songs. The revue, which is what the show had become, moved quickly until a scene from Langston Hughes's 'The Emperor of Haiti' brought the first note of seriousness. Hugh Hurd, playing the title role, reminded us all that although as black people we had a dignity and a love of life, those qualities had to be defended constantly." It wasn't simply happenstance to end with Hughes and Haiti. The insurgency of the Haitian revolution still influenced the black American political imagination, as did Hughes's figure as a leading artist of the New Negro era. History was ever-present in black protest. At the conclusion of the show the cast stood in a straight line and sang the song that would resonate most deeply with them all, "Lift Every Voice and Sing." Angelou wrote, "The audience stood in support and respect. Those who knew the lyrics joined in, building and filling the air with the song often called 'The Negro National Anthem.' After the third bow, Godfrey hugged me and whispered, 'We've got a hit. A hit, damn, a hit.'"

Weeks later, Maya Angelou signed on to be a local coordinator for the growing civil rights organization. But months later, at the 1961 SCLC convention, although the participants closed the proceedings by singing the first and the third verses to "Lift Every Voice and Sing" as usual, they also listened to Guy Carawan and Harry Belafonte sing folk songs of the sort that would soon become known as "freedom songs" for their association with the civil rights movement. Like the SNCC youth, the convention participants were gifted with a remixed version of past sounds for their future protests. This meeting of old and new ways of performing political protest foreshadowed that "Lift Every Voice and Sing" would be slowly but surely bypassed.

That fall, three young SNCC activists arrived in Albany, Georgia, to conduct a voter registration drive. But it grew to be much more. Albany activists dedicated themselves to an effort to desegregate the entire city. Bernice Johnson Reagon, an Albany native serving as the NAACP youth secretary when SNCC came to town, had come of age singing "Lift Every Voice and Sing." In an interview decades later, she said, "I learned that in elementary school. So one of the aspects of growing up in the South in these schools is we got a repertoire that really had something for us in terms of sustaining us in what was a segregated society. So that song has been a part of my repertoire since I was about seven years old."[15] Reagon soon would join SNCC. So did a white woman named Faith Holsaert, who came from New York to join the movement. Holsaert described her coming of age and how it also led her to SNCC:

My sister and I grew up on James Street in a Greenwich Village household headed by two women, our Jewish birth mother, Eunice Spelman Holsaert, and Charity Abigail Bailey, our African-American mother by affection. When I was seven, we spent a year in Haiti where my sister and I were in the racial minority, and our female household was noteworthy. Scene of a historic slave uprising, Haiti, the first Black-run republic in the Americas, prompted a pride in Charity that I took on, because I loved her so much. In my child's heart, Haiti and Blackness and rebellion were one. . . . My 10-year-old classmates and I studied Negro history, so-called Negro history. We learned "Lift Every Voice and Sing," the Black national anthem, in which the stormy past gives rise to hope.[16]

Just as Holsaert had grown up an organizer, so had Reagon. They began to work together. At the first rally, Reagon began by singing "Lift Every Voice and Sing" but didn't get the reaction she expected:

I remember being surprised that everybody in Albany State College gym at that time didn't know the Negro National Anthem, which in Albany you learned from the time you were born. That was one of my first awarenesses that all black people didn't grow up like we did in Albany. After this first march, we're at Union Baptist Church, Charlie Jones looks at me and said—Bernice, sing a song. And I started, *Steal Away*. By the time I got to, troubled—where "trouble" was supposed to bell I didn't see any trouble, so I put "freedom" in there. And I guess that was the first time I really understood sort of using what I'd been given in terms of songs.[17]

Cordell Reagon, a SNCC worker who married Bernice Johnson in 1963, worked with her as one of the Freedom Singers during the movement. He describes the transition in this way: "Charles [Sherrod] and I brought with us the music we had been doing on the freedom rides, and when it mixed with that rich Baptist and African tradition in Albany, something happened. Before we came, the kids might have been singing the Negro National Anthem—we brought something to them and they gave something to us, a spirit, a power that made us less afraid. Together we all made something unbelievable, a total spiritual experience."[18] The transition to freedom songs was major. And, as Reagon remembers, their sound, which traveled from churches to bus stations, lunch counters, and southern streets, became an essential element in the movement:

Most of the mass meeting was singing, in Albany—there was more singing than there was talking. And uh, so most of the work that was done in terms of taking care of movement business, had to do with nurturing the people who had come, and there would be two or three people who would talk but basically songs were the bed of everything . . . and I'd never seen or felt songs do that. . . . I'd had songs in college and high school and church, but in the movement—all the words sounded differently. *Steal Away*, which I'd sung all my life, said something very different—"all in the street, I'm going to let it shine."[19]

"Lift Every Voice and Sing" had once been the primary freedom song, but the SNCC Freedom Singers, along with the other student activists and members of SCLC and CORE and the multitudes who joined marches, sang new freedom songs. The Freedom Singers, in addition to singing at mass meetings, demonstrations, and rallies, also toured and recorded songs as fundraising endeavors. And so the songs circulated beyond the sites of protest. Moreover, freedom songs invited people in who didn't sing well, those who were on their first trip down south, and those who had no familiarity with black institutions or culture but were joining the movement in droves.

The aesthetics of the student movement shifted away not just from "Lift Every Voice" but also from black formalism. SNCC workers, the vanguard and the pulsing heart of the freedom movement, wore overalls day in and day out, like the fieldworkers in the Mississippi Delta that they joined. They became part of local communities. Their work was not primarily in churches or marches, where the features of black formalism were often most pronounced. More important, however, the times called most insistently for strategizing and fighting, not self-defining and narrating. Though the movement relied upon black formalism, and with it the anthem, the move away from them both in the midst of the period's most pressing demands made a great deal of sense.

But through the détentes, crises, and standoffs of the movement, freedom songs were there. The songs emboldened organizers and protesters as they faced down deadly racism. But they also kept spirit intact, not unlike the spirituals and work songs of the past. Organizers sang them in Albany, Birmingham, the Mississippi Delta, Atlanta, and many other sites of movement. And the youth who revived and reinterpreted the traditional purposes of song remained at the forefront. Even its most prominent "elder," Martin Luther King Jr., was only in his twenties and thirties during his leadership days. Still, SCLC and SNCC members butted heads over SNCC's resistance to traditional hierarchical organizing models, and these felt like generational conflicts. Young activists, and their allies, stepped out in courage and with a more diffuse and democratic leadership philosophy that was echoed in how they sang for freedom.

Although Albany's activists weren't successful in achieving the goal of desegregation, Birmingham's benefited from the knowledge garnered from both successes and failures, and they succeeded in desegregating their city. Moreover, the Birmingham's Children's Crusade of 1963 awakened the nation to the brutality of the Deep South. Birmingham's segregationist political leaders were shaken by the black youth of their city, who displayed all the self-regard, interdependence, and courage that had been socialized in black children by teachers, community activists, and families for generations. Organizers in Birmingham were both local, such as Fred Shuttlesworth's Alabama Christian Movement for Civil Rights, and regional, like the SCLC. The youth there, however, as in Greensboro, acted on their own behalf, at times betraying their elders' wishes in order to join and shape the movement.

During the civil rights movement, southern black radio stations often used their transmissions to share information and provide forums for discussion among diffuse black communities that were cut off from each other by the boundaries of segregation and geography. They served as an extension of the historic role of the black press. In Birmingham, Tall Paul White of WEDR drew praise from Martin Luther King Jr. and other prominent African American leaders for supporting student protesters. His coded language told students when to walk out and which streets to take. Their demonstrations, arrests, and confrontations with dogs and fire hoses, televised on national TV news, led to an agreement in May between the city's African American leaders, the SCLC, and the mayor to integrate public facilities.

The balance between understanding that the young activists benefited from the transmission of tradition, on the one hand, and that youth were breaking into a new phase of the freedom movement, on the other, must be treated with care. Deborah E. McDowell describes an intergenerational community event that took place earlier in 1963 in her memoir *Leaving Pipeshop: Memories of Kin.* That February's Lincoln Douglass Birthday Banquet, hosted by the Bessemer Voters League, was an impassioned occasion, Mc-

Dowell writes: "For months schools and churches throughout the Birmingham area had been preparing for the ceremony. . . . The *Birmingham World* headlined speakers and black radio stations broadcast a veritable Who's Who of civil rights personalities, who flowed in and out of Birmingham throughout 1963."[20] This was the centennial year of the Emancipation Proclamation, and the formalism of the occasion was befitting such an important event. Rev. Manfred McKinley, a preacher and a leading voting rights organizer, delivered the keynote address. "A royal blue banner billowed on the church's front façade and you could see the gold lettering EMANCIPATION—100 YEARS, all the way from the Bessemer Super Highway. The women of the Deaconess society cooked all day for the event, and the girls of the junior choir helped to serve the collard greens, mustard yellow scoops of potato salad, fried chicken, corn bread and sweet potato pie."[21] Consistent with the tradition, McDowell, then eleven years old, was also a participant in the program. She delivered a portion of the Gettysburg Address, a "speech that I can still recite almost verbatim now, thirty plus years hence. I had practiced it over and over again . . . but none of the rehearsals had prepared me for the overwhelming emotion I felt that evening in the basement as the candles flickered on the paper covered tables and the room grew very still."[22]

Several months later, girls and boys as young as McDowell would be attacked by police dogs, knocked down by fire hoses, and jailed at the fairgrounds in Birmingham. Moments like the one McDowell described prepared them for the transformation to the new mode of organizing. The Lincoln Douglass Banquet concluded with "Lift Every Voice and Sing." But at the fairgrounds the children sang the freedom songs. While "Lift Every Voice and Sing" was integral to the socialization that enabled organizers and activists in Birmingham and elsewhere to confront Jim Crow so courageously, the musical resources they looked to now, for the most part, were songs like "We Shall Overcome" and "We Shall Not Be Moved." In the anticipation of dangerous encounters, short insistent verses worked better. When the police descended, and some marchers would fall, punchy and powerful lines bolstered their courage. The immediacy of danger called forth music that could echo the shouts of field hollers and the wails of spirituals of supplication. Protesters were moving outside of the zones and rituals of black associational life when they began daily and dangerous confrontations with American public space, declaring it no longer "whites only."

In a 1963 article for the *Chicago Defender*, columnist Dave Potter declared "We Shall Overcome" to be the "New Negro Anthem." He described it as "the theme song of America's militant Negro" that was displacing "Lift Every Voice and Sing": "Until the civil rights movement got into full swing in Montgomery, Alabama, with the famed bus boycott led by the Rev. Dr. Martin Luther King and his Southern Christian Leadership Conference, the acknowledged Negro National Anthem was 'Lift Every Voice and Sing,' written by James Weldon Johnson."[23]

That may have been an overstatement or perhaps too early a declaration. On March 28, 1963, over 100 high school students marched to the downtown businesses in Rome, Georgia, to protest segregation. The students held sit-ins and were refused service at G. C. Murphy Co., Keith-Walgreen Drug Store, Redford's Variety Store, and Enloe Drug Store. Police were called, and about sixty students were arrested and sent to jail for the next several days. Their young age did not spare them punishment. Their families who came to bring them provisions were turned away. At night the guards made the teenagers cold by turning on the air conditioners and opening windows, and during the day they made them roast by keeping the windows closed and the air conditioners off. To keep their spirits up, the youth sang freedom songs like "Go Down, Moses," with lyrics modified to replace Pharaoh with the local police chief. On Sunday, however, the day before their court hearings, they recited the Lord's Prayer and sang "Lift Every Voice and Sing."[24] Though not a freedom song, it still had a treasured meaning.

Some people blended freedom songs with "Lift Every Voice," holding on to tradition and embracing the renewed passion for freedom fighting at once. A letter to the *Defender*'s editors by Bessie Hughes, just a few weeks prior to the Rome protests, commented on a televised debate between James Baldwin and James Kilpatrick, the editor of the *Richmond News Leader*. Kilpatrick was an advocate for segregation who argued that black people were biologically inferior to whites. Baldwin responded to him with characteristic poise and brilliance. In her letter, Hughes responded to Kilpatrick's assertion that Negroes had not contributed to Western civilization by referencing Percy Julian, Adam Clayton Powell, Ralph Bunche, W. C. Handy, and Martin Luther King Jr. She concluded the letter with a mixture of the two anthems: "Sing a Song Full of the Faith that the Dark Past has taught us, Sing a Song, full of the hope that the present has brought us. Facing the Rising sun of our new day begun for WE SHALL SURELY OVERCOME!"[25]

That summer, over twenty years after A. Philip Randolph and Bayard Rustin had begun to plan their March on Washington, it finally happened. Toward the end of the march, a star-studded, televised, and relatively sanitized display of movement energies, Benjamin Mays began his benediction with the first words of the third verse of "Lift Every Voice and Sing": "God of History of all mankind. God of Abraham and Moses, Amos and Isaiah, Jesus and Paul. God of our weary years, God of our silent tears." It was a subtle warning and reference, modest and barely noticeable to the untrained ear. Other things were clearly noticeable, though. DuBois had died mere hours before the march began, as an expatriate living in Ghana. Both women activists and more radical voices of the movement in general were absent from the program. And notwithstanding the power of Martin Luther King Jr.'s gorgeous speech, and the national attention the march garnered, the federal government was still failing to adequately support the members of SNCC working under harrowing conditions in the Mississippi Delta and Alabama.

Mays's prayer to the "God of our weary years" was a prophetic supplication in advance of the tragedy to come. In the early morning of Sunday, September 15, 1963, just shy of three weeks after the March on Washington, members of the Ku Klux Klan planted a box of dynamite with a time delay under the steps of the Sixteenth Street Baptist Church in Birmingham, near the basement. At a little after 10:00 that morning, Sunday school children walked into the basement assembly room to prepare for the day's sermon. It was titled "The Love That Forgives." The bomb exploded, killing four girls: Addie Mae Collins (age fourteen), Denise McNair (age eleven), Carole Robertson (age fourteen), and Cynthia Wesley (age fourteen). Addie's younger sister Sara and twenty-one other people at the church were injured. A gaping hole was left in the rear wall. The back steps were blown away. All but one of the stained glass windows were shattered. The one that remained showed Jesus Christ with a group of little children.

Black Birmingham furiously took to the streets in response. Abraham Wood, pastor of the Metropolitan Baptist Church of Birmingham and president of the local branch of the SCLC, described how he "dashed to that scene. . . . I found a group of young blacks with a pile of rocks and every car that passed with a white driver in it, they were tearing it up."[26] The boys rejected his pleas that they maintain "nonviolent resistance." One child protester, thirteen-year-old Virgil Ware, who is today barely remembered, was also killed by a group of white men in the uproar.

The tragedy in Birmingham revealed that nonviolent resistance required extraordinary discipline and courage. It faced barbaric attacks against the very idea of black citizenship. And at times it felt like too high a price to pay. That day Wood said to himself, "Not going to be long till this thing is going to take a new turn," a turn away from forms of resistance that required forbearance in response to obscene violence. This shouldn't have been surprising to anyone. The three-story Sixteenth Street Baptist Church in Birmingham had been a rallying site. It was where the students who were arrested during the 1963 Birmingham campaign's Children's Crusade were trained. It was where two generations of black communities had met, organized, socialized, and developed plans for freedom. That September morning it became the site of a terrorist attack on the black community, a violent punishment for asserting their long overdue rights to citizenship.

Congress passed the Civil Rights Act in 1964. The act was supposed to guarantee equal application of voter registration requirements and finally ban racial segregation in schools, workplaces, and facilities that served the general public, under the authority granted to Congress through the Constitution's Commerce Clause. For several years, the U.S. Department of Justice had brought lawsuits to support black voting rights, but local judges and voting registrars consistently thwarted these efforts. And they continued to do so even after the passage of the Civil Rights Act. Concurrently, the Student Nonviolent Coordinating Committee worked with local black organizations to promote voter registration in various parts of the South. Again, local authorities were intransigent. However, black people in the Selma area, more rural and less resistant historically than those in Birmingham, were becoming more organized and militant. They wanted to ratchet up their movement and bring more people to Selma to wage struggle. Selma residents invited Martin Luther King Jr. and the SCLC to their city in January 1965. Soon thereafter daily marches began. They were focused in particular on voting rights. Although the Selma community had been organizing for years prior to King's arrival, his presence drew more attention to the small city than it had ever received before. When King was arrested in Selma, the *New York Times* published an open letter he sent to them that dramatically asserted, "THERE ARE MORE NEGROES IN JAIL WITH ME THAN THERE ARE ON THE VOTING ROLLS."[27]

Mass rallies were held in churches and schools. Groups of teachers protested, students protested, and families protested. The activists had a series of confrontations with the violent agents of white supremacy, including police who routinely beat and sometimes killed protesters. The passion these state actors had for racism made those charged with upholding the law appear to be the lawless ones. And the presence of television cameras, witnesses for the nation, helped the organizers shift national public opinion to their cause.

On March 3, King announced a plan to march from Selma to Montgomery, the state capital. The marchers were confronted on the Edmund Pettus Bridge, somewhat appropriately named after a Confederate army general. As the confrontation began, ABC was showing the film *Judgment at Nuremberg*. It depicted the trials of Nazi war criminals. The movie was interrupted to report on the scene in Montgomery. State troopers beat 600 unarmed marchers with billy clubs, fists, and feet. They blinded them with tear gas, and chaos ensued. Forty-eight million viewers witnessed America's homegrown fascism for fifteen uninterrupted minutes.

The next day, a call was sent out by Selma organizers for clergy from across the country to come and support them. Approximately 450 people arrived quickly, including the Unitarian minister James Reeb of Boston. The night of his arrival, he ate dinner at an integrated restaurant with two of his colleagues, Clark Olsen and Orloff Miller. They walked into the balmy Selma night and were accosted and beaten by a group of white locals. Reeb was driven to a hospital in Birmingham, where he died from his injuries two days later. His funeral was held in Selma on March 15.

Representatives of various religious traditions came to Selma to pay tribute to James Reeb. Some of the speakers at the funeral, unfortunately, treated Reeb, a white man, as an exceptional victim. In truth, his story was yet another tragedy. He was one of a very long line of victims, including Jimmie Lee Jackson, a twenty-six-year-old black organizer who had been killed two weeks prior to Reeb. Reporters described the funeral in general as more than a little disorganized. It was filled with a motley crew of people, many of whom had had no part in the movement but who had just come down to partake in its latest devastation.

When King took to the podium, however, he made meaning of the gathering. He called them all to accountability, asking rhetorically, "Who killed Jim Reeb?" A few ignorant men, he answered. He then asked, "What killed

Jim Reeb?" An irrelevant church, he answered, an indifferent clergy, an ir-responsible political system, a corrupt law enforcement hierarchy, a timid federal government, and an uncommitted black population.

He encouraged everyone to put their bodies on the line to destroy segre-gation. He challenged them to see that Jim Reeb's death wasn't in vain and that his work would continue.

King's eulogy began with references to *Romeo and Juliet* but ended with *Hamlet*. He took the mourners from romance to tragedy, from idealistic hope to reckoning. According to the program, the benediction of the service was supposed to be offered by a rabbi, after which the congregation would sing "We Shall Overcome." A *Life* magazine reporter noted this didn't quite happen:

> In everyone's combined weariness and exultation things got a bit mixed up. We were all on our feet, holding crossed-over hands, swaying and singing before the rabbi could reach the pulpit. The surprises overwhelmed me as I watched [a] bearded primate intoning the moving Negro anthem: felt the two men on either side tugging my crossed arms, even heard my own voice seem to soar. Then suddenly as we were all humming the final verse the rabbi got started. Over the throbbing church filled ecumenical hum of more than 400 nuns and clerics, we could clearly hear him intone the Kaddish, the ancient Hebrew prayer for the dead.[28]

The "Negro anthem" they intoned was not "Lift Every Voice and Sing." The congregation sang "We Shall Overcome." In some ways this signaled the ultimate displacement of "Lift Every Voice." "We Shall Overcome" was in the eyes of the nation, and in the lungs of protesters, the anthem of the civil rights movement. The day of Rev. Reeb's funeral, President Lyndon Johnson addressed Congress and announced that he would introduce a Voting Rights Act for African Americans in the South. Seventy million Americans watched his announcement on TV. Johnson used the phrase "We Shall Overcome" as a refrain, saying, "It is the effort of American Negroes to secure for them-selves the full blessings of American life. Their cause must be our cause, too. Because it's not just Negroes, but really it's all of us, who must overcome the crippling legacy of bigotry and injustice. And *we shall overcome*."

Later in the speech he added, "These are the enemies: poverty, ignorance, disease. They are our enemies, not our fellow man, not our neighbor. And these enemies too—poverty, disease and ignorance—*we shall overcome.*" But the conclusion to his speech reveals much more: "At the real heart of the battle for equality is a deep-seated belief in the democratic process. Equality depends, not on the force of arms or tear gas, but depends upon the force of moral right—not on recourse to violence, but on respect for law and order."

The law had only rarely and recently been on the side of civil rights protesters. This legislation was the exception, rather than the rule. In many if not most other instances, "order," when it came to black communities, was nothing more than a streamlined system of racial domination. Whereas movement people had adopted the Augustinian principle that "that which is not just, is not law," or at least not binding upon people of conscience, President Johnson revealed what would be the constrained scope of this landmark civil rights legislation.

The march resumed in Selma, from March 21 to 25. This time, President Johnson provided federal troops to protect the marchers. This protection required disabling three bombs that were set along the route. Violent racism wouldn't die easily. Once they arrived in Montgomery, the marchers gathered for a festival-like rally. Harry Belafonte; Peter, Paul, and Mary; Odetta; and Joan Baez all performed. Nina Simone sang "Mississippi Goddam," reflecting the rebirth of militancy.

But before the party, King spoke to the crowd, which numbered around 25,000 people. He was poignant and impassioned; he recalled the loss of life and the hardship of the past several years of struggle:

> We've come a long way since that travesty of justice was perpetrated upon the American mind. James Weldon Johnson put it eloquently. He said:
>
> > *We have come over a way*
> > *That with tears hath been watered. (Yes, sir.)*
> > *We have come treading our paths*
> > *Through the blood of the slaughtered. (Yes, sir.)*
> > *Out of the gloomy past, (Yes, sir.)*
> > *Till now we stand at last*
> > *Where the white gleam*
> > *Of our bright star is cast. (Speak, sir.)*

"Lift Every Voice and Sing" became antiphonal as King recited it and the people responded:

Today I want to tell the city of Selma. (Tell them, Doctor.) Today I want to say to the state of Alabama. (Yes, sir.) Today I want to say to the people of America and the nations of the world, that we are not about to turn around. (Yes, sir.) We are on the move now. (Yes, sir.)

Yes, we are on the move and no wave of racism can stop us. (Yes, sir.) We are on the move now. The burning of our churches will not deter us. (Yes, sir.) The bombing of our homes will not dissuade us. (Yes, sir.) We are on the move now. (Yes, sir.)

At the conclusion, his dance with the Negro National Anthem shifted to the phrasing at the end of the first verse, "Let us march on":

Let us therefore continue our triumphant march (Uh huh) to the realization of the American dream. (Yes, sir.) Let us march on segregated housing (Yes, sir) until every ghetto or social and economic depression dissolves, and Negroes and whites live side by side in decent, safe, and sanitary housing. (Yes, sir.) Let us march on segregated schools (Let us march, Tell it) until every vestige of segregated and inferior education becomes a thing of the past, and Negroes and whites study side-by-side in the socially healing context of the classroom. Let us march on poverty (Let us march) until no American parent has to skip a meal so that their children may eat. (Yes, sir.) March on poverty (Let us march) until no starved man walks the streets of our cities and towns (Yes, sir) in search of jobs that do not exist.

By most accounts, Selma marked a victory. But King's citation of the second verse of "Lift Every Voice and Sing" revealed his more nuanced feelings about the moment. This was no mere sentimental or poetic gesture toward the old anthem in the midst of a new day. King went to a resource, a verse, that spoke particularly to grief. The Selma march led to a legislative victory, yes, but at such a heavy price: the deaths of Jimmie Lee Jackson, Jonathan Daniels, a New England Seminarian–turned–civil rights protester who was murdered in Alabama, and James Reeb. Soon the triumphant protesters would learn that Viola Liuzzo, a white woman who had come south to support the movement, was shot to death by Klan members on that day of celebration. And after her death her reputation would be sullied in the press by those who could not imagine anything but a prurient reason for a white mother joining the freedom movement. For years, and even generations, death had been the response the society offered in response to black freedom dreams. The triumphalist narrative that is generally offered of Selma minimizes how tortured the time actually was, and how the Voting Rights Act, as King and so many other organizers knew, would not solve the hunger, joblessness, exploitation, and police brutality that black Americans experienced in a racist society.

Less than two weeks after Lyndon Johnson signed the Voting Rights Act, Watts, a working-class black neighborhood in Los Angeles, was in flames. The conflagration began when a policeman pulled over a young black male driver, Marquette Frye. His brother, Ronald, who was riding in the car with Marquette, left the scene to get their mother from home two blocks away. Marquette argued as the officer tried to arrest him. It was a warm night, so people were outside, and they began to gather around Marquette and the police officer. Ronald returned with his mother. The officer was unsuccessful in getting Marquette to submit to arrest. A scuffle followed. Ronald and his mother tried to protect Marquette. The officer called for back up and the group arrested Marquette, Ronald, and their mother. As the crowd of onlookers, now numbering close to 300 gathered at the scene, their collective anger at police officers who routinely harassed, arrested, and brutalized them, bubbled up into outrage. This set off a six-day rebellion. Enraged citizens overturned and burned automobiles. They broke into grocery stores, liquor stores, department stores, and pawnshops. Over 14,000 California National Guard troops were mobilized to descend on South Los Angeles. Thirty-four people died, the majority of them black and at the hands of the National Guard and the Los Angeles Police Department. The casualties included 118 people shot and over 1,000 injured. There were approximately 4,000 arrests. This was Johnson's beloved "law and order." Voting had not solved the problems of black life in the West, and the problems of black life in the West were national problems. They beleaguered black people in the North, South, and Midwest as well. Police brutality, poverty, and systemic marginalization were the lot of black people all over the nation. Racial liberalism did not provide solutions for this.

The failure of racial liberalism was dramatically rendered at the 1964 World's Fair. As with the 1939 fair, there was a nod to black contributions in the form of an art piece dedicated to "Lift Every Voice and Sing." James Ira DeLoache had been commissioned by the NAACP to do a mural named and inspired by the words "Our New Day Begun." This mural was selected for display at the World's Fair. At 48 × 8 inches, it was an inspiring, flowing, and captivating twelve-section mural.[29] The tableaux depicted the seizure of Africans as slaves, the slave system in operation, and the rise of King Cotton. The Underground Railroad; abolitionists John Brown, Harriet Tubman, and Frederick Douglass; the Negro flight to the Union during the Civil War; a lynching; the NAACP silent protest march on Fifth Avenue in 1917; the facade of the Supreme Court building; and the spirit of the contemporary "direct action" tactics were depicted chronologically from left to right. DeLoache, a graduate of Booker T. Washington High School in Norfolk, Virginia, went on to study at both Howard University and Cooper Union. His work was often historically based and concerned with the black freedom struggle. He had previously presented a painting of Harriet Tubman to President William Tubman of Liberia, and one of Crispus Attucks to President Sylvanus Olympio of Togo. The Brooklyn PTA had commissioned portraits of John Brown and Benjamin Banneker from him. DeLoache was thus an apt choice of artist to depict the "Negro in the World." *Our New Day Begun* was finished in 1964 and hung at the New York World's Fair in the Hall of Education. Later it would become part of the Schomburg Collection in the New York Public Library before being gifted to Dillard University in Louisiana in the 1980s.

The phrase "New Day Begun" suggests hopefulness. But given the national energy in the throes of the civil rights movement, "March on 'til Victory Is Won" would have been a more appropriate title. The theme of that year's World's Fair was "peace through understanding." And it was expected to bring a great deal of money to New York City during the two years the exhibition was to be up. It was also expected to bring good publicity to the city. Plans were made for portions of the opening ceremony to be televised, and President Johnson announced that he would attend the festivities to deliver the keynote address.

Black New Yorkers, however, did not seem to be particularly moved by the World's Fair, and they paid little attention to DeLoache's contribution to it. They were at best ambivalent, and many were outraged about the whole enterprise. The more than 1 million black people in the city suffered from racial inequality in every arena: substandard housing and schools, employment discrimination, and poverty were widespread. The Brooklyn branch of CORE planned a massive protest of the fair, which they considered too expensive and indulgent given the dire conditions under which black New Yorkers lived. CORE had been founded in 1942 by the Fellowship of Reconciliation. From the outset, it had embraced nonviolent direct action rather than the litigation and persuasion that the NAACP was known for. CORE had been a direct influence upon the SCLC. However, the organization had floundered as a result of red-baiting in the McCarthy era. In 1964 CORE had only recently been revived and revitalized by the model of the southern movement. The Brooklyn branch of CORE was more militant than most. The other New York branches of CORE discouraged plans to disrupt the World's Fair. No matter. Brooklyn CORE announced a plan for a massive protest at the opening of the World's Fair during a press conference held at the historic Hotel Theresa in Harlem, where the Johnson brothers, Malcolm X, and other black artists, intellectuals, and activists had traditionally gathered when they were in New York.[30] At the press conference CORE boasted that 1,800 drivers pledged to stall on the roadways and would block bridges, subway cars, and all traffic going in and out of the fair on its opening day. In response to these plans, the mayor sent 1,000 police to guard the fair.

But very few people—protesters or patrons—actually showed up. It was raining, and the threat of a conflict scared visitors away. Nevertheless, President Johnson delivered a speech at the opening and was directly confronted by young protesters who found his civil rights record wholly insufficient. They shouted "Jim Crow Must Go!" and "Freedom Now!" directly at the president. One sign read, "A World's Fair Is a Luxury but a Fair World Is a Necessity," while another invited attendees to "See New York's Worse Fair—Segregated Schools for Negroes, Puerto Ricans and Rats."[31] Johnson was alarmed. He described his Great Society initiative to a crowd that included loud freedom movement hecklers.

Their sentiment was shared in many parts of black America. Before Watts there were the Harlem Riots, a six-day uprising that followed a police lieutenant's killing of a black child. The years between 1964 and 1965 were not simply bloody for Selma and Birmingham: Harlem, Chicago, and Los Angeles also ached and roared against injustice. Black America was dissatisfied and rightly so, notwithstanding congressional acts that were necessary but also insufficient. The acts didn't change economic disenfranchisement, police violence, deindustrialization, and underfunded schools. Black America also grieved the death toll of the struggle that had been waged. And then raged. Black power was coming, and it would reclaim one of its noblest inheritances: "Lift Every Voice and Sing."

CHAPTER SIX

All Power, All Poetry, to the People

From "Negro" to "Black" National Anthem

There's been so many things that's held us down
But now it looks like things are finally coming around
I know we got, a long long way to go
And where we'll end up, I don't know

—GENE MCFADDEN and JOHN WHITEHEAD,
  "Ain't No Stoppin' Us Now"

James Meredith began walking on June 6, 1966. He started in Memphis, Tennessee, and planned to go all the way to Jackson, Mississippi, on foot, a distance of 220 miles. Meredith was frustrated. Four years after he'd integrated Ole Miss, two years after the passage of the Civil Rights Act, and a year after the Voting Rights Act, little progress had been made to lift the heavy burden of racism on the backs of African Americans. In September 1962, he'd been escorted by federal marshals into his dorm room. In response, several thousand protesters attacked the marshals. President John F. Kennedy had to send 1,400 troops from Fort Dix to protect him by morning. Meredith knew firsthand how hysterical the commitment to white supremacy was and yet confronted it again anyway.

On the second day of his Memphis to Jackson "March against Fear," Meredith was shot by a white gunman. With Meredith recovering in the hospital, activists from various organizations committed to continue the walk in his stead. On the way they registered over 4,000 black people to vote in various counties. They were joined and celebrated at some places, yet also jeered and threatened. The marchers camped out each evening, usually at schools. But when they arrived at the Street Elementary School in Greenwood, Mississippi, where they planned to stay the night, Stokely Carmichael, the young SNCC leader, was arrested for trespassing on public property. After his release, he went to a park where the marchers had gathered. Carmichael took to a speaker's platform that was set up and delivered his historic "Black Power" speech. Just a day before he had been encouraged by another young activist, Willie Ricks, to adopt the slogan. They'd gone back and forth in a call and response with one asking, "What do you want?" and the other responding, "Black Power!" Carmichael's speech that night connected domestic racism to America's imperialist foreign policy and demanded that his listeners hold themselves both accountable and worthy:

We have to talk about wars and soldiers and just what that means. A mercenary is a hired killer and any black man serving in this man's army is a black mercenary, nothing else. A mercenary fights for a country for a price but does not enjoy the rights of the country for which he is fighting. A mercenary will go to Vietnam to fight for free elections for the Vietnamese but doesn't have free elections in Alabama, Mississippi, Georgia, Texas, Louisiana, South Carolina and Washington, D.C. A mercenary goes to Vietnam and gets shot fighting for his country and they won't even bury him in his own hometown. He's a mercenary, that's all. We must find the strength so that when they start grabbing us to fight their war we say, "Hell no."

Like Malcolm X, Carmichael preached self-love and community care in addition to radical and complete liberation.

There is a psychological war going on in this country and it's whether or not black people are going to be able to use the terms they want about their movement without white people's blessing. We have to tell them we are going to use the term "Black Power" and we are going to define it because Black Power speaks to us. We can't let them project Black Power because they can only project it from white power and we know what white power has done to us. We have to organize ourselves to speak from a position of strength and stop begging people to look kindly upon us. We are going to build a movement in this country based on the color of our skins that is going to free us from our oppressors and we have to do that ourselves.[1]

The black power call was SNCC's answer to Malcolm X, who had been murdered in February 1965. Malcolm was a leader many members of SNCC had embraced as the voice of a new radicalism, and they saw themselves continuing his work. A group of them had traveled across Africa with Malcolm in 1964 and, like earlier generations, had recognized that their struggle in the United States was tied to the liberation of African people globally. The rift between two ways of doing protest became clear during the Meredith march.

King arrived in Mississippi on Friday. He came from Chicago, where he had faced a brutal white mob that responded to his Open Housing marches in ways that exceeded in both tenor and force much of the nastiness he'd experienced in the Deep South. Out from the Chicago mob a bottle flew and hit him in the head midstride, causing a stream of blood to pour down his face. Now in Mississippi, King and Carmichael walked alongside each other, debating. They were in tactical and ideological conflict but showed mutual care. Some SNCC marchers chanted "Black Power," while SCLC members shouted their slogan "Freedom Now." All of them were tear-gassed and attacked by the Mississippi state police, again, when they tried to camp on school grounds in Canton. Although the governor had promised to protect them, he didn't. And federal forces were nowhere to be found, either. The marchers continued and finally were able to stop, rest, clean up, and replenish on the campus of the historically black Tougaloo College, outside of Jackson. The next day they entered the state capital. The crowd by then was massive. Among the roughly 15,000 people were celebrities, including James Brown, Dick Gregory, and Marlon Brando. A partially recovered James Meredith stood on the front lines with Martin Luther King Jr. Jackson-bred R&B performer Maybelle Smith sang "Lift Every Voice and Sing."

It was to be remembered as the last great march of the movement. There was dissension in the ranks for sure, but the spirit of the time was changing as well. Black organizers were battle-weary and fully awakened to the horrific depths of American racism. People began to reach even more deeply into the cultural repertoire to find what kept the enslaved and their spirits alive. Transcendence had already been appealed to, black people had attempted to rise above the veil by taking the moral high ground, and they were murdered and beaten in the process. Now the deepest recesses of resilience and resistance had to be called forward and championed. That process was called by many names: black power, black consciousness, black is beautiful, and soul.

In May 1964, two years prior to Meredith's March against Fear, Sargeant Gerald Westbrook published an article in *Negro Digest* that sought to capture "The Essence of Soul": "The dictionary gives several definitions for this particular essence," Westbrook writes, "history identifies those who possessed it; the bible reveals from whence it came. The song that begins 'Lift Every Voice and Sing' portrays it. Violent death often takes he who displays it—Medgar Evers he conveyed it. Many more died, but the essence lives on and on."[2]

Westbrook goes on to describe the manifestation of soul in James Meredith's fight against Ole Miss, pianist Mary Lou Williams's compositions, and at the March on Washington: "Soul combines strength and a feeling of helplessness, faith and a feeling of hopelessness, an awareness of living and suffering, a love for loving, an urge for laughing, and the need to cry. Soul is to each of us what it is unto itself, a reflection of life's miseries and a mirror for its joys. We have caught that reflection, we have looked into that mirror. Such is Soul, the essence we feel."[3] From the mid-1960s to the mid-1970s, soul was foregrounded alongside black power, and together, along with Pan-Africanism, these sensibilities birthed the cultural and social movements known as black power, black consciousness, and black arts.

In the February 1965 issue of *Negro Digest*, an article by Donald Henderson, then a faculty member in the Sociology Department at the University of Akron, titled "Negro Militancy Is Not New: A History of Protest in America," gave context to the growing sense of militancy among young black Americans that would be on display in Watts, Newark, and Jackson in the near future: "The rather general belief that the Negro passively accepted his position as slave and later as second-class citizen is hardly the case."[4] Henderson gives an account of slave insurrections, maroon colonies, Garveyism, and the New Negro–era NAACP. Among his examples of militancy in literature are James Baldwin's *The Fire Next Time*, Paul Laurence Dunbar's poem "Sympathy," and Langston Hughes's "Song for My People," as well as James Weldon Johnson's Negro National Anthem, and Claude McKay's "If We Must Die."

The reference to "Lift Every Voice and Sing" in both discussions of militancy and soul is much more than an invocation of the song's once-powerful influence. In the mid-1960s the emotional energy of the battle-weary movement's foot soldiers became bolder, and freedom fighters embraced blackness, both literally and figuratively. Evidence was all around that the aspiration to integration would fail. Black people in northern cities were caught in ghettoes. The white South had resisted and murdered black people with every step they took closer to full citizenship.

Acquiring property and the control of institutions had always been elusive for northern and midwestern African Americans, particularly because of the history of redlining and restrictive covenants. Although blacks in some of these cities lived without de jure segregation, and could always vote, black people in the North experienced pervasive disenfranchisement and had fewer civic institutions than those in the segregated South. The new black nationalist organizations and movements that sprung up in the late 1960s were deliberately institution building. They imagined revolution and independence, at home and abroad. In parallel to postcolonial nations in Africa and the Caribbean, they envisioned new economic systems and political structures, and they built intentional communities. These included programs for children that provided both after-school and before-school care, and even schools in some places. Cooperative living arrangements cropped up, and black college students on predominantly white campuses protested to gain their own black living spaces, while those at historically black colleges protested the conservative rules of administrations and boards. In some ways, this was also an effort to reimagine black associational life. It couldn't be the same as it once was. Television, the social and sexual revolutions, and increased options, opportunities, and mobility for educated black young adults meant that even the most passionate activists were unlikely to find a world as highly networked as that of their parents' generation. That said, the imagination of young people about what they could do, and how they might live, and the various ways they could fashion their futures, expanded beautifully. In these spaces, "Lift Every Voice and Sing," which just a few years earlier was dying on the vine of "We Shall Overcome," came roaring back. Artist Gwendolyn Knight Lawrence, a native of Barbados who migrated to New York, first encountered the song in the 1960s in Harlem in the midst of the freedom movement. "It was very moving to find yourself in a massive audience of hundreds or even thousands and have them rise about you as one body when the introductory strands of the song were played. The music was so compelling! Then, as their voices were lifted in song, the words seemed to be their very own, and were uplifting powerful and strong."[5]

In the midst of all this blossoming, King was in trouble. He was caught between and betwixt. The other prominent civil rights leaders—Whitney Young, Roy Wilkins, and Bayard Rustin—decried black power. King resisted the slogan, but he also understood it and in some ways shared the sensibilities that led to it. He spoke out against the Vietnam War even though his peers warned him to stick to civil rights. King listened to the young people (SNCC had opposed the war from the outset) and to his own conscience. In April 1967, King led a 125,000-person rally against the war in New York's Central Park. Ralph Bunche, Bayard Rustin, and Carl Rowan all spoke out publicly against the rally.

King retreated to Jamaica. In a house with no telephone, he sat with his thoughts and put together his final manuscript, *Where Do We Go from Here?*

Later that year, he delivered a speech before the SCLC convention based upon portions of that book. In the book, King criticizes Western colonialism, neocolonialism, and economic exploitation. He calls for a movement to end poverty and debt. In the speech, he focused on the United States and the particular moment in the movement. Although he rejected communism theoretically, the speech was unabashedly critical of capitalism.

> I want to say to you as I move to my conclusion, as we talk about "Where do we go from here?" that we must honestly face the fact that the movement must address itself to the question of restructuring the whole of American society. (Yes.) There are forty million poor people here, and one day we must ask the question, "Why are there forty million poor people in America?" And when you begin to ask that question, you are raising a question about the economic system, about a broader distribution of wealth. When you ask that question, you begin to question the capitalistic economy. (Yes.) And I'm simply saying that more and more, we've got to begin to ask questions about the whole society. We are called upon to help the discouraged beggars in life's marketplace. (Yes.) But one day we must come to see that an edifice which produces beggars needs restructuring.[6]

King's reckoning with the depth and complexity of racism, as interlocked as it was with the workings of capital, geopolitical relations, and the ideals of empire, had to be overwhelming.

> I must confess, my friends (Yes, sir), that the road ahead will not always be smooth. (Yes.) There will still be rocky places of frustration (Yes) and meandering points of bewilderment. There will be inevitable setbacks here and there. (Yes.) And there will be those moments when the buoyancy of hope will be transformed into the fatigue of despair. (Well.) Our dreams will sometimes be shattered and our ethereal hopes blasted. (Yes.) We may again, with tear-drenched eyes, have to stand before the bier of some courageous civil rights worker whose life will be snuffed out by the dastardly acts of bloodthirsty mobs. (Well.) But difficult and painful as it is (Well), we must walk on in the days ahead with an audacious faith in the future. (Well.) And as we continue our charted course, we may gain consolation from the words so nobly left by that great black bard, who was also a great freedom fighter of yesterday, James Weldon Johnson (Yes):

Stony the road we trod (Yes),
Bitter the chastening rod
Felt in the days
When hope unborn had died. (Yes)
Yet with a steady beat,
Have not our weary feet
Come to the place
For which our fathers sighed?
We have come over a way
That with tears has been watered. (Well)
We have come treading our paths
Through the blood of the slaughtered.
Out from the gloomy past,
Till now we stand at last (Yes)
Where the bright gleam
Of our bright star is cast.

Let this affirmation be our ringing cry. (Well.) It will give us the courage to face the uncertainties of the future. It will give our tired feet new strength as we continue our forward stride toward the city of freedom. (Yes.) When our days become dreary with low-hovering clouds of despair (Well), and when our nights become darker than a thousand midnights (Well), let us remember (Yes) that there is a creative force in this universe working to pull down the gigantic mountains of evil (Well), a power that is able to make a way out of no way (Yes) and transform dark yesterdays into bright tomorrows. (Speak.)

Let us realize that the arc of the moral universe is long, but it bends toward justice.

Again, the second verse of "Lift Every Voice and Sing" came to King in a moment of confusion and crisis. He was demonized by the mainstream press and politicians for his stand against imperialism and the Vietnam War. His nonviolent tactics were ridiculed by younger militants who found the idea of sitting still while your brothers and sisters are being beaten and murdered unconscionable. And more than that, King was beginning to think that assimilation into American society, with its dangerous mores and questionable priorities, might be impossible to do with principle, and might even be undesirable.

But he continued his work. While organizing a Poor People's March on

Washington, King was drawn to Memphis. There, the all-black corps of sanitation workers were on strike. The sanitation workers suffered daily indignities and unfairness. In the 1950s and early 1960s garbage was collected in Memphis on flatbed trailers, meaning the sanitation workers were forced to sit in trash as they collected it. The trucks also lacked heaters. Because they weren't allowed to stop and get a drink the men carried a cooler filled with ice water on hot days, but the water routinely became infested with maggots that crawled in from the garbage. The black workers had no place to relieve themselves, so they urinated in the garbage piles. And if the weather was bad, and they couldn't collect garbage, black workers were sent home without pay, while white workers were allowed to spend the day at the work site without collecting trash and yet still receive full pay.[7]

But one particularly horrifying day precipitated the strike. Two men, named Cole and Walker, were standing in the truck's barrel to protect themselves from the rain. "As Cole and Walker stood inside the cylinder designed to smash refuse mechanically, an electrical wire shorted and the compressor began to run. The button to stop the machine was on the outside of the truck, far from their reach. Before they could escape, the steel packer used to mangle the city's garbage pulled Cole and Walker inside. Within seconds they were crushed to death."

The families of the victims received $500 toward burial pay, one month's salary, and nothing more. In the aftermath of this tragedy, and in light of years of abuse and exploitation, the sanitation workers decided to go on strike. Of the city's 1,300 workers, 1,200 did not report to work on February 12. It was Lincoln's birthday and the traditional beginning of Negro History Week.

The union demanded a pay increase, overtime pay, official recognition, and improved job safety as well as a procedure for grievances to be addressed. They began daily marches, with placards that poignantly read, "I AM A MAN." There were some skirmishes. On February 23 a police car ran over the foot of a protester, Gladys Carpenter, who had been at the Selma to Montgomery March as well as the March against Fear. The men around Carpenter reacted by pushing against and rocking the police car. The police sprayed mace into the crowd and began hitting the demonstrators with nightsticks.

Soon the national press began to cover the strike. And civil rights leaders came down to support the workers, including Roy Wilkins and Bayard Rustin. After them, King arrived. Like Wilkins and Rustin, he expressed his support for the strike, and he promised to return soon. He spoke words that captured the energy of the historic moment. In the speech, he talked about the injustice of Vietnam abroad and poverty at home. He encouraged black citizens of Memphis to stand strong and refuse pressure to end their protests until their demands were met. He even talked about power, and though he didn't use the term *black power*, he both signified on the slogan and recognized the need for it. "Power is the ability to effect change. We need power. What is Power? Walter Reuther once said that power is the ability of a labor union like U.A.W. to make the most powerful corporation in the world, General Motors, say yes when it wants to say no."[8] King was unflinching in his indictment of the hypocrisy of the American dream, and he asserted that when the Poor People's Campaign descended upon Washington, people would come from every sector of the country, "and we're going to take a shack by the Smithsonian Institute, so that it can stand there as a symbol of American life. Then we're going to build a shanty town in Washington. We're going to call it our City of Hope."[9] The next day, March 28, 1968, King led a march of thousands of African American protesters down Beale Street in Memphis. They took the same path that the cavalcade celebrating W. C. Handy had once taken. But the spirit was far from festive in 1968. Some of the younger marchers ripped their "I Am a Man" signs off the sticks and used the sticks to smash storefronts in the commercial district. The police responded with tear gas and nightsticks. Young people threw rocks. The police killed sixteen-year-old Larry Payne. The marchers never made it to City Hall.

The National Guard was called into Memphis and a curfew was ordered. King left and returned six days later to finish his work. King delivered his famous Mountaintop speech the night he returned to Memphis. "Well, I don't know what will happen now. We've got some difficult days ahead. But it really doesn't matter with me now. Because I have been to the mountaintop. . . . And I've looked over. And I've seen the Promised Land. I may not get there with you. But I want you to know tonight that we as a people will get to the Promised Land. I'm so happy tonight. I'm not worried about anything. I'm not fearing any man. Mine eyes have seen the glory of the coming of the Lord."

The next day, standing on the balcony of the Lorraine Motel, King was murdered. Nina Simone would name the tragedy this way: "The King of Love Is Dead."

Uprisings ripped through black America. What hope was there, if even the King of Love was murdered? The aftermath was grief and rage. The Monday after King's assassination, in Roxbury, a predominantly black Boston neighborhood, several thousand people gathered at White Stadium in Franklin Park. They took the American flag down and put up the Black Star flag of Ghana. Rev. Virgil Wood, the Boston representative of the SCLC, stood before the microphone: "We took down the flag that has dishonored us . . . and raised the flag which honored us. Now, we will not sing the anthem that has dishonored us but we will sing the one that has honored us."[10] The crowd sang "Lift Every Voice and Sing," facing the Black Star.

The people reached for black power. It was philosophically inchoate, but it called for black people to imagine independent and protected black life. For some people this meant a journey of return to the black associational lifeworlds that had prepared them for the struggle. That, as far as they were concerned, was better than the fool's gold of nominal integration. Geronimo Ji Jaga Pratt of the Black Panther Party described how his coming of age in Morgan, Louisiana, prepared him to join the Black Panther Party for Self-Defense, the most widely remembered, and most broadly attacked, of the black power organizations that grew in the mid- to late 1960s: "Morgan City was a very rural setting and very nationalistic, self-reliant, and self-determining. It was a very close-knit community. Until I was a ripe old age, I thought that I belonged to a nation that was run by blacks. And across the street was another nation, a white nation. Segregation across the tracks. We had our own national anthem, 'Lift Every Voice and Sing,' our own police, and everything. We didn't call on the man across the street for nothing and it was very good that I grew up that way." Communist Party activist and scholar, and Black Panther Party ally, Angela Davis, whose mother had been part of the Southern Negro Youth Congress, recalled the pride with which she sang the lyrics of "Lift Every Voice" at Tuggle Elementary School in Birmingham: "I always sang the last phrases full blast: Facing the Rising Sun, of a New Day Begun, Let us march on Til Victory is Won!"[11] (Davis also sang it, in a very different setting, at the Little Red School House in New York, which she attended for high school.) In a 1975 interview that Maya Angelou conducted of her for a New York television show, *Assignment America*, Davis said, "If you went to a predominantly black school in the North and asked a particular class to stand up and sing the Negro National Anthem, there would be many children, many students who wouldn't even know about the existence of the Negro National Anthem and would not recognize the name James Weldon Johnson. But when we were growing up, whenever there was an assembly, if we sang 'The Star-Spangled Banner' or 'My Country 'Tis of Thee,' we also sang the Negro National Anthem and we learned that from the time we were 6 years old, or earlier than that actually."[12] Then, together, Angelou and Davis sang the first verse.

Sonia Sanchez, also a Birmingham native and a central figure in the Black Arts Movement, also recalled the importance of "Lift Every Voice and Sing": "During my early school years we sang 'Lift Every Voice and Sing' at all weekly assemblies. . . . I vividly remember . . . the music teacher at the Parker School in Birmingham opening every event in town by saying 'Spread the word . . . Lift Every Voice and Sing.' That meant everyone rose and began singing."[13] When Sanchez moved to New York and the students at her school were asked to stand and sing the anthem, she and her sisters were the only ones who sang "Lift Every Voice and Sing," while the rest of the auditorium sang "The Star-Spangled Banner." A 1930 newspaper account of the music directors at Parker High School captures the memories that both Davis and Sanchez brought to their visions of 1960s black radicalism. The title is "Untwisting All the Chains That Tie the Hidden Soul of Harmony" and it reads, "They untwist them in chapel every morning at the Birmingham Industrial High School, when the 2,500 Negro boys and girls sing their 'spirituals' under M. L. Wilkerson's lilting leadership there is nothing hidden of the soul for harmony which lives in their race. It pours from their throats, floods their faces, swells the vast chapel auditorium with a mighty volume and vitality of sound."[14] It was that register of soul and liberation that the turn to black power reimagined.

In retrospect, Andrew Young, a member of the SCLC who would become the U.S. ambassador to the United Nations, then mayor of Atlanta, described the shift in the early 1960s from "Lift Every Voice" to "We Shall Overcome" (and ultimately back to "Lift Every Voice" again) not so much as a displacement but rather as a reflection of the distinct applications of each song: "'We Shall Overcome' was always the closing song, expressing the prevailing hope that someday, things would be all right. But 'Lift Every Voice and Sing' laid out the road map through tragedy and triumph. For it is the God of our weary years and silent tears who points the way through the storm under the rainbow sign."[15] Connie Curry, the first white woman to serve on the executive committee of SNCC, described how the once-prevailing hope expressed by "We Shall Overcome" was dashed by persistent white violence in response to organizers, "those early sit-inners and SNCC people . . . really believed that they were going to win. It was the whole thing of 'We Shall

Overcome.' They really sorta thought there was an end in sight, and when they would sing 'God is on our side,' I would never sing that verse. . . . I don't think that anybody ever envisioned the long years of struggle and violence and everything—anguish."[16]

A return road, and a distinct forward movement were taken up at once with the shifts of the late freedom movement. In the late 1960s and early 1970s black organizers repurposed the cultural resources of the Deep South as well as those of continental Africa and used them to envision autonomous and liberated black living and thriving.

One of the limitations of the standard description of the post-1966 freedom movement as the black power era is that it can obscure how much of the energy of that period was devoted to the development of black consciousness, a term primarily associated with the philosophy of South African freedom fighter Steven Biko, and which he describes in his book, *I Write What I Like*: "At the heart of Black Consciousness is the realization by blacks that the most potent weapon in the hands of the oppressor is the mind of the oppressed. If one is free at heart, no man-made chains can bind one to servitude, but if one's mind is so manipulated and controlled by the oppressor then there will be nothing the oppressed can do to scare his powerful masters." The strategies for developing that consciousness in the U.S. movement consisted of a simultaneous looking backward at the past while moving forward, a restoration of tradition while expunging the aspects of it associated with fear and internalized racism, and an explicit embrace of blackness itself.

Amiri Baraka, the Black Arts Movement artist, activist, and intellectual, reflected on the significance of the anthem for him as someone who blossomed as a creator in the context of black power and black consciousness:

> "Lift Every Voice and Sing" was part of my growing up. Very early in my expanding perception I understood that at certain programs my parents took me to, the Negro National Anthem would be sung. . . . When we went down to Tuskegee, where my mother had attended normal school, and I saw a statue of Booker T. Washington pulling the cover of ignorance off the prototype slave, there was the anthem loud and heartfelt. . . . When we went down to Tennessee to visit Fisk, where she'd gone to college, where there were also those dynamite murals by Aaron Douglass, I remembered all my life, "Lift Every Voice" was sung further animating that gathering with the heap of heavy vibra-

tions from the folks I saw, and I felt, black angels hovering invisibly, rah-rahing the proceedings.[17]

However, Baraka's 1967 short play *Home on the Range*,[18] first written to be performed at a fundraiser for the Black Panther Party when he was still called LeRoi Jones, made irreverent use of the anthem. The entire play was performed with avant-garde saxophonists performing strange improvisations in the background. In it, a black character named CRIMINAL breaks into the home of a white family as they're watching television. CRIMINAL is frustrated that all their words to him sound like gibberish, and he yells and shoots the TV silent in response. Midway through the play, CRIMINAL morphs into a conductor: "He begins with great fanfare . . . with . . . now very haughty demeanor, turning to acknowledge an invisible audience to conduct the FAMILY singing; first a version of 'America the Beautiful' then a soupy stupid version of the Negro National Anthem, 'Lift Every Voice and Sing,' which comes to a super-dramatic climax, with the CRIMINAL having been moved to tears, finally giving a super-military salute. As they reach the highest point of the song, suddenly a whole crowd of BLACK PEOPLE pushes through the door."[19] The play reads at once as an indictment of a certain form of sentimentalism attached to the song (somewhat consistent with Countee Cullen's satire) and as a recognition of how deeply felt it was among all sorts of black folks, even those breaking into people's houses and shooting them up. Later in his career, Baraka returned again to "Lift Every Voice and Sing," this time more reverently, as a reference point in "Funk Lore," a piece by his performance group Blue Ark that told the story of black music and art from the Middle Passage to Malcolm X, backed by the playing of the anthem.

The practice of black consciousness-raising urged a reconnection with African continental culture, and Pan-Africanist solidarity. The forward-looking imagination, to a different state, was rooted in a remix of traditions and an explicit rejection of the false hope of integration. So now when black people gathered to sing "Lift Every Voice and Sing," they did so in bell bottoms, with large afros and fists raised in the sign of black power. They moved from black formalism to insistent demands for black liberation.

On February 23, 1973, the newsletter of the Oakland branch of the Black Panther Party announced a play performed by the elementary school the party had recently founded: The Inter-communal Youth Institute. The program was held in honor of Chairman Huey P. Newton. It was also a celebration of what had recently become Black History Month (rather than Negro

History Week).[20] This was their third special program of the year. The children, aged two to eleven, began the program by singing "Lift Every Voice and Sing," now designated the Black (rather than Negro) National Anthem. Next the Youth Band, directed by Brother Charles Moffett—an accomplished free jazz drummer who often worked with such distinguished contemporaries as Ornette Coleman, Archie Shepp, and Pharaoh Saunders—followed with three selections: "Skin Tight," "Peace on Earth," and "Caravan," played in honor of the late jazz great Duke Ellington. After the musical performances, Institute students Nyota Archibald and Valerie Wilson read selections from *The Insights of Huey P. Newton*. Interspersed throughout the program were songs from Jamaican singer Jimmy Cliff's soundtrack to the movie in which he starred, *The Harder They Come*. *The Harder They Come* was a cult classic for activists inspired by Cliff's portrayal of Ivan, aka Rhygin, the hero of the film who begins his life in the countryside and after his mother's death migrates to the big city of Kingston. Rhygin tries to make a respectable living at first but finds himself becoming a glorious outlaw.

In this period, elements of the classical tradition that were once de rigueur for black formalist performance spaces were traded in for variations upon the theme of unapologetic blackness in all of its diversity and complexity. "We Shall Overcome" seemed naive and even insipid in comparison to the reach for soul and the deliberate invocation of the African continent and diaspora. An example of this is found in the work of James Thomas Jackson, a Temple, Texas, native who became a poet in the Watts Writers Workshop. He published a piece in the early 1970s titled "Daybreak." It riffs on both Langston Hughes's poem "Daybreak in Alabama" and Sam and Dave's song "Hold On!," which has the boisterous energy of the contemporary social movement. In the poem he expresses his disaffection with "We Shall Overcome":

I'm tired.
That weary old song . . .
"We shall overcome . . . "
Has no fascination for me,
Hell no, I didn't like the damn thing
In the first place
I'm writing some brand new
Lyrics for it as of right now
So you can remember and

The words are:
"Hold on, I'm coming, hold on, I'm coming . . . "
And I am too![21]

In contrast to "We Shall Overcome," Jackson remembered "Lift Every Voice and Sing" fondly:

I was first introduced to their work by my high school music teacher, who was a beautiful black rebel in her own right. She had us sing the Johnson brothers hymn—The Negro National Anthem—"Lift Every Voice and Sing" before "The Star-Spangled Banner." She did that, that is, if none of the white faculty members were present. She tried to get us to sing it softly if she thought they were anywhere near, but her efforts always failed terribly.

Francis Scott Key's lyrics were all right with us, but not in the same league with the Johnson Brothers' soul-ensnaring bombast:

Sing a song full of the faith that the dark past has taught us
Sing a song full of the hope that the present has brought us
Facing the rising sun, of our new day begun,
Let us march on, til victory—is won.

After we had put our voices into that with fervor, there was never a dry eye in the classroom.

"Lift Every Voice and Sing" was commensurable with the turn to black power and black consciousness in a way that "We Shall Overcome" was not. Part of its insurgent appeal had to do with the conditions under which it had been written and first shared. It was a song that resisted the dominant society's depiction and treatment of black Americans. It was a song of fortitude not hope, and the intimacy of black community rather than the dashed dream of interracial unity through integration. A graduate of the segregated Dunbar School in Tucson, Arizona, remembered the loss of the song as one of the painful costs of integration:

Instead of singing "The Star-Spangled Banner," we would sing the Negro National Anthem. And they thought that that was not the thing to do. So, when White people came, we would sing "The Star-Spangled Banner" and then "Lift Every Voice and Sing." I talked to my friends. It was done all over the country. At segregated schools they would sing the Negro National Anthem. I know the words to the Negro National

Anthem, but I do not know the words to "The Star-Spangled Banner." So, we would all sing the Negro National Anthem. The superintendent did not like that at all. . . . When the schools became integrated, we said we would no longer sing the Black National Anthem. We stopped singing it when the schools became integrated.[22]

Partly because there was a sharp sense that too much had been lost and too little gained with desegregation, renewed energy was focused upon the task of nurturing young black people in the late 1960s and early 1970s. The networks were not as robust as they had been during Jim Crow. Black people had a much wider range of professions available to them as access to college increased and businesses and professions stepped away from Jim Crow practices. No longer were they limited to black institutions in pursuing their careers. But more than that, associational life diminished for Americans generally during the 1960s and 1970s. The cultural revolution ripped asunder the traditional intergenerational transfer of habits and memberships. Rather quickly though, even the rebelling youth understood changes that seemed necessary weren't all good. And there were still important efforts to reimagine black associations and institutions especially given that school integration had failed badly. Adelaide Cromwell, a scion of Boston black elites, whom she would later term "the other Brahmins,"[23] drew on resources from the past to articulate the needs of black children within the context of the black nationalist politics in the 1970s. Cromwell argued that black people ought to revive the ethos of institutions like the Dunbar School of Washington, D.C. And, anticipating the criticism of Dunbar as bourgeois, she wrote that Dunbar was not a factory for the creation of "Uncle Toms," despite what some might surmise. Rather, Cromwell wrote, Dunbar was unapologetically black: "There were no 'Black Studies' for in a sense there was no real need for Black Studies. Well-trained black teachers taught the subjects in ways black students with proper education understood. The black experience in terms of persons and content was ever present. All students knew and sang, with regularity and more feeling than the manner in which they saluted the American flag, 'The Negro National Anthem.'"[24] The anthem was, according to Cromwell, a sign of black nationalist sensibilities in this most elite of black schools. "Black teachers in Black schools can teach and develop superior black students" more effectively than other teachers in other contexts, she argued, making her skepticism regarding integration clear and unflinching. As a Dunbar graduate, she had good reason to be skeptical. By 1973, when

Cromwell's essay was published, Dunbar had been integrated and almost wholly evacuated of its impressive tradition. Following desegregation, the demolition of the original facility, and, with the upheaval, the loss of the traditional school culture, Dunbar's prestige dropped notably. Through the 1980s, Dunbar High School continued to perform below the standards. But the losses of desegregation were already being acutely felt in the early 1970s.

Joanne Peerman, who integrated a high school in North Carolina, chose to attend a historically black college precisely because as a student at a predominantly white high school she missed the things that made her first high school, a segregated one, so special. An interviewer asked Peerman, "What did it mean to you, going to an all-black school in college?" And Peerman responded,

> It just felt so good. I felt like I was returning to my roots. I felt like integration had been forced upon me and now that I was able to choose what school I could go to I was going to choose to return back to my community where I knew that academics would be stressed in a totally different kind of way. Learning would be received and taken in a very different kind of way. Black schools have such rich heritages. They have such bonds, such togetherness, such—the activities, the bands, the choruses, the football. I wanted to return to that whole feeling. . . .
> The proudest I ever was of my Dad, at a high school assembly for Black History Week, those assemblies always started with the singing of the Black National Anthem, "Lift Every Voice and Sing." When he stood there and raised his fist along with all the rest of the black students, I just really got a chill. I was just very emotional because he showed that he was with us and he understood what we were going through. He looked just like the guys at the Olympics that first raised their fists when the National Anthem was being played. That was a very memorable moment for my dad sharing with the black community.[25]

Peerman's nostalgia, and that of many others who integrated white institutions, was pointed. It was not only for the warm communities they left but for a space where the intransigence of white America on the question of true integration wasn't felt in every moment of one's educational life. They longed for a time when they didn't attend schools where as a black student you could only be a visitor, not a member. Their yearning was for a place to belong again.

That Peerman mentions "Lift Every Voice and Sing," then, isn't surprising. It was a song of membership and community. And it seemed that full membership in what it meant to be American hadn't been fully granted, despite the difficult civil rights struggle, and even after black people had let go of so many of the institutions in which their membership had been deep and meaningful in order to pursue that ever-elusive vision of integration.

In light of the disappointing transition to technically integrated schools—ones that allowed black pupils but also ones that white students fled, ones without black teachers and principals, athletic directors, and choir directors, ones that had black populations but could not be described as black schools in the tradition of black education—some black activists and educators tried to teach the white adults who increasingly taught black youth how to engage with them in a culturally appropriate manner. A 1972 article titled "More 'Soul' Needed in White Teachers," Kenneth Fish begins with the voices of black children: "It seems that some dig black people, but others—they're just prejudiced." After several additional examples, Fish summarizes:

> The foregoing quotes of black youths show that there are different kinds of white teachers in their world: a few who are empathetic and aware, but more who seem insensitive, hostile or indifferent. . . . The responsibility to appreciate the personal strengths of black people and to interpret the positive values of their society to the white majority is an awesome one. This is a task that must be undertaken by all who are in a position to do so, including America's teachers. . . . For starters, how many readers of this article would recognize the song title, "Lift Every Voice and Sing"? If this is less familiar than "God Save the King" or "The Marseillaise" then something is seriously wrong. How odd that one should recognize the national anthems of European nations more readily than the song known by 20 million of our fellow Americans as "the Negro National Anthem."[26]

While the recommendation to acquire some knowledge about the culture of one's pupils was undoubtedly a good one, such lessons could not lead to a restoration of the contexts in which "Lift Every Voice and Sing" had its greatest impact. Diversity additions to curricula and cultural awareness lessons are not the same thing as cultivated school cultures and rituals. They don't take root or inspire in the same way. But some new schools with explicit black consciousness philosophies sought to rebuild the kind of school cultures that were destabilized and even destroyed with desegregation. At the Nairobi Day School in East Palo Alto, California, the educators were concerned with making sure their white volunteers had a culturally appropriate approach to black children, but they were also dedicated more broadly to building a school culture that nurtured the identity and honored the traditions of black American youth. The "Nairobi Method" developed out of the workshops that had been led by the school's founders to orient and train its volunteer tutors, most of whom were European Americans with no previous experience teaching African American youth. . . . During the attitude workshops it was made clear to tutors that they were required to have "high expectations and a nonpatronizing attitude toward Nairobi Day School's predominantly African American students."[27] The workshops sought to instantiate what was standard practice for black teachers in the segregated South—believing in the ability and possibilities of black children—in all faculty, black and white.

The Nairobi Day School was one example of how even as many black schools were closed others were founded that blended the current political moment with older traditions. Established in 1966, Nairobi was an example of the community school movement that emerged from black nationalist thought and the philosophy of black consciousness. Mary Rhodes Hoover, a teacher at Nairobi whose husband was its founder, described the school's beginnings: "On the first day of school in 1966, founders of the day school expected a handful of high school students and tutors. However, approximately 200 students (mostly elementary) and 200 tutors arrived! Saturday morning and Wednesday evening classes were held until 1969, when Nairobi Day School became a full time school in conjunction with its Saturday school."[28] In the first couple of years Stokely Carmichael, who had transitioned from being a leader of SNCC to brief membership in the Black Panther Party before moving to Guinea, came to visit the students frequently. Contrary to mainstream media depictions of Carmichael as terrifyingly militant and violent, he showed to the Nairobi students a great tenderness that many who knew him recalled. He preached a doctrine of self-love to them, saying on one occasion, "Before you learn to read and write and learn mathematics and chemistry you've got to learn to love yourself . . . because if you don't love yourself you won't want to learn about mathematics and chemistry."[29]

The daily program of the Nairobi Day School was described as follows: "At the Day School we use the assembly for motivation. Assembly begins with the singing of 'Lift Every Voice and Sing.' . . . We continue with motivational songs, many of which are old familiar hymn tunes and spirituals with new words to stimulate the student in developing a positive attitude . . . 'I'm a Learning Man' 'Good News! Freedom's Coming!'" The teachers encouraged respect for black vernacular language and used rhyming poems based in African and African American history to support literacy skills. One in particular captured the political moment rather dramatically:

Genocide
Genocide, Genocide
A hundred million Black folks died.
Imhotep
Imhotep
Built the pyramids, step by step.
Malcolm X
Malcolm X, Malcolm X
Read so much he needed specs . . .
Loved his people, loved the Blacks
Taught us how to speak up loud
Taught us how to stand up proud . . .[30]

This blend of tradition and the new radicalism emerged out of the initiative of a native North Carolinian, Robert Hoover, who had traveled west for graduate studies at Stanford. With his wife, Mary, as his professional and intellectual partner, Hoover founded both Nairobi Day school and Nairobi College, although the two schools were independent from one another. The story of Nairobi College is like that of the day school, a study in black nationalism, black consciousness, and a renewed commitment to black institutional life and rituals.

The College of San Mateo, a public junior college, first hired Robert Hoover to recruit minority students. His program served over 500 students and sent over fifty students to four-year colleges in two years. But when a new president came to San Mateo two years into Hoover's tenure, he slashed funding for the program. The students responded by accusing the administration of racial discrimination. Campus protests resulted in conflicts with local police. Hoover was fired, and many of his students quit in protest. But he had a plan. With $80,000 raised from private sources, Robert and Mary Hoover and a handful of others opened Nairobi College in an East Palo Alto five-room frame house. By 1969, a year after it opened, Nairobi was accredited as a junior college with over 100 students taking classes in houses around the area taught by a volunteer faculty drawn from neighboring institutions. None of the instructors received a salary. The curriculum was standard in some ways and radical in others. Classes included black English, which was taught as a sociolinguistic course and imparted knowledge about the unique phonology and syntax of African American vernacular speech. Students could also take courses in Swahili, black psychology, leadership development, and political awareness. Communications courses included Shakespeare and comparative mythology.[31] Students over eighteen were admitted to Nairobi College without regard to their academic records and, consistent with the school's radical democratic philosophy, students were involved in institutional decision making. By 1972, the college served 300 students, whose average age was twenty-five. The tuition was $600, but 95 percent of students received financial aid.[32] Orde Coombs, a freelance writer, described his experience visiting Nairobi in 1972 for an all-college meeting. Before things began, "Stokely Carmichael, dark glasses on his handsome face, comes through the door." Carmichael milled about with students before the program began.

> The mistress of ceremonies is listed as Sister Denise Armstrong, and she asks everyone to stand and sing the black national anthem. It is "Lift Every Voice and Sing" by James Weldon Johnson, and it has replaced "The Star-Spangled Banner" at many black meetings with any pretense to nationalism. As the young pianist strikes the first note, over two hundred voices rise to carry the words out of the auditorium and into the seedy but hopeful ghetto of East Palo Alto. . . . The moment of catharsis over, Sister Armstrong now leads the assembly in repeating the Nairobi College Code: The Seven Principles of Blackness.[33]

The Seven Principles of Blackness they recited were what are more generally referred to now as the Seven Principles of Kwanzaa, the holiday founded in 1966 by a cultural nationalist, Maulana Karenga. While critics of the celebration of Kwanzaa have often derided it for being a contrived holiday—and a signal of the cultural deprivation or insecurity of African Americans; who according to detractors confusedly mimic West African harvest celebrations while using East African language, alongside "Lift Every Voice and Sing"—a counterinterpretation rapidly emerges. Like the pageants of the early twentieth century, the Nairobi College program was a blend of past and present, a collage of identity that spoke to the political moment and buoyed the commitment of those who would wage it.

Coombs concluded his essay with a moving reflection on Nairobi:

As the week ended I thought that the Nairobi experiment was really a naked call to ferret out the seeds of black pride that lie dormant in an abused people. And it is this call, really, that gives these students their bearing and their confidence in themselves. They come, after all, from ghettoes in which black men give up early, but it is their current realization that black life in this country is truly triumph over tragedy that pushes them, now, to give substance to that triumph. It is no wonder, then, that in the college catalogue a pantheon of black heroes are quoted. Patrice Lumumba: "A man without nationalist tendencies is a man without a soul." Marcus Garvey: "Look for me in the whirlwind or the storm, look for me all around you, for . . . I shall come and bring with me countless millions of black slaves who have died in American and the West Indies and the millions in Africa to aid you in the fight for Liberty, Freedom and Life."[34]

Like Nairobi Day School, Nairobi College merged traditional forms of celebration found in black southern institutions with the radicalism of black politics of the late 1960s and early 1970s. As Martha Biondi writes, "Nairobi adopted rituals that celebrated both African and African American culture and history. School holidays included Nigerian Independence Day on October 1, the founding of the Black Panther Party on October 17, Rosa Parks' resistance to segregation on December 1, Ghanaian Independence on March 6, and Malcolm X's birthday on May 19. Of course, Kwanzaa was celebrated from December 25 to January 1."[35]

"Lift Every Voice and Sing" was not merely a song of black affirmation in the age of black power, it was also a song of black protest. The protest politics ranged from the revolutionary socialism of the Black Panther Party to a new stage of arguments for inclusion, ones that did not romanticize integration yet demanded seats in predominantly white colleges and high schools. This inclusion was not the same as the inclusion sought by SCLC- or NAACP-style protest. It was an inclusion which insisted that black nationalist politics, aesthetics, and boldness had to be part of black people's sitting at the proverbial table. In colleges and universities it was part of calls for black studies in the curricula and black dorms on campus. It emerged in some unlikely areas as well. When the National Convention of Black Lay Catholics met in Philadelphia in 1970, it passed a resolution insisting that the American Catholic Church respond to the needs of black Catholic parishes and seek and support vocations among black congregants. Black Catholics delivered this resolution to the apostolic delegate of the United States by motorcade and, once arrived at his residence at Catholic University in D.C., they burst into an impromptu singing of "Lift Every Voice and Sing."

In Newark two years later, black students in public high schools walked out of classes and demanded an increase in the number of black teachers and black history courses. They also demanded the right to sing "Lift Every Voice and Sing" each day (a practice that was adopted and continued for many years in some Newark schools). Black youth in Newark were the descendants of migrants and for the most part hadn't had the institutional experiences black children from the South had. Many also didn't have Newark artist Baraka's immediate connection to a southern past. Now they were demanding part of what their parents had left behind to come along with them in integrated spaces.

Similar confrontations arose in Richmond, Virginia, specifically around the anthem. Black composer Hale Smith was enlisted to respond. He recalled that "at the time there was trouble going on between white and black students . . . that had started when some black students had walked out rather than sing 'Dixie.'" The next day white students walked out when the teacher, in compensation, wanted the students to sing 'Lift Every Voice and Sing.' The discord was spreading all through the state at that time."

Smith responded by putting together an orchestral arrangement of "Lift Every Voice and Sing" for the Richmond Symphony Orchestra. "The audience [at concerts where the orchestra performed it] was very much mixed," he observed, "and this particular anthem closed the program. It begins with a big orchestral introduction which leads into an orchestral treatment of the first part of the song. Therefore, the recognition of the piece was somewhat gradual. However, as soon as the audience caught on to what was going on they stood up . . . then the chorus started, unaccompanied. By the time they got to the second verse, everybody would be singing. . . . The sound was coming from the stage and from the audience. It ends big."[36]

Smith's arrangement would become one of the most popular of the end of the twentieth century, particularly for commemorative events celebrating the life of Martin Luther King Jr. Another classic arrangement that came out of the early 1970s was that of Roland Carter, whose arrangement of "Lift

Every Voice and Sing" is also often used today, particularly when it is sung collectively at ceremonial events. Carter's arrangement has made it easier for untrained audiences to sing by bringing the piece down to a lower register.

Other musicians reinterpreted or simply reengaged the song in light of the spirit of the black power movement. Art Blakey's Jazz Messengers played "Lift Every Voice" at shows throughout the 1970s. Bobby Watson describes the sensibility of these performances:

> When I was in the Jazz Messengers, Art had us play "Lift Every Voice and Sing"—the Black National Anthem—at the opening of every show. That was his musical statement. He didn't go to the mic and talk about why he was doing this song; he just did it. He never made any speeches, but we all knew why. He was very political, and there was always an undercurrent of social awareness and black pride in the music. Art also demanded respect by the way he had us dress in the band. We wore overalls, and it was because as black men, off-stage, you could not just walk around free and get any respect dressing that way. But Art would not allow perceptions to dictate anything. He was saying, "You're going to respect me for who I am, because I'm great at what I do."[37]

The Roy Haynes Hip Ensemble also played "Lift Every Voice," but they placed it at the end of their shows. Haynes describes one powerful performance on the anniversary of the composer and arranger Billy Strayhorn's death:

> When I had the group Roy Haynes Hip Ensemble, which was started in the late '60s, we were once playing at the Jazz Vespers at St. Peters, and it was during the period when I had George Adams and Hannibal Peterson in the front line. We used to close with the "Negro National Anthem" as ["Lift Every Voice and Sing"] was called back in the early days; Lift every voice and sing, 'til earth and heaven ring. . . . and I would come out of this drum solo and go into that. . . . Dr. Logan, who was my doctor for a while, was Duke Ellington's doctor, and they had just gone to the Hudson River to throw flowers in the water because [Strayhorn] was cremated; he was one of the first Blacks I know to say, "throw my ashes in the river," and it was the Hudson. They came by the church afterwards and the church was packed. I went into this drum solo, then "Lift Every Voice and Sing" and [Logan and Ellington] stood up and the whole congregation stood up, and that was one of the most

exciting things of my career—to have Duke Ellington in the audience, standing![38]

There were distinct emphases in the various interpretations. Some musicians used the anthem primarily as a springboard for imagining the new terrain upon which black life would or should be built. For example, in 1969 pianist Andrew Hill released an album titled *Lift Every Voice*, and in 1971 bandleader and drummer Max Roach titled an album *Lift Every Voice and Sing*. Each blends an instrumental ensemble with a choir. But neither album actually has "Lift Every Voice and Sing" on it. Hill's work is more abstract. The title track, "Lift Every Voice," is filled with word repetition: free free free, song song song, we will not go back, move on to the stars . . . ascension—voice and sing—sun will shine. . . . Sometimes the vocalizations of the choir are chants, other times they holler. But the singers remain largely in the background, while the band is primary. The album is intertextual if not citational. He draws out elements from "Lift Every Voice and Sing," makes them unfamiliar, and reconsiders them in mantra-like form. The entire album has a searching quality to it, appropriate for the late freedom movement.

Max Roach's album is the better known of the two. It is a reintegration of forms (gospel, blues, jazz, and spirituals) and coalesces as a journey through the emotional and creative spectrum of black music. By then, Roach had been making political music for over ten years. In 1960 he recorded *We Insist! Max Roach's Freedom Now Suite*. The record was originally intended to celebrate the 1963 centennial of the Emancipation Proclamation. But Roach found his inspiration in black student activists instead. The lunch counter sit-ins were the impetus for his earlier release of the album. The sleeve notes to *We Insist!* begin, "A revolution is unfurling—America's unfinished revolution. It is unfurling in lunch counters, buses, libraries and schools." Roach played on the album with jazz greats Coleman Hawkins, Babatunde Olatunji, and the singer (and Roach's future wife) Abbey Lincoln. After the release of *We Insist!* Roach declared, "I will never again play anything that does not have social significance." He then went on to produce a series of powerful albums dedicated to the struggle for black emancipation—*Members Don't Get Weary, It's Time, Speak Brother Speak*, and finally *Lift Every Voice and Sing*. Over these years he performed benefit concerts for Malcolm X, the NAACP, and Martin Luther King's SCLC. Clearly when he called his album *Lift Every Voice and Sing*, Roach was signaling his allegiance to something greater than himself. It was a commitment to blackness. On the album, Roach painted a sonic portrait of black cultural and spiritual life that echoed DuBois's 1903 book *The Souls of Black Folk* and yet was thoroughly modern.

Likewise, Aretha Franklin's 1972 album *Aretha* both reached back and moved forward. She recorded it over two days at the New Temple Baptist Missionary Church in Los Angeles, backed by the Southern California community choir directed by gospel great James Cleveland. It was a traditional gospel sound, coming from a great migration community. On the album cover, she attired herself in a traditional West African gown and head wrap. The cutting edge of black music reached back and way back with a new boldness. The same year, Aretha Franklin sang the anthem at the first Whitney Young Classic football game. The Classic was established in 1971 after Young, executive director of the Urban League, died unexpectedly while in Nigeria. It became an annual football game between two Louisiana HBCUs, Southern University and Grambling, but it was held in New York at Yankee Stadium and televised. Post-desegregation, historically black colleges and universities were the one type of educational institution where one could be assured that ritual singing of "Lift Every Voice and Sing" remained. At HBCUs, it was part of weekly chapel services, graduations, and programs when honored guests visited campus. Black Greek letter fraternity and sorority members were expected to learn all three verses. The Whitney Young Classic brought the culture of HBCUs into the public arena. And with that, along with a series of other key events, "Lift Every Voice and Sing" was heard in the American mass-culture mainstream.

Ray Charles's 1972 album *Message from the People* opened with "Lift Every Voice." Although Charles was a music icon, this was a period of decline for him. In the 1950s and 1960s he had been one of the most popular artists in the nation. But by the early 1970s his fame was eclipsed by fresh styles and younger performers. He tried something new with this album, more in line with the energy of the newer artists. *Message from the People* would be Charles's first and only explicitly political album. This turn was in part a reflection of how the social climate politicized artists, and also a sign of the demands audiences made upon artists of that era to produce politically relevant work.

Doing publicity for the album, Ray Charles performed his rendition of the anthem on the *Dick Cavett Show*. This performance, like his recorded version, was buoyant, even joyful. As Charles rocked and played, standing behind him were four soulful background singers in pastel-colored evening gowns. Two had afros and two wore straight bouffant wigs, as though they were spanning the styles of two decades at once. They swayed with spirit, in harmony with Charles's lead voice. In the interview following the song, Cavett, known as the thinking man's interviewer, was somewhat uncomfortably fixated on Charles's blindness and seemed to deliberately avoid the obvious politics of his performance. But they were readily apparent. Charles was celebrating blackness.

"Lift Every Voice" appeared on various other television shows. In 1969 Bill Cosby sang it with the Art Reynolds Singers for the finale of his eponymous show. A week later, in a letter to the editor of the *Amsterdam News*, Vivian Williams responded to the finale: "At the End of Bill Cosby's show last week I was caught speechless. I have two teenage sons, 17 and 18 years of age, and they were watching the show with 8 of their friends, girls and boys, all teenagers. At the end of the show the Negro National Anthem was sung but not one of the teenagers knew what it was. Three said they had heard of it. One boy said it should be printed and put around so we can hear it more. Dear God what is happening and what is going to happen to our Black children?"[39] Her anxiety was symptomatic of both the losses wrought by desegregation and the demands for a renewed black public sphere. The performance itself was a sign that black people were taking up more space in the mainstream public sphere.

Black people, particularly activists and educators, pursued institution-building along with black consciousness. This was an internal job but one that was also publicly visible. Black faces moved into mainstream public life at an unprecedented rate in the early 1970s. For the first time, largely in response to the urban rebellions of the late 1960s, there was local black television programming in various cities in the early 1970s. Several of these shows were named *Lift Every Voice*, and they covered black arts, history, and contemporary social and political issues.

The spillover of black consciousness and black power politics into the public sphere ignited the imagination of nonblack artists as well. For example, "Lift Every Voice and Sing" was part of the soundtrack to director Robert Altman's 1970 film *Brewster McCloud*, which can be described as a mix of apocalyptic fantasy and existential crisis. It tells the story of a young white man living in a fallout shelter in the Houston astrodome. Brewster tries to build a pair of wings that will allow him to fly away from everything, a goal he ultimately fails in achieving. In the midst of the film a black band is playing "The Star-Spangled Banner," poorly. The conductor stops them and fusses. They begin again and then ultimately overtake her direction and start playing "Lift Every Voice and Sing." As with Baraka's *Home on the Range*, the scene is thick with the tension of black people taking over or overtaking the scene. Soul singer Merry Clayton performed "Lift Every Voice and Sing" for the film, and Roger Ebert's review offered particular praise for Clayton's rendition, which he said "makes you want to jump up and run around the theater."[40] The expansiveness of blackness spreading into the public sphere was a play upon the treatment of black people as a threat, dangerous and pestilential. It was a play on the fear that produced white flight to the suburbs. But the aesthetic beauty of these artists' performances rendered blackness enchanting and compelling, rather than fearsome.

Even James Brown, the Godfather of Soul, spread "Lift Every Voice and Sing." In 1975, a white boxer named Chuck Wepner challenged Muhammad Ali for the heavyweight boxing title. Ali was guaranteed $1.5 million for the fight, and Wepner, a relative unknown, signed for $100,000. It was Wepner's big break. He trained for eight weeks straight. The fight was held on March 24 at the Richfield Coliseum outside of Cleveland. Before the fight began, James Brown was invited to sing "The Star-Spangled Banner." He began accordingly. But then when he got to the phrase "the land of the free . . . ," his voice lingered and slowed down. He repeated, "Free. Free. We wanna be free." The crowd screamed its approval. Then he changed the melody and sped up, singing the first line, "Lift Every Voice and Sing, till earth and heaven ring," and finished up "and the home of the brave." The moment crackled with the intensity of black insistence. It was classically 1970s. Ali won that fight, and Chuck Wepner became the inspiration for Sylvester Stallone's Rocky.

While "Lift Every Voice and Sing" was compellingly revived by many artists in the 1970s, the most significant recording of it in this period was that of Kim Weston, a singer whose voice was described as "ranging from black chiffon to shimmering velvet."[41] In May 1970 Kim Weston, a Motown alum and Motor City native who would also record for Stax Records, was a guest on the *Tonight Show*. She sang "Lift Every Voice and Sing," which she had included on her 1968 album *This Is America*. The album also included a version of "The House I Live In," the song Sonny Rollins had ended with a brief quote of "Lift Every Voice" in 1956. Weston's archive and sensitivity to the politics in music was apparent.

After Weston's performance, the guest host for the *Tonight Show*, Flip Wilson, a popular African American comedian, announced to the audience that Weston had just sung the Negro National Anthem. The audience laughed in response. Wilson, however, went on to say: "I'm very serious. This is the Negro National Anthem. The Rev. Jesse Jackson of the Southern Christian Leadership Conference has requested that radio stations all over the nation play the anthem as we rededicate ourselves to nonviolence as advocated by the late Dr. Martin Luther King."[42]

Wilson was making a clear reference to the urban uprisings, often referred to as "riots." They were dramatic responses to dire economic conditions and political frustration and rage. To call upon "Lift Every Voice and Sing" as a disciplining tool against riots was interesting, but also rather ineffectual. The formalism once attached to the song, the socialization into grace, discipline, "good home training," and knowing how to "act right" was waning. Young activists in the early 1970s, across the lines of race and class, were rejecting such social conventions and demands for appropriateness, at least when it came to political protest. They were also experimenting with radically expressive self-identification and presentation. Even the way Weston sang "Lift Every Voice and Sing," swinging and full-throated, was more defiant than decorous.

In August 1972, a concert was held in Los Angeles to commemorate the seventh anniversary of the Watts rebellion. This concert had been held annually, but this year was different. Stax Records and Schlitz Brewing Company were cosponsoring the event and filming it for a documentary. This would become Wattstax, popularly considered to be black America's response to Woodstock. The radical potential of the concert was immediately diminished by the sponsorship of a beer company, a sign of things to come.

In the 1960s, corporations began to recognize black buyers as a desirable and long neglected consumer base and began to court them. Black-owned advertising agencies were hired to create ads specifically for black publications like *Ebony* and *Essence*. Without the help of black agencies, things could go poorly. For example, in 1967, Maier Brewing in Los Angeles introduced the racially targeted Soul Stout Malt Liquor and Soul Mellow Yellow Beer. The release of these targeted "soul" beers was met with ire-filled NAACP-led protests, and Maier pulled the brands. Beer corporations would have to be a bit more subtle. Hence Wattstax.

At the beginning of the show, Jesse Jackson shouted out into the concert audience: "This is a new day. This is a wonderful day. It is a day of black awareness. It is a day of black people taking care of black people's business.

Today we are together . . . and together, we got power!" The concert footage is interspersed with narration from Richard Pryor, and shots of the decaying Watts streets. The first song that we hear is "The Star-Spangled Banner" sung by Kim Weston. The camera pans a wholly uninterested crowd. Next, Jesse Jackson has the audience stand and raise their right fists in the black power sign. He leads them in a call and response of William Borders's poem "I Am Somebody," which Jackson would recite frequently throughout the 1970s and 1980s. Then, Jackson asks the crowd to stand for "OUR Black National Anthem." Kim Weston returns to the stage to sing "Lift Every Voice and Sing." The stands are now filled with erect and focused people. Their fists remain raised. It does not appear that most are singing, perhaps because the lyrics weren't well known by young black people born and raised on the West Coast, but the crowd is nevertheless rapt and at attention. They are patriots to blackness.

Their refusal of "The Star-Spangled Banner" was symbolic of the era. Black people were tired of the broken promises of the American dream. Their feelings were appropriate. In Boston, the school busing crisis revealed that even the reputedly most liberal parts of the nation could be frighteningly hostile to black Americans. Black children who were sent to white schools were trapped on buses with white mobs surrounding them, throwing bottles and yelling slurs. Actress and activist Victoria Rowell recalls that in the midst of this violence "Lift Every Voice and Sing" was sung at organizing meetings: "I can remember sitting as a child . . . at an assembly for the desegregation of schools in Boston. Suddenly, everyone stood up and sang this glorious song. . . . I'd never heard it before. My mother told me it was the Black National Anthem. A chorus of beautiful black voices resonating throughout the hall. One had to believe that God heard them."[43] As with conflicts of the past, the busing crisis in Boston revealed that solidarity between black and white working-class people was often thwarted by antiblack racism, and not just in the South. Black nationalism could be both bulwark and affirmation in the face of that reckoning. A number of observers noted that the white South Boston and Charleston residents who believed they were protecting their kids from black encroachment, already sent their children to schools that were under-resourced just like those in predominantly black communities. Black students weren't being bused to better schools, and the white protesters weren't protecting anything of material value. Their reaction was simply racism. Rather than join black parents in demanding better from the Boston school department, they retaliated against black children. Similarly, black desegregation activists in Boston soon realized that busing would not be a path to either educational equality or integration.

By the late 1970s it was clear that the black nationalists, along with youthful revolutionaries of all races, antiwar activists, feminists, and communists, despite their passion and purpose, had been soundly defeated in their ambitions to radically transform the society. COINTELPRO, the FBI's surveillance and counterintelligence program that targeted black nationalists, pushed the most radical branches of the black freedom movement into disarray. Beginning in the mid-1970s, federal courts were rolling back the legislative gains of the civil rights movement. The antiwar movement had gone from radically challenging the status quo to a general melancholy that settled across America as thousands of coffins holding the corpses of American teenagers returned from a war that most Americans believed was at least misguided and at worst completely unjust.

Concessions to activists were made, but they fell far short of revolution. Individual gains among people long excluded were apparent, championed, and even celebrated, at the same time as the bigger dreams of so many radicals were eroded. Women and people of color began to experience the benefits of affirmative action programs in employment and education. Gender and ethnic studies programs were available to those who had access to higher education. "Lift Every Voice and Sing" in this context became a signifier or symbol of blackness, rather than a ritual. It marked identity rather than practice.

That is not to say it was meaningless. It became a part of a renewed interest in archiving black history, now often with the support of predominantly white universities and publishing companies. For instance, in the early 1970s publishers released several children's book versions of "Lift Every Voice and Sing." And since that time, there have consistently been illustrated children's book versions of the song and many books in general either named "Lift Every Voice" or named after another phrase in the song, such as "Stony the road we trod" or "Let us march on 'til victory is won." The assertion of identity and the enshrining of the history of the anthem along with important figures in black history was significant. But this enshrinement coincided with the steady loss of rituals for many black Americans.

In 1976 the Association for the Study of African American Life and History, formerly the ASNLH, officially expanded Negro History Week to Black History Month, whose celebration has become a key part of how mainstream educational institutions acknowledge racial diversity and the heterogeneity of the United States. But even some fifty years later, it is the rare institution that has pursued fundamental transformation of curricula to make it deeply inclusive of African American and African history and culture. Truly racially integrated institutions are few and far between, and traditionally black institutions that have maintained a deep commitment to the study of African American history and culture as well as black formalism are just as rare.

Some black thinkers grew skeptical of Black History Month soon after its institutionalization. They worried about how it quickly became a means for selling consumer goods, and how superficially it was celebrated. In 1997, a group of scholars published essays in an issue of the *Journal of Negro History* about the danger that Black History Month in the post–freedom movement era had become merely an empty reason to buy and sell black ephemera rather than the pedagogically and politically meaningful ritual of teaching black history that once existed in black schools. The steady erosion of black associational life had hastened this decline. In his contribution to the issue, Allen B. Ballard wrote nostalgically about the past:

> Black history month will always be associated in my mind with Miss Nelly Bright, principal of the Joseph E. Hill School, the segregated elementary school in Philadelphia that I attended as a child in the 1930s. Throughout the year, the halls and classrooms of that school were decorated with pictures of such notables as Harriet Tubman, Frederick Douglass and Alexander Dumas, and each of our weekly school assemblies began with the singing of the Negro National Anthem. But to Nelly Bright, Negro History Week, its name then, was something special. It was a time for skits about the Underground Railroad, poetry readings of the works of Paul Laurence Dunbar, art contests for the best Negro history poster and a special chorus to sing such spirituals as "Walk Together Children" or "Steal Away." The week was always climaxed by the appearance of a famous local black person—I remember so well the time that Marian Anderson came and sang and then bent down to sweep a bunch of us little children into her arms. When Nelly Bright finished with her kind of celebration we knew that we were important people, that great things were expected of us, and that we had a tradition of honor, excellence and perseverance to uphold. That meant a lot to us as we daily walked by the spanking brand-new white school with its high wire fences on our way to the Hill School three blacks past it. The purpose of Negro History Week

was clear—to give us an intellectual and emotional anchor in the midst of overt racism, legal segregation and the attendant myths of white superiority.[44]

When Ballard wrote his essay, the most overt forms of racism were in decline, legally enforced segregation was no more, and institutional racism was harder to apprehend and ward oneself against. Might those rituals he missed be passé in light of that shift? Could they be replicated in institutions that weren't black-controlled and ensconced in black communities? It was hard to say. These scholars were undoubtedly right, however, to be concerned with the commodification of black cultural practices. Increases in disposable income and leisure time that went along with a growing black middle class and black peoples' entry into new labor markets and higher education in unprecedented numbers meant that black people didn't just participate in the culture of black power and black consciousness, they bought it with identity artifacts: Afro-sheen hair spray, picks with fists at the end, and mass produced dashikis. These were commodities. Kwanzaa, a holiday that began as an anticonsumerist project, fell prey to commodification, too. The holiday was intended as a ritual that would reconnect and reaffirm African American culture with continental African culture by means of seven principles for living. In the beginning Kwanzaa was also intended as an alternative to Christmas, a holiday overwhelmed by commercialism.

From the outset, Kwanzaa ceremonies often included a singing of "Lift Every Voice," which was a nod to black history in the United States, but most of it was more akin to a pageant or pantomime of West African harvest holidays. As I have noted, this structure is, in its own way, a continuation of the pageant traditions of the early twentieth century. Soon, however, Kwanzaa cards, Kwanzaa clothes, and Kwanzaa artifacts threatened to turn it into the very commercialism against which it was meant to serve as an antidote, and to distance it from the community-building pageant tradition from whence it grew. That's not surprising. A new economic philosophy emerged in the late 1970s. Neoliberalism is a riskier form of capitalism. As it descended upon the U.S. economy, it encouraged everyone to become an entrepreneur and allowed money to move even more easily across borders. Exploited laborers in former colonies increasingly produced goods to serve the consumer desires of people in the West, while the poor in Western nations found work disappearing. The entrepreneurial impulse that defined this economic turn coincided neatly with the ideal of ownership that had long been embraced in black communities as people sought some degree of autonomy from white bosses. The self-creation aspect of this new economic philosophy was readily embraced by many in the black community who believed in the gospel of black entrepreneurship as they thought ruefully back to the independent economic spheres of black towns and some black commercial districts of an earlier era. The other side of neoliberalism, however, was that alongside this advocacy of autonomy came the marketization of everything, as well as a sink-or-swim philosophy that would devastate the poorest people in this country.

Yet optimism ran high in many sectors of the black community during the 1970s, before all this became apparent. Black radio ownership expanded rapidly. The number of black-owned stations grew from sixteen to eighty-eight in the 1970s. Two black-owned and operated radio networks were established in the 1970s as well: Mutual Black Network and the National Black Network. The trend in radio during this period was to deemphasize news and public affairs programming and focus on standardized formats with a lot of music. This threatened the rich tradition of political commentary on black radio when it was smaller or more local. Fortunately, however, this change didn't fully depoliticize black radio, because popular black music was frequently overtly political in the first half of the 1970s. So much so that a series of songs emerged to claim the status of new anthems of black America: Parliament Funkadelic's "One Nation under a Groove," McFadden and Whitehead's "Ain't No Stoppin' Us Now," Marvin Gaye's "What's Goin' On," and many other generational odes. Nina Simone even said she hoped that her "(To Be) Young, Gifted and Black," inspired by her late friend Lorraine Hansberry, would displace "Lift Every Voice and Sing" as black America's anthem. And it was the closest in succeeding. "Young Gifted and Black" was declared the new Black National Anthem by CORE in 1971.[45] Originally recorded and released by Simone in 1969, it was featured on her 1970 album *Black Gold* and rose to number eight on the R&B chart. Subsequently a number of other artists covered it, including Donny Hathaway, the Heptones, and Aretha Franklin, who also named one of her albums after it, *Young, Gifted and Black.*

The passionate embrace of blackness was in some sense an attempt to recover feelings that couldn't be recovered, and to hold on to hopes that proved to be fragile. The society had not become equal, but it had become more accessible. Black life was more diffuse. There was increased opportunity, though never nearly enough. People strayed from the tight-knit communities and the networked organizations. The black institutions that remained still held on to the anthem, but there were fewer of them. Black newspapers began to disappear, unsustainable because they drew inadequate advertising funds and mainstream newspapers covered some of the news pertaining to black people.

Among the most resilient institutions when it came to black formalist practice, however, were black colleges and universities, which continued to educate the majority of the black professional classes and embraced tradition even when other colleges were become assiduously casual places. Students at HBCUs still had to dress for chapel, observe parietals, and sing the anthem ritually when they weren't talking about revolution or taking over campus buildings like their counterparts at predominantly white institutions. In a 1975 letter to high formalist fellow poet Robert Hayden, Michael Harper described a visit to Southern and Jackson State Universities:

> Just returned from New Orleans, Baton Rouge (Southern U), and Jackson State, where I saw Margaret Walker. The trip, on the whole, was very good, but some mindless performances by our people, the students who don't read or think, but "politic"—questions from the gallery about how poems relate to the people, and faculty catering to this nonsense, an attack on May Miller (Kelly's daughter), and Mari Evans saying she could only write the political poem—consciousness is political! At the same time Mari admires your work enormously, told me about a story when you two met at the bus station in Chicago, and her continued joy at your poems. Margaret's been ill, had a no. of operations, bad kidneys and other ailments, and slow of energy. She was gracious, and just as worried as ever, about her writing, her inability to concentrate, finish her autobiography, and other projects she's had stored up for weeks on end. The students were mostly demoralized, and into student elections—in fact, I fear that we've lost the major battle re schools and education, raising class upon class of illiterates, who have no appreciation of the struggles we waged. I was still inspired by the nat'l anthem: "Lift Every Voice and Sing," which was the opening of the convocation at Jackson State. Then the southern lunch, with the president, scheduled, but absent. I did meet him in the 9 story building on the 9th floor. I like your comments about the Dunbar poem—you know that the "double-conscious brother in the veil" recalls not so much DuBois, as the tradition, the fusing of Dunbar's sensibility, and

promise, his hopes to draft poems that would speak to both traditions, Afro-American and American, and his failure to do such as he bantered for an audience, for a market.⁴⁶

The generational gap between Harper and the students is palpable in the letter. He dismisses their explicitly nationalistic politics and their boldness. He holds fast to "the tradition," that striving black formalist pursuit of excellence. Years later, the friend to whom he wrote, Robert Hayden, would write an epic poem answering Stephen Vincent Benét's call for a black-skinned epic response to his 1928 book-length poem *John Brown's Body*. Hayden's endeavor, in relation to Benét's poem, was akin to the relationship between "Lift Every Voice" and "The Battle Hymn of the Republic." Hayden, like the Johnson brothers, depicted black life in epic terms. His work stood in contrast and complement to a white-authored vision of the struggle for democracy.

Tellingly, then, in 1975, a moment Harper describes as one of generational conflict, the only point of connection that the curmudgeonly Harper felt with this new black generation and the brash form of their struggles with white supremacy, the only tie binding these rakish young people with their elders, was through the anthem. He assumed that the similarly formalist poet Hayden would understand. Harper was "still inspired" by "it," that "it" being not just the song but the collective voice with which the anthem was sung. It was alive, even as formalism was gasping.

By then, however, the "we" to whom the song referred wasn't secure. The idea, though sometimes fantastical, of belonging to a black world had been sustained for most of the twentieth century. But after independence was gained by many black nations (and neocolonialism settled in), and black nationalist movements within Western powers were either crushed or incorporated into the status quo, the common thread that stretched across the black world seemed to have been lost or at least worn so fine as to be nearly invisible. Some individuals maintained the connections. Carmichael, along with some other former members of SNCC and the black power movements, migrated abroad. They went to Tanzania, Ghana, and Guinea, or joined efforts to build a revolutionary black nation in Grenada, while others went to graduate school to build lives as university professors, and others still were locked behind bars as political prisoners. Many of them labored to sustain the tradition of transnational black political communities. But these were for the most part individual bonds, or tiny networks, not movements.

Within those fine threads of black internationalism, however, "Lift Every Voice and Sing" often reappeared, quieter and yet still, for some, a signifier of black identity that transcended the nation-state. In 1976, the military president of Nigeria, Olusegun Obasanjo, called for a National Arts Theatre to be built in Lagos. Nigeria had oil, and therefore wealth. At the National Arts Theatre, Nigeria hosted the Second World Festival of Black Art, from January 15 to February 12, 1977. Attended by more than 17,000 participants from over fifty countries, it was the largest cultural event ever held on the African continent. Such festivals were planned as Pan-African celebrations and ranged in content from performance—particularly dance and theater—to debate. Paule Marshall, the Barbadian American novelist and short story writer, described attending this festival, called FESTAC 77, in her memoir *Triangular Road*. Marshall traveled to Nigeria to come to terms with her "tripartite self": American, Barbadian, and African. There she was at once inspired to connect with her Africanness, and yet dismayed at what her presence and that of other American black people who had come to Nigeria for FESTAC revealed about their struggle. She described them as "Unprepared. Unrehearsed. Improvised. Disorganized." In one scene, the group she has traveled with marches aimlessly through Lagos, some singing "Lift Every Voice and Sing," others singing "Amen."[47] The confusion she depicts is vaguely reminiscent of the divergent energies of the March Against Fear, and the crisis after King's death. What it portended this time was not a shift in the movement but rather its dissipation.

CHAPTER SEVEN

A Piece of the Rock

Post–Civil Rights Losses, Gains, and Remnants

There's a lot of chocolate cities, around
We've got Newark, we've got Gary
Somebody told me we got L.A.
And we're working on Atlanta
But you're the capital, cc
Gainin' on ya!
Get down
Gainin' on ya!
Movin' in and on ya
Gainin' on ya!
Can't you feel my breath, heh
Gainin' on ya!
All up around your neck, heh
—Parliament, "Chocolate City"

One of the more tangible outcomes of the late 1960s freedom movement was the rise of black leadership in electoral politics. Carl Stokes became the mayor of Cleveland in 1967, the same year Richard Hatcher was elected mayor of Gary, Indiana. Between 1967 and 1995, approximately 400 black mayors were elected in American cities, a remarkable transformation in local leadership that began just over a decade after Jim Crow had been declared unconstitutional. Hatcher hosted the National Black Political Convention in 1972. In attendance were activists, nationalists, revolutionaries, and politicians from across the political spectrum. The convention was declared an all-black space, with no white speakers and no white reporters. The NAACP and the Urban League chose not to attend because of this racial exclusivity, although there were many political moderates in attendance alongside radicals. The convention's cochairs were Hatcher, U.S. Representative Charles Diggs of Michigan, and Newark's Imamu Amiri Baraka, who was at that time the program chairman for the Congress of African People. Forty-two states were represented. Jesse Jackson, Coretta Scott King, Roy Innis (CORE), Haki Madhubuti, and Nixon aide Robert Brown were all present.

The convention's theme was "Unity without Uniformity." One attendee recalled, "Of course, not everyone was there. Not every group was represented at high levels. For example, although members of the NAACP participated, I don't recall representation by anyone in a senior leadership position of that organization. Nevertheless, the Convention was a hopeful sign. I was there and found the proceedings extremely moving. The dialogue was heated at times, uplifting at others. When the audience rose to sing 'Lift Every Voice and Sing' with fists raised in the air (yes, even Coretta had her fist raised and I have the photo to prove it!), it was amazing."[1] They'd come together bringing along a history of political and ideological differences, and yet by singing the Black National Anthem with fists raised, they celebrated the militant energy of the historical period as they sought to answer the question King had posed some years prior: "Where do we go from here?"

Discussions held over three days focused primarily on whether it was better for black people to achieve within existing power structures or create new ones altogether, ones built specifically for and by black people. Eight thousand people, 3,000 of them delegates, grappled with this question together. They talked about eliminating capital punishment, nationalizing health care, and community control of schools, among other timely issues. Although many attendees would complain that the gathering was disorganized and overwhelmingly male, it was a collective confrontation with the fork in the road.

The call for black political power was met, even in the heart of Dixie. In 1973 Atlanta's Maynard Jackson was elected the first black mayor of a large southern city. The successful mayoral campaigns of black politicians were widely understood as part of the black freedom struggle. That doesn't mean that political unity was commonplace among these representatives. Ambitions differed, as did personalities, ideologies, and circumstances. But the campaigns of this new pool of black politicians were generally facilitated by the white flight to the suburbs that followed desegregation and ramped up in the aftermath of urban uprisings. And the black political class was larger and more powerful than it had ever been before.

Stella White's memory of the first Congressional Black Caucus (CBC) dinner in 1971 marked it as an unquestionable extension of the movement. She described how "nails of four fingers dug deeply into the palm of my hand as a surge of emotion was held aloft in that right hand. Closing words of the

Negro National Anthem crescendoed to a close—3,000 voices, as one filled with hope. No longer is the anthem sung in a slow tempo, cadence is faster, more lively, a new dignity punctuating its rhythm."[2] Each year the dinner maintained a commitment to racial identity and yet also became fancier. In 1974, with a theme "A Tribute to Strong Black Women," Aretha Franklin performed for guests. In 1975 the annual CBC dinner featured the Newark Boys Choir singing "Lift Every Voice and Sing" and the black Republican Massachusetts senator Edward Brooke presenting the awards. Tickets by then were $100 each and the popular R&B group the O'Jays provided entertainment. Guests of honor included the widows of Malcolm X, Martin Luther King Jr., and Medgar Evers. It was a lavish event. Speakers preached the gospel of self-reliance and encouraged guests to fundraise for the CBC in their home communities. Pageantry and pomp in the black political class was taking on new forms, more exclusive and at a greater remove from their constituents.

But black communities continued to be deeply invested in black politics. And over the 1970s the ceremonial singing of "Lift Every Voice" became a symbol of chocolate cities with black power brokers and elected officials. The anthem was played at the inaugurations of Maynard Jackson in Atlanta and Harold Washington in Chicago. At Washington's ceremony "he straightened his shoulders, upwardly tilted his chin, positioned his arm for the arm of his fiancée and walked the ceremonial 300-foot stretch to become inaugurated as the forty-second mayor of the city of Chicago."[3] Cardinal Joseph Bernardin offered the invocation. Gwendolyn Brooks read her poem, "Chicago: The I Will City," and writer Studs Terkel spoke. The Chicago Children's Choir led everyone in singing "The Star-Spangled Banner," "Lift Every Voice and Sing," and "Jesus Cristo, Hombre y Dios." Brooks's poem echoed the themes of the anthem, but placed them in the soul of the city rather than black people generally, saying, "Now the way of the I will city is on this wise: ripe roused ready: richly rambunctious, implausible: sudden, or saddle-steady. In the jamboree jounce and jumble of our Season of Senselessness the I Will City is ready to rise. Toward robust radiance. Valid! Away from hunger, anger, and from dread. Toward health and difficult splendor. Toward immense creative indignation and defense. Toward, verily, the level land beneath the solid tread."

Harold Washington was a beloved mayor, and during his first term, on February 4, 1986, the Bulls game against the Detroit Pistons was dedicated to Black History Month and began with not the conventional "Star-Spangled

Banner" but "Lift Every Voice and Sing," performed by the Wendell Phillips High School A Cappella Choir.[4] Chicago, with its long history of ghettoizing and marginalizing much of its substantial black population, was symbolically in a new era. But it was also one in which appeals to racial equality were made by companies as marketing devices. David Rosengard, the vice president of marketing and broadcasting for the Bulls organization, stated in explanation, "The Chicago Bulls are proud to acknowledge black history month."[5] This was a savvy move in a city that was half black, with an organized black political class. Margaret Burroughs, founder of Chicago's DuSable Museum of African American History, said in response, "I think it is very important that the song expresses past struggles of our people and our hopes and determination to attain a better future is exposed. . . . I hope it will be sung up tempo as a fighting song and not a funeral dirge."[6] Certainly, under the leadership of Harold Washington, the political spirit of black Chicago was on an ascent even as the economic conditions of black people across the nation declined.

U.S. Representative Barbara Jordan of Texas also used the song as a symbol of black aspiration and attainment. Elected to Congress in 1972 and 1974, Jordan made a widely viewed and highly regarded speech before the House Judiciary Committee in support of Richard Nixon's impeachment. Two years later, she became the first African American woman to deliver the keynote address at the Democratic National Convention. Five years later Jordan retired from public life. In the first year of her retirement she was invited to record a version of "Lift Every Voice and Sing." Jordan narrated the song accompanied by the Royal Philharmonic Orchestra of London as part of an album titled *Symphonic Spirituals*, which also included the Negro spiritual "Swing Low, Sweet Chariot" and the Negro-spiritual-turned-freedom song "This Little Light of Mine." Jordan's improvisations on "Lift Every Voice" made the song explicitly Christian, but she also brought to mind the Augusta Savage sculpture in her riffs "Praise him with the Harp, praise him with stringed instruments."

A time of praise turned soon into a time filled with lament. Black mayors and politicians of the 1970s and 1980s came to power having to confront the issues of communities that had suffered from generations of neglect. In many cities the hopes held by mayors and their constituents were simply unrealizable. Unemployment, urban decay, and deindustrialization, combined with a diminished tax base, were challenges enough, but soon the country would swing dramatically to the right with the election of Ronald Reagan, making their work even more difficult.

In 1979, Sam Attlesley, a black politician from Dallas, described black voters as "an army without a general," saying, "I am not convinced we have reached the point where we can sing Lift Every Voice as doxology rather than an exhortation for continuing action."[7] Furthermore, the mainstream of the country was no longer with black people's struggles (if it ever was). The tide had turned, and the exhortation might just fall on deaf ears.

In 1980 Ronald Reagan, the Hollywood actor and former California governor, soundly defeated the incumbent president, peanut farmer and former Georgia governor Jimmy Carter. Reagan swooped in promising further deregulation of businesses and the diminishment of civil rights in favor of "states' rights." He began his presidential campaign with a "states' rights" speech delivered in Philadelphia, Mississippi, near the site where civil rights workers Andrew Goodman, Michael Schwerner, and James Chaney had been murdered, sending a not-too-subtle message of hostility toward the civil rights movement and its gains.

A report on the 1980 Urban League Convention captured the sentiment of black political organizations in the midst of the rise of Reagan: "The perception of a national stampede to the right, severe recessionary damage in black neighborhoods, the end of a 12 year respite from major urban riots and the recent shooting of Urban League President Vernon E. Jordan were cited by many delegates as the reason for one of the league's most joyless conventions in a long time."[8] Jordan, who had survived a sniper attack in Fort Wayne, Indiana, made a surprise appearance during the convention. He was wheeled to his hospital auditorium and "received a two-minute standing ovation as he rose from the wheelchair and firmly strode across the stage to the podium. He began by reciting a stanza of the Negro anthem, 'Lift Every Voice and Sing,' and offering a short prayer."[9] Raised in Atlanta, where he sang the song at Emancipation Day programs and played it in his high school marching band, Jordan was strongly aligned with the Democratic Party. He was wise to be worried about the impact of Reagan.

Jordan had frequently been criticized by black leftists for his connection to the Carter administration. For example, William Sales wrote of him, "To place the stamp of validity upon this testimonial to the 'American Dream'

Jordan rhetorically wraps himself in the red white and blue, calls upon God and country while singing the last stanza and chorus of 'Lift Every Voice and Sing' to the tune of 'Yankee Doodle.' . . . This emerging black bureaucratic petty bourgeoisie is beginning to see that it will have to play out its role within the confines of the status quo." Sales went on to comment on Jordan's willingness to criticize rioters but not exploitative gas companies and big banks. However, with Reagan's election, both black party-line Democrats and far leftists were out of favor and out of luck.

In 1980 black political leaders gathered yet again, this time in Richmond. They wanted to shape a black agenda for the decade. Again the gathering, sponsored by the Urban League and the Congressional Black Caucus, brought together a cross-section of black leadership, including Richard Hatcher, Cardiss Collins, Andrew Young, Vernon Jordan, Ron Dellums, Jesse Jackson, Coretta Scott King, Dorothy Height, Dick Gregory, Joseph Lowery, William Gray, and Mickey Leland. There were also lawyers, doctors, business people, and academics from across the country. They held a slew of workshops and drafted a series of white papers. The representatives from the business sector dedicated themselves to gathering resources in order to widely distribute information about the agenda that the group had agreed upon. A primary focus of the gathering was closing the employment and income gaps between black and white Americans. Delegates also believed a national voter registration drive would facilitate a steady increase in the number of black elected officials, and they dedicated themselves to that pursuit as well. Further, they advocated a boycott of South Africa, an end to police brutality against black people in the United States, and an increase in aid to Caribbean and African nations. For black youth, they planned to form a national youth coalition that would support young people in educational and employment goals, and prevent drug abuse and violence in the black community.

These were lofty goals and proved too difficult to bring to fruition. This had a good deal to do with Reagan's power and his Congress. Once elected, Reagan made good on his vision to eradicate much of the success of the civil rights movement. He described poor black women as "welfare queens" who were too heavy a tax burden. Having opposed the landmark Civil Rights Act of 1964 when it was passed, as president he sought to limit the Voting Rights Act of 1965. Reagan claimed that such protections for black voters were an unconstitutional infringement on "states' rights." His backlash against civil rights didn't end there: Reagan was also an outspoken critic of affirmative action, condemning "racial quotas" as a form of reverse racism only two decades after the end of legally mandated racial segregation. Reagan consistently appointed conservative justices to federal courts as part of his bid to dismantle the practice.

Reagan's rejection of the politics of the black freedom movement was international as well. In 1983, during his first term, the U.S. military invaded Grenada, a small black island that had a friendly relationship with Cuba and a community of black American radical expatriates. In contrast, Reagan maintained a friendly relationship with South Africa, notwithstanding its practice of racial apartheid, and he vetoed a bill for sanctions against South Africa that Congress had passed and a majority of Americans supported.

Reagan's administration also reduced funding for critical social welfare programs like the Comprehensive Employment and Training Act (which trained citizens and provided them with public sector jobs), the Equal Employment Opportunity Commission, and the Civil Rights Division of the Justice Department. This meant investigations and prosecutions of school and housing discrimination were effectively null and void under his administration. Wages and employment dropped, and incarceration dramatically increased during his two terms.

Reagan had a few black allies on the right wing. One was Tony Brown, who was well known for a multidecade-running PBS talk show *Tony Brown's Journal* and often sounded like a Booker T. Washington redux. Brown believed that African Americans had to earn social membership with economic development. His uplift politics included advocacy for historically black colleges, and his show routinely featured a wide range of black guests who, to his credit, represented the entire political spectrum and often did not share his beliefs. In 1985, Brown founded the Council for the Economic Development of Black Americans with the motto "Buy Freedom." It was intended as a "buy black" initiative to support black free enterprise. Participating businesses were supposed to display a "freedom seal" that would be a sign to consumers that the businesses would give discounts, offer competitive prices, and be active in supporting the local community.

Brown's campaign began with a "Call to Freedom," during which participating black radio stations across the country played "Lift Every Voice and Sing" simultaneously.[10] However, Brown found few stations, businesses, or individuals willing to participate. He didn't adequately account for how vulnerable black-owned businesses actually were. They needed capital, far more than a seal, to be competitive in the 1980s. To say that Brown was naive, and more than that, that Ronald Reagan was bad news for black America, however, is not to say that Reagan defeated black American political aspiration. Jesse Jackson's two presidential campaigns, while not garnering him the Democratic nomination, were remarkably successful. Under the banner of the Rainbow Coalition, a term first used by slain Chicago Black Panther Party leader Fred Hampton, Jackson built a multiracial constituency of voters who cared about the lot of working people and minority populations.

Furthermore, beyond electoral politics, the student antiapartheid movement was robust in the United States, notwithstanding Reagan's declaration that Nelson Mandela, the imprisoned leader of South Africa's African National Congress, was a terrorist. In the spring of 1985, 211 people were arrested at Cornell University after students occupied the main administrative building. They demanded that the university divest from its holdings in South Africa. At Harvard, antiapartheid activists set up shantytowns on the Yard in the center of campus to represent the conditions black South Africans lived in under apartheid. Students at Swarthmore College marched into a Swarthmore board meeting to protest the school's financial investments in South Africa, and at Haverford students held a two-day sit-in at one of the administrative offices. Students at Georgetown and Howard University joined forces to create a Washington, D.C., antiapartheid student organization, as did students at Fisk and Vanderbilt in Nashville. In Atlanta, student protesters at Morehouse were visited by Bishop Desmond Tutu and Andrew Young, and Spelman College brought South African youth speakers to campus to inform students about life under apartheid. Students at Columbia, Penn State, Yale, and Occidental, among other universities, were successful in leading their institutions to disinvest partially and sometimes even wholly from South Africa. By 1988, 155 schools had done so.

"Lift Every Voice and Sing" was often sung at antiapartheid protests in the United States, on campuses and in the streets, along with another song, "Nkosi Sikeleli iAfrica." "Nkosi" was written in 1897 by Enoch Sontonga, a South African Methodist minister. Just as "Lift Every Voice" had been a song of freedom in the early years of Jim Crow, "Nkosi" was an important freedom anthem as apartheid took root in South Africa. For a time it also served as the national anthem of Zambia, Tanzania, Namibia, and Zimbabwe. The twinned performances of two black anthems in the 1980s were a sign that despite the failure of Pan-Africanism to develop into a sustained global movement, some of its threads remained. Apartheid would not be dismantled until 1994, after a long struggle. Yet in South Africa, other independent African nations, the United States, and the Caribbean it seemed that the centuries-long global system of white supremacy was intransigent, and even the most extraordinary victories still didn't unsettle racial inequality.

Between the rolling back of civil rights legislation and the U.S. government's support for South Africa, it would be easy to simply state that the freedom movement had completely failed by the 1980s. But in truth, some of its principles had taken root in the profession of the United States to be an egalitarian and "color-blind" country. But practice and profession were mismatched. As a result, a distinctive form of racial discourse emerged in those years, one that reflected the tension between the rightward drift of the nation and the lingering energy of the antiwar, feminist, indigenous, and black liberation movements.

Even Reagan with his coded segregationist language understood he had to at least pay lip service to the promise of racial equality. Americans were not supposed to be racist anymore. And so racial animus had to be displaced. Instead of traditional claims that black people were inherently inferior, it became commonplace to hear that the suffering of the black poor was caused by their deficient character and anti-American ways of being. This allowed white Americans to avoid both charges of racism and the responsibility to atone for the persistence of American racism. This shift was clear during President Reagan's remarks at a 1982 National Black Republican Council Dinner. Reagan asserted that he would not write off the black vote, because for too long black people had been taken for granted by one party and written off by the other. He described the Republican Party as an ally of black people, citing his placement of 130 blacks in "top executive policy making positions" on the basis of merit rather than race. He spoke about supporting black business but decried Great Society and social welfare programs as bad for business and the nation. He rejected "throwing tax money" at a problem and claimed that dependence upon public assistance was the cause of black poverty. It was an elaborate doublespeak, praise for black people in each moment coupled with standard racial narratives of black inferiority, dependence, and laziness.

Reagan concluded his remarks with a nod to, and an interpretation of, "Lift Every Voice":

Earlier in the program you sang, "Lift Every Voice and Sing." The third verse to that beautiful hymn ends with the words, "May we forever stand true to our God and our native land." Tonight, let us make that pledge. Let us be true to our God and native land by standing by the ideals of liberty and opportunity that are so important to our heritage as free men and women. Let us prove again that America can truly be a promised land, a land where people of every race, creed, and background can live together in freedom, harmony, and prosperity. And let us proclaim for all to hear that America will have brotherhood from sea to shining sea.

It was as though, at least according to Reagan, marketing had fully displaced content. Marketing themselves as "black friendly" was supposed to stand in for substance, at least for the National Black Republican Council. Consumer culture was not simply expanding, it was also beginning to define American identity and politics. How politicians marketed themselves and the degree to which they actually represented the interests of the constituencies they claimed increasingly diverged.

For black politicians, there were a greater array of choices about alliances and allegiances, especially given that their actions could diverge from the desires of their voting constituents, if they had enough financial or institutional support from other sources. This dynamic became evident in Cleveland. For many years, Carl Stokes, mayor from 1967 to 1971, was at odds with the president of the Cleveland City Council, George Forbes. Both men were black. Stokes grew his support by making explicit appeals in the black community's interest, whereas Forbes was a more conventionally loyal Democrat. Forbes was ultimately more powerful in the city, as his interests were often aligned with those of business elites. He supported tax abatements and incentives for the business class, and while he spoke out on issues like police brutality, his criticism of structural racism was modest at best.

In 1987, many years into their conflict, there were two separate Martin Luther King Jr. Memorial breakfast ceremonies in Cleveland. One intimate gathering took place under the leadership of Stokes. The other, under the banner of Forbes, featured the Cleveland Orchestra and most of the city's black leaders. Stokes claimed to be the one who stood in the tradition of King. But he spoke to a much smaller audience. At both breakfasts the audience was asked to sing "Lift Every Voice and Sing." It had always been embraced regardless of political perspective. The song was not aligned with a politics, it was aligned with a people. But the sense of linked fate that was once an integral part of the singing couldn't be assumed. And the rival breakfasts were just one indication of that.

Black Americans were increasingly included in the media marketing landscape of the late 1970s and 1980s, and the black middle class was pulling away from the black poor. This distance was evidenced in electoral politics as well as mass culture. Black magazines increasingly featured the black elite, who were largely distinguished by their fancy cars and vast homes rather than by their achievement or work as race men and women. They came to represent the aspirational image of black America. One black advertising firm, Mingo-Jones, was particularly successful in tapping into black markets with aspirational imagery. Their clients included American Express and the National Urban League. In 1979, the agency developed the slogan "We Do Chicken Right!" for Kentucky Fried Chicken. Even beer advertising, which was historically white, white, and more white, learned to market to blacks more successfully by hiring Mingo-Jones. When Miller Brewing launched Miller Lite in the 1970s, it wanted to convey a manly image (with the subtext that "lite" beer was not a girly diet drink). With Mingo-Jones they had already created a memorable, and successful, string of TV ads that featured retired black professional athletes, and Miller returned to them to sell its new beer.

Miller wanted a special, targeted campaign to woo black drinkers to Miller High Life. So Deborah McDuffie, the first female composer in the advertising industry, was approached to write a Black History Month jingle for the brand. McDuffie had worked with many popular musicians and could enlist a wide array of talent. She arranged what she termed "a celebratory, contemporary version of 'Lift Every Voice and Sing'" and recorded it with a host of prominent singers including Al Green and Deniece Williams backed by Patti Austin, Roberta Flack, Melba Moore, and Deborah herself. She used the Blues Brothers band, and Leon Pendarvis was the musical director. The album they produced was distributed to select groups. For example, all the attendees at the Delta Sigma Theta Sorority Convention that year received copies. In addition to the record, Miller printed up colorful posters with the words "Lift Every Voice" boldly printed across the top. The blue background was covered in Matisse-like abstract black bodies, with the first verse of the anthem written in multiple colors from top to bottom. Stamped in the bottom right corner was the logo "Miller High Life." The brand manager of Miller Lite, Barren Barrett, said, "The anthem is about faith hope and above all the pride and dignity of a people. Like the spirituals which are so much a part of America's diverse culture, the message of the anthem is universal."[11]

In this era, to be "for" black people, nominally, could mean absolutely nothing of substance. It might simply mean somebody was trying to sell something, or, in the tradition of Reagan, it might actually mean a paternalistic damnation. Frank speech was needed to clear away the underbrush of race in America.

Then came hip-hop.

In the final year of the 1980s, Spike Lee, a young, brilliant, brash, and black film director, released his second feature, *Do the Right Thing*. It is the story of a sweltering day in New York and a racial conflagration that begins when a young black man, played by Lee himself, complains that there are no images of "brothers" on the wall at the Italian-owned pizzeria he frequents. It concludes with the murder of another young black man by means of a police chokehold. The film was inspired by a series of racially charged deaths in New York: the Howard Beach death of Michael Griffith, who was struck by a car as he ran from a violent white mob, and the police murders of Eleanor Bumpers and Michael Stewart. Spike Lee asked Chuck D, the frontman for the socially conscious rap group Public Enemy, to create a hip-hop version of "Lift Every Voice" for the film, but Chuck D declined. He had come of age in the black power era and considered the song sacred. Instead the group came up with a new anthem, "Fight the Power."

The movie begins with a solitary horn playing strains of "Lift Every Voice and Sing," and then suddenly actress Rosie Perez bursts on to the screen, dancing hard and fast to "Fight the Power." The sharp lyrics—"Elvis was a hero to most, but he never meant shit to me, a straight up racist the sucker was simple and plain, mother fuck him and John Wayne! I'm ready, I'm hyped cause I'm amped, most of my heroes don't appear on no stamp!"— were an example par excellence of the newest and most energetic form of popular music: hip-hop. Hip-hop was irreverent, bold, sacrilegious when it came to formalism, and relentlessly vernacular. Hip-hop artists wore the casual clothing of quotidian life in urban centers, not the tailored suits and ball gowns of performers in the 1940s, 1950s, and 1960s, or the elaborate and wild costumes of performing artists of the 1970s. As R&B music lost nearly all of its political content in the 1980s, and became increasingly sentimental and "smooth," hip-hop was unflinching and explicitly both hard and political, even when it didn't have an overt political message. It was the music of the young people dispossessed by the Reagan era. It was the music of migrants and their descendants, from the Caribbean and the South, from the country to the city, who arrived to far less opportunity than hoped for, and with only their resilience and rich cultural archive to rely upon.

The introduction of hip-hop into black popular culture must be understood alongside the diminishing sphere of black institutional life. Hip-hop's transgressions against norms of what it meant to be respectful and appropriate spoke to its frankly adolescent sensibilities. It also was indebted to the black power era, and the "rapping" and poetry of the Black Arts Movement. It was street. It was a resourceful collage, a threading together of technology and bits and pieces of the world surrounding the youth and their languages. It was the music made in the shadows of Reagan, crack cocaine, and COINTELPRO, and without paternalistic oversight.

Melba Moore recorded a version of "Lift Every Voice and Sing" in 1990, the throes of the hip-hop era. It was somewhat popular and brought together a panoply of stars with a beautiful music video. Her choice to rely upon the visual in addition to sound belied an awareness of the growing importance of the visual in popular music with the rise of music television and videos. Yet despite its beauty, Moore's song honestly sounded old-fashioned in comparison to the newer and harder-hitting form of music.

Although it always had a multiracial audience and artists, hip-hop remained primarily popular with black and Latino communities until 1992, when the West Coast gangsta rap album *The Chronic* became a massive crossover success. For years, mainstream moral panics had been ginned up about hip-hop due to its explicit and profane content. But the rise of gangsta rap alarmed even older black folks, who were familiar with gutbucket hits and blues ballads of lawlessness but nothing so explicitly vulgar and antisocial. However, the widespread generalization of all hip-hop as "gangsta" simply because that was the style most popular with white audiences was a gross mischaracterization. The music developed a range of regional, political, and aesthetic variations. There were hip-hop Afrocentrists and revolutionaries, middle-class suburban kids, language lovers, bookworms, and counterculture hippies, along with those who spread the gospel of street hustling.

Despite this wide variation and many excellent hip-hop acts of various sorts, when the Fugees burst on the scene, they were distinctive. Their name was short for "refugees," and they turned the sensationalistic and racist representations of Haitians in popular media upside down by embracing the term *refugee*. These artists refused shame and expressed allegiance to the least of these. The trio, Haitian Wyclef Jean, Haitian American Pras Michel, Lauryn Hill, and producers Jerry Wonder, Salaam Remi, and John Forté created a magnificent sophomore album, *The Score*, which earned them a Grammy Award and multiplatinum sales. During live shows, the Fugees often began their performances with Wyclef Jean playing "Lift Every Voice and Sing" on the electric guitar with his tongue. It wailed and moaned, reminiscent of how Jimi Hendrix once played "The Star-Spangled Banner" but also suggestive of how Marvin Gaye interpreted the national anthem, both sensual and erotic. One such performance was at the 1996 BET awards. Clef's rendition of "Lift Every Voice" breaks up. It is choppy and ephemeral. Then he smashes the guitar into pieces. Almost immediately, the driving beat of Mary J. Blige's hip-hop soul classic "Real Love" follows, and Hill emerges from backstage rhyming, alto-voiced, and supremely confident. The crowd screams its approval.

Hip-hop uttered its farewell to the Black National Anthem. Once upon a time, this was a song around which black immigrants and migrants articulated shared identity and forged it, too. Once it was a part of a ritualistic sphere of black life. But that sphere ceased to exist for many young black people when legal desegregation and middle-class mobility took hold. For someone like Wyclef Jean, who had emigrated from Haiti to New York in the late 1970s, it is easy to imagine that the song would have no particular significance at all. But it is worthwhile to contemplate why he treated it as something to rework, and not simply to leave behind. This new fabric of "Lift Every Voice" was tattered and much, *much* smaller but never completely forgotten.

In 1988, the U.S. Postal Service issued a twenty-two-cent James Weldon Johnson stamp as part of its Black Heritage series. Underneath an image of his face are the words and notation of the first line of "Lift Every Voice and Sing" along with the designation "Black Heritage USA." It was a symbolic achievement, but merely that: symbol. Likewise, when Stevie Wonder snuck it into his "Star-Spangled Banner" performance at the 2005 NBA All-Star game, it was sweet but not particularly moving, and certainly little more than a blip in comparison to his substantial corpus of works devoted to profound depictions and expressions of black life and consciousness.

The culture wars raged through the late 1980s and 1990s. Affirmative action was diminished and in some places disappeared. So did many black spaces—dorms, cultural centers, programs—that had been hard earned on college campuses in the 1970s. Black unemployment remained chronic, black imprisonment skyrocketed, and transiency as a result of eviction and gentrification weakened community ties in many cities. "Lift Every Voice and Sing" was still sung here and there, mostly as part of Black History Month programs or at black college graduations, but not nearly as frequently.

Bill Clinton was elected president in 1992. Clinton was referred to as "the First Black President" by Toni Morrison, in a manner that was at once tongue in cheek but also a commentary upon the right wing's use of tropes usually applied to black people to attack Bill Clinton. But no matter how much sneering there was at his poor background, his single mother, and his drug-addicted brother, Clinton, like all U.S. presidents, was ultimately implicated in a system that sustained racial inequality. While his affinity for and appeal to black people was widely noticed, his welfare reform legislation both deepened poverty in black communities and created more precarious conditions for people living in cities who had relied on public assistance when employment had disappeared. Clinton's Violent Crime Control and Law Enforcement Act—that is, his version of "law and order"—was the largest crime bill in U.S. history and led to dramatic increases in incarceration, even as crime rates were steadily decreasing. These policies further damaged black associational life by weakening social ties and stability. It is somewhat ironic, then, that Bill Clinton not only knows the words to "Lift Every Voice and Sing"—all three verses. Vernon Jordan once recalled that Bill Clinton sent him a photograph of the two of them singing the song at a party on Martha's Vineyard in 1993. The president inscribed the picture with the words "from the only white man in America who knows all the words."[12]

When Bill Clinton awarded Rosa Parks the Congressional Medal of Freedom, Jessye Norman led the audience in singing "Lift Every Voice and Sing." Tom Joyner remembered that "every living black dignitary was in the audience that great day and everyone stood and sang the first verse loudly and proudly. . . . As we got to the second verse, the singing got faint. Most of us left it up to Miss Norman, who had the words in front of her. The only person in the room who sang every word of every verse by heart was Bill Clinton. By the third verse he and Jessye Norman were doing a duet."[13] Clinton's intimacy with rituals of black space, one that he was afforded by virtue of his many years in the South living with close ties to black communities, one that earned him a good deal of trust from black constituents, was increasingly unavailable to young black people who came of age during his presidency.

That said, in the 1990s, black organizations continued to try to revive and revitalize the political energies and social organization of the past. In

1995, the Million Man March on Washington was called for by the leader of the Nation of Islam, Louis Farrakhan. Under the banner of the Nation, various civil rights organizations joined the march. Even though the national NAACP refused to participate due to a number of Farrakhan's controversial statements regarding Jewish and white people, the Washington, D.C., branch was present. One controversy regarding the march was Farrakhan's insistence that it be only for men. This seemed to some observers to be a sign that the marchers were advocating for black male patriarchy rather than black people's freedom writ broadly. After the march a number of the attendees criticized Louis Farrakhan, whose very long concluding speech veered into a stream of consciousness about numerology and cosmology incomprehensible to the majority of the participants who were not members of the Nation of Islam. And there were conflicts over the size of the crowd. Conference organizers said 1 million people attended. The U.S. Park Service put the numbers at about 400,000. The Park Service was accused of racism and of making a deliberate effort to diminish the magnitude of the gathering. A back-and-forth debate was waged on television and in newspapers.

Over the course of the actual march day, many prominent speakers, including the national director of the march, Benjamin Chavis, spoke to the massive crowd. The speeches were lengthy and often meandering. There was very little music, although at one point an adoring crowd surrounded Isaac Hayes, who stood on top of his tour bus, arms outstretched, in an elaborate caftan reminiscent of his 1971 *Black Moses* album cover. The march preached self-help, a renewed commitment to the health of black communities, and dedication to shifting the negative public image of black men. But the follow-up strategy quickly lost momentum.

Two years later, black women held the Million Woman March in Philadelphia. This march was principally organized by grassroots activist Phile Chionesu. It was held on the Benjamin Franklin Parkway in Philadelphia's Center City. The Million Woman March focused on social, political, and economic development in black communities, as well as on nurturing a global sisterhood of black women. Marchers called for healing from conflict and enmity among black women, and the restoration of family and community bonds among black people. Approximately half a million people attended, and the women sang "Lift Every Voice and Sing" at the end of the day. Notwithstanding the gravitas of the moment, it also did not translate into sustained political mobilization.

The Million Family March was smaller than the previous two marches and was called by the Nation of Islam like the first. The focus was again on personal improvement. The marchers were encouraged to eat healthfully and, reflecting the Nation's social conservatism, were told to marry and stay married, and to maintain strong communities. They also raised money to pay off the mortgage for the Washington, D.C., headquarters of the National Council of Negro Women (NCNW). Organizers noted that the NCNW headquarters was the only black-owned building in the nation's corridor of power. The group of thousands sat or stood on the lawn in front of the Capitol. Together, those who knew it sang "Lift Every Voice and Sing."

Certainly these marches were significant. They showed a continued dedication by large numbers of people to the goal of thriving black communities. They subverted dominant images of black people as apathetic. However, these marches did not lead to social movement, or any systematic institution-building. Perhaps because of their large size, they also lacked the sophisticated analyses of domestic and foreign policy that characterized the Pan-African congresses and other national and international black meetings of earlier generations. The marches and meetings of earlier generations could do more with more sustainable agendas, in large part because they relied upon a thickly networked associational life. They didn't need a single dramatic mobilization of thousands to reach thousands, because the networks could carry news and ideas to smaller gatherings with extended deliberations. But by the late 1990s, black associationalism was not simply largely absent but also unpracticed for black adults who had come of age after desegregation. They could go to a march, be moved, and then never think about it again. Easily.

Afterword

The end is bitter with only the slightest sweetness. After eight increasingly frustrating years of the second Bush presidency, marked by September 11 and the continuing toll of two long wars, candidate Barack Obama stood as a beacon of hope: hope for new beginnings, for the possibility of a changed course in our national political vision, and for a refuge from the painful politics of race. That hope was unrealistic, premature, and sophomoric at best.

One hint of how overinflated this hope was could be found in the furor around singer Rene Marie. In July 2008, she stood onstage in advance of the Denver State of the City address. Charged with singing "The Star-Spangled Banner," she adhered to its melody but sang the words to "Lift Every Voice and Sing."[1] This was less than a month before the Democratic National Convention would be held in Denver. The widespread quick and impassioned denouncement of Rene Marie by many public commentators included fears that her gesture threatened the candidacy of Barack Obama, who in a few short weeks would be named the Democratic Party's candidate for president. Marie's singing smacked of black nationalism to many listeners, and more than that, disloyalty to the nation. Candidate Obama echoed the patriotic words of earlier critics: "If she was asked to sing the national anthem, she should have sung that. 'Lift Every Voice and Sing' is a beautiful song, but we only have one national anthem."

The idea that any explicit articulation of blackness, of black fidelity or black identity, would be understood as hostile to "America" and "Americana" would continue to dog and even hinder President Obama and further stymied the pursuit of racial justice and equality by black communities in general. Having a black president was supposed to be enough. And his election *was* overwhelming for Americans and especially black Americans. For some it seemed to be a sign that we had finally scaled our way to "the mountaintop" King had once prophesied. For many others it simply was an extraordinary event in this country, where the original sin of slavery still shapes so much of our lives. At his inauguration, held on a cold, wet Washington morning, hundreds of thousands thronged as breathless witnesses to history. After President Obama was sworn into office, Joseph Lowery, a veteran of the civil rights movement, offered the benediction, echoing Benjamin Mays in 1963.

Like Mays, he began with the final verse of "Lift Every Voice": "God of our weary years, god of our silent tears . . . " But, unlike Mays, he continued. This was not a subtle gesture but a fully formed homage to the anthem:

> . . . thou, who has brought us thus far along the way, thou, who has
> by thy might led us into the light, keep us forever in the path we
> pray, lest our feet stray from the places, our god, where we met thee,
> lest our hearts, drunk with the wine of the world, we forget thee.
>
> Shadowed beneath thy hand, may we forever stand true to thee,
> oh God, and true to our native land.
>
> We truly give thanks for the glorious experience we've shared
> this day.
>
> We pay now, oh Lord, for your blessing upon thy servant Barack
> Obama, the 44th president of these United States, his family and his
> administration.

The moment was weighted with a particular history, a black history, and a particular message to black America. The third verse is the one that warns and prays. It reminds the people to stay the course toward freedom.

But what exactly was the course? Pundits speculated incessantly that Obama's presidency promised to make us finally "postracial." This postracial formulation seemed to many of us who write and think about race, and to the many more who experienced the daily impact of racial inequality, to reflect a desire to be rid of having to think about racism rather than an actual commitment to eradicating racism. Racial inequality was everywhere. And it deepened after the economic crisis of 2008 and 2009, a crisis that was produced by a deregulated and racially discriminatory mortgage market. But there seemed to be very little political will among politicians of any rank to respond to the persistence of American racism.

Even as most black people, and many others as well, rejected the fiction that we were postracial, there was a more remote theory of race in the twenty-first century that advocated a more nuanced understanding of the moment in black life, and that was "postblackness." Thelma Golden, the distinguished curator of the Studio Museum in Harlem used the phrase in the context of the 2001 exhibition *Freestyle* at the Studio Museum. It was an extraordinary show, and one of its installations so inspired me that I chose stills from it for the cover art for my first book, *Prophets of the Hood: Politics and Poetics in Hip Hop*. *Freestyle* featured twenty-eight black artists, who were "postblack" in that they were not defined by a singular idea of blackness. They were individual artists with particular stories, and yet each was steeped in black cultural practices and traditions. These were the post–civil rights "children of hip-hop" looking for ways of describing themselves that resisted the traditional categories of race men and women, or conventional civil rights notions of uplift and dignity. These artists with varying experiences and influences were joined under the general category of blackness, yet they also had enough distinctiveness that they rejected the idea that they could easily be identified by a single tradition. Postblackness was porous, and at times amorphous.

Writers and visual artists who could be classified as part of postblackness have since played with the Black National Anthem. The protagonist in Paul Beatty's satirical novel *Slumberland* is a black deejay in East Germany named Ferguson W. Sowell who goes by the appellation DJ Darky. Along with the conceit of having a phonographic memory, DJ Darky is obsessed with Charles Stone, aka the Schwa, a musician who disappeared into East Germany in the 1960s. In the novel Darky is gifted with an already-scored tape that is so stunning and transformative that he believes it must be the work of the Schwa. So he makes his way to Slumberland, a bar in Berlin where he determines it was recorded. In advance, DJ Darky has put together "the perfect beat," which he hopes will be played over by the Schwa. Darky's search for meaning and music, in the midst of the Cold War's demise and the exportation of black popular culture across the globe, is rendered satirically and provocatively. When he finally encounters the Schwa, however, Darky's race mettle is tested.

> He was switching up the tempo. Seguing from a frenzied fortissimo
> to a languid legato by quoting from "Lift Every Voice and Sing," the
> Negro National anthem. It's a beautiful yet trepidatious song, and
> especially so in his hands. Musical mason that he was, the Schwa
> erected a series of African American landmarks upon the foundation
> I had laid down. . . . Despite the tune's genius, in my mental landscape
> where blackness is passé quoting the Negro National anthem was a
> blatant violation of the zoning laws. By constructing a new black Berlin
> wall in both my head and the city, he was asking me to improvise. . . .
> He was daring me to be "black."

DJ Darky refuses the challenge, but the Schwa goes on to sonically deconstruct "Lift Every Voice and Sing": "He cannonballed into his own tune, unleashing a voluminous splashing salvo of triplets that shattered and scattered the song into a wave of quarter, half, whole notes that fluttered to the floor in wet, black globular droplets."[2]

The post–civil rights urge, expressed by DJ Darky, to declare blackness "over" reads as naive and stubbornly misguided. But the Schwa's performance of "Lift Every Voice and Sing," and his deconstruction and rearticulation of it in a scattered landscape seems right. It is not intact as it once was. The pundit Touré argued in his book *Who's Afraid of Post-Blackness?* that blackness was being redefined in the twenty-first century, such that everything that any single black person did constituted black culture. But that couldn't be right. That definition would make black culture essentially meaningless and too dependent upon the technical "fact" that someone was defined as black, an individualistic form of essentialism, rather than the stuff of black life. Beatty describes postblackness better. The Schwa's droplets display molecular cohesion, they both gather and splatter in different directions.

Visual artist and musician Sanford Biggers has performed "Lift Every Voice and Sing" with his band Moon Medicine. In one performance, they wore white hazmat jumpsuits splattered with neon paint: "Their faces were hidden behind gold rubber masks that were bent out of shape with large lips protruding ominously. But even if their faces were hidden, it was clear they were having fun. At one point, they spoke the lyrics of 'Lift Every Voice and Sing' to the tune of Prince's 'Controversy,' flashed the lyrics, the word 'controversy' and all sorts of found footage, from vintage war clips to Miley Cyrus grinding against Robin Thicke at [the] Grammys."

One of Moon Medicine's recordings of "Lift Every Voice and Sing" has been incorporated into Clifford Owens's performance art pieces. Owens teaches the audience the history of the anthem, why it was written, and then tries to teach them to sing it. Although this seems rather straightforward, in the larger performance piece he responds to other scores as well, and the result is both layered and provocative: "Another score was contributed by Senga Nengudi, who instructed Owens to scatter and sweep coloured sand into the centre of the room. The most controversial of scores was provided by Kara Walker, who ordered Owens to 'French kiss an audience member. Force them against a wall and demand sex. The audience/viewer should be an adult. If they are willing to participate in the forced sex act abruptly turn the tables and assume the role of victim. Accuse your attacker. Seek help from others, describe your ordeal. Repeat.'"[3]

In each vignette the provocativeness of the performance becomes an explicit challenge to the piety and formalism traditionally attached to the anthem, and yet in some ways the piece as a whole reminds the viewers of the song's significance. In Owens's piece, the performance of "Lift Every Voice and Sing" was the least incendiary of the bunch. Or maybe not. Perhaps asking audiences, in particular white audiences, to sing a black anthem is as much of a challenge as the others. In any case, the question remains, it seems, whether the implied significance of the song is merely in memory or current.

The anthem certainly remains here and there: as inspiration for fabric artist Gwen Magee, as a feature of black banquets and Black History Month events. Touré's call for "Lift Every Voice" to be displaced by Marvin Gaye's "Troubleman" as the anthem of black America elicited little reaction or interest. But Paule Marshall's description of FESTAC was a foreshadowing. The course is unclear. Racial inequality has persisted. It has morphed but remained. Yet there don't seem to be tangible remedies in law or elections for the persistence of the color line, even as a few black people seem to have escaped its grasp. Something more fundamental about the United States has to be addressed in order to get rid of its deep racism, and we haven't figured that out at all.

"Things were so much better before desegregation." Many of us have heard this from black elders, an ironic formulation given how hard they fought to make sure the society's doors were open to us. Such romantic renderings of the pre-desegregation past as "better" often seem too simplistic. Life was difficult under Jim Crow. Exclusions were pervasive and systematic. Though the society has never come close to achieving racial equality, having the right to vote, to attend schools without explicit legal barriers, to enter into a wide variety of professions, to go to the public library and sit at lunch counters and drive the nation's roads largely without incident, these are important transformations in our society, hard fought for by black Americans and other believers in racial justice. The nostalgia, however, is real and much of it, I would argue, has to do with the perception that the loss of black associational life and black formalism was the cost of the freedom movement. And it might have been too high a cost. But it wasn't just desegregation that led to their loss. Americans' associational life is diminished generally. We are less likely to go to church or to belong to a community group than our grandparents were. We are increasingly private citizens. But it is also the case that the rich interior life of black communities grew thinner as black mobility increased, as did the demands for private rather than community striving. At the same time, the vulnerabilities associated with deindustrialization and mass incarceration and transiency due to eviction that are ever threatening in the life of the black poor also diminish social networks. Longing for what once was—black formalist rituals, black associations, and a fabric of meaning, values, and identity that were solidified with singing "Lift Every Voice and Sing"—is more than understandable. It is to be expected.

Today, it often seems, our impulse to memorialize landmark marches and civil rights heroes isn't forward looking. Looking to the past often isn't a means for understanding the present. Rather, memorialization stands in lieu of the burden of figuring out our time. So it was with the 2010 celebration of civil rights music at the White House. It was a star-studded and televised event, beautiful in its array of talent, and stunning in its symbolism. Morgan Freeman served as the master of ceremonies, Yolanda Adams sang Sam Cooke's "A Change Is Gonna Come" and concluded the song by saying, while looking at the president, "A change has come!" The story of this presidency, she seemed to say, was to be thoroughly ensconced in our national mythology of steadily moving toward a more perfect union. The performers sang freedom songs. "This Little Light of Mine" and "Abraham Martin and John" were both led by Smokey Robinson. But then it came time to sing "Lift Every Voice and Sing." The initial plan was for the Howard University Gospel Choir to perform it, but the producer decided at the last minute that it would be more appealing to the television audience if it were sung by celebrities. And so they did. The president, who had been standing in the front, introduced the song and then moved to the back. The celebrities were still jubilant and swaying. But they stumbled over the words. Many hummed, or stopped singing in moments of confused silence. They simply didn't know it.

In August 2014, Mike Brown, a young black man, was shot in Ferguson, Missouri. His body was left on the ground for four and a half hours, a harrowing repetition of the long American tradition of racial terror, but with his black body splayed on the concrete instead of swinging in a tree. After so many deaths of black people at the hands of police officers, over and over again, black youth in Ferguson said, Enough. They stood in the street, refused, and resisted. They faced down military-grade weapons and tear gas and ignited the imagination of a nation.

In the age of Ferguson and beyond, the freedom songs of the 1960s don't seem to work. They ring as naive when they were once strong, and as hokey where they were once defiant. Perhaps that is why on one night in Ferguson, protesters sang "Lift Every Voice and Sing." And then, when Howard University students protested in Washington, D.C., in solidarity with Ferguson, they sang it, too, while wearing shirts and placards that read "Justice for Mike Brown" and "Black Lives Matter." As students at a historically black college, they are some of the few who today still carry the torch of black formalism. The moment was profound and insistent, but it was nevertheless on unsure ground. How to protest today, how to prepare for struggle, who is in the community of the struggle? These questions are urgent in the twenty-first century. Many of us know we have to act. But the "how" behind it is fitful.

When it was announced that the grand jury failed to indict Darren Wilson for killing Mike Brown, people were already gathered at the Westside Missionary Baptist Church in St. Louis. Upon learning the news, they elected to remain silent for four and a half minutes: a minute for each hour Mike Brown's body lay in the street. The pastor read a prayer of forgiveness written by South African bishop Desmond Tutu, and the congregation sang "Lift Every Voice and Sing" in advance of a twenty-four-hour prayer vigil.

In Baltimore, less than a year later, Freddie Gray was arrested for possession of a switch blade. After a "rough ride" to the precinct, Gray was in a coma. He died seven days later from his injuries. Again, people took to the street. The choreography of the aftermath of his death was a truncated dance of black American politics from the mid-1960s to the present. We saw black political power in the form of elected officials who were unable to address the pervasive poverty and marginalization of their constituents. We saw violent and enraging policing. We saw media that demonized the least of these when they wailed their frustration and pain. We watched. Prince went to do a benefit concert. The Baltimore Symphony Orchestra put on a special performance called "One Baltimore" that included "The Star-Spangled Banner," Harry Belafonte's "Turn the World Around," pop star Rihanna's "Stay," as well as an audience participatory version of "Lift Every Voice and Sing."

In 2015, during Black History Month, convocations, and memorial services, the song came back with the melancholy and steeliness of the moment, but also with trepidation. There was some hopefulness in response to the way black people and others, in both the United States and abroad, were choosing in this, the second decade of the twenty-first century, to publicly refuse waves of racist violence, persistent inequality, and economic despair by organizing and protesting. The digital age has made the world smaller. Having political concerns that are global can reinvigorate, and is being reinvigorated. And yet, those who *care* are heartbroken again each time they witness the next tragedy, and the next, and the next. I, like many other people, find singing "Lift Every Voice and Sing" alongside other people of conscience to be one bulwark against a pessimism that threatens to descend at every turn. But when I look around the room and see so many closed mouths, or eyes focused on the page, nervous gestures, I am reminded not to be deceived about the moment in which we live, grasping somewhat randomly into traditions and their archives and yet in desperate need of rebuilding tradition, or building anew.

There is no song that touches me so deeply, but while the Black National Anthem (or Negro National Hymn), "Lift Every Voice and Sing," is powerful, we should not be sentimentally attached to it or any other composition just for tradition's sake. Despite the fact that I have spent an entire book on this song, I cannot conclude with a call for us to revive "Lift Every Voice and Sing." Rather, the ways of being that appear in the traditions of singing the anthem continue to matter. The features of black formalism matter, too, though I suspect the "form" of formalism will continue to change and perhaps won't merit the same title. Perhaps it won't be rooted so firmly in a national racial identity and will instead be based at the crossroads of local concerns and collectives. Or maybe there is something to be developed from the growing interest in international black politics and a shrinking globe. I am not a prophet. My point is, however, that people need interdependence and community that affirms their value and position in the world, counterpublics and public arenas that set values that contest the inequality and injustice that continue to fester. As social beings we flourish when all of this is part of our regular life rituals. We learn to be through repetition. We are who we are through the regularity of our doings. And so, I conclude with a call for a return to an active associational life, to deliberately being and doing together. That is what must be encouraged and revived. The path is rugged, the lantern light dim. That ritual community, that deliberate meaning-making and learning, that repetition, meditation, and fellow feeling, that epic story, that sense of courage, inspiration, promise, and resilience, that love and beauty that once sustained black struggle in song—we need them now just as much as we did in 1900. May they, may we, forever stand.

Acknowledgments

To borrow from the inimitable Alabaman Margaret Walker, this book is for my people. And it is of them. I mean specifically the black South and its diaspora. This book is also a "but for my people" work, meaning it exists because of the grace of others as much if not more than as a result of my own labor.

My editor, Mark Simpson-Vos, has been an absolute delight to work with, and I couldn't imagine better hands for bringing it to the world.

My wonderful, generous, and brilliant colleagues and students in the Department of African American Studies at Princeton University have talked and thought with me through this research and writing journey. I must express especial gratitude to our chair and my friend, Eddie S. Glaude Jr., for reading every draft and asking probing and powerful questions about both substance and form, every step of the way.

The generous feedback I've received about this project from people at various colleges, universities, and high schools that have invited me to speak has been wonderful: particular thanks to the faculty, students, and community members in the Program in Law and Public Affairs at Princeton University, in the University of Pennsylvania Departments of English and African American Studies, in the Carter G. Woodson Center at the University of Virginia, in the Stanford University Department of African American Studies, and at Rowan University. Beyond those in-person encounters, scholars working in the field of the history of black education, especially James D. Anderson, Heather Andrea Williams, Michael Fultz, Vanessa Siddle Walker, and the forerunner Thelma D. Perry (along with the many others cited in this book), have provided me with essential models for the methodological approach I have taken here. This book rests on their shoulders, and on the many others who have devoted their lives to mining, culling, and sharing black institutional, cultural, and social history.

So many friends encouraged me as I wrote this book, too many to name but all remembered. Among them, Michele Alexandre, Ashon Crawley, the late Byron Davis, Farah Jasmine Griffin, my coparent Christopher Murphy Rabb, Nate Thompson, Cheryl Jones Walker, and Simone White, who listened so intently and offered sources and stories that mattered.

My extended Perry family, along with my mother, gave me the tools to know what I should be looking for in order to bring this story to life. They are a group of people who are intellectually sharp, deeply loving, soulful, imaginative, creative, and hard-working. I hope to make them proud.

I have learned that after the deaths of beloveds, grief never leaves, but thankfully that means neither do the departed: I am grateful every day for the presence of my grandmother Neida Garner Perry, my father, Steven S. Whitman, and my aunts Phyllis Perry Paxton and Barbara Harris.

To my children, Issa Garner Rabb and Freeman Diallo Perry Rabb: Your kindness, brilliance, and luminous spirits lift and encourage me every day. You are my greatest gifts and my deepest inspirations. May you both soar and find gentle and enchanting landings. May we, as a family, always remember those who made a way for us and honor their legacy in both word and deed.

Notes

PREFACE

1. *Ebony Jr.* magazine was a children's magazine published from 1973 to 1985 by the Johnson Publishing Company, which also published the popular black magazines *Ebony* and *Jet*.

2. Though in the original verse and composition the song title is written "Lift Ev'ry Voice and Sing," I refer to it in this book as "Lift Every Voice and Sing," primarily because references to the song in literature and news over the past 115 years more often refer to it this way.

3. Shana Redmond, *Anthem: Social Movements and the Sound of Solidarity* (New York: New York University Press, 2013); Timothy Askew, *Cultural Hegemony and African American Patriotism: An Analysis of the Song* (Ronkonkoma, N.Y.: Linus, 2010); Keith Cartwright, *Sacral Grooves, Limbo Gateways: Travels in Deep Southern Time, Circum-Caribbean Space, Afro-Creole Authority* (Athens: University of Georgia Press, 2013); Julian Bond and Sonya Kathryn Wilson, eds., *Lift Every Voice and Sing: A Celebration of the Negro National Anthem, 100 Years, 100 Voices* (New York: Random House, 2000).

CHAPTER ONE

1. James Weldon Johnson, *Along This Way* (Boston: Da Capo, 1933).

2. See generally Michael Craton and Gail Saunders, *A History of the Bahamian People from the Ending of Slavery to the Twenty-First Century* (Athens: University of Georgia Press, 2000).

3. See generally Christopher Linsin, "Black Mobility in Florida in the Decades following the Civil War," *Florida Conference of Historians Annual Proceedings* 2 (September 1994): 58–80; http://fch.fiu.edu/proceedings.html (retrieved July 9, 2015).

4. Rudolph Byrd, ed., *The Essential Writings of James Weldon Johnson* (New York: Random House, 2008), iii.

5. Civil Rights Cases, 109 U.S. 3 (1883).

6. Manning Marable, *Race, Reform, and Rebellion: The Second Reconstruction and Beyond in Black America, 1945–2006*, 3rd ed. (Oxford: University of Mississippi Press, 2007), 7.

7. *Plessy v. Ferguson*, 163 U.S. 537 (1896).

8. Johnson, *Along This Way*, 143.

9. James B. Crooks, "Changing Face of Jacksonville, Florida: 1900–1910," *Florida Historical Quarterly* 62, no. 4 (April 1984): 439.

10. Rayford Whittingham Logan, *The Betrayal of the Negro: From Rutherford B. Hayes to Woodrow Wilson* (Boston: Da Capo, 1965), 52.

11. Ibid., 52, 53.

12. Marable, *Race, Reform, and Rebellion*, 6.

13. Alexis de Tocqueville, *Democracy in America*, book 2, chapter 5 (1835), University of Virginia, "Tocqueville's America" project website, http://xroads.virginia .edu/~hyper/detoc/ch2_05.htm (retrieved December 13, 2015); de Tocqueville, *Democracy in America*, vols. 1 and 2 (New York: Floating, 2008 [1840]), 929. Also see Arthur Schlesinger, "Biography of a Nation of Joiners," *American Historical Review* 1, no. 1 (October 1944): 1–25, for an extended discussion of associational life in the United States.

14. This is a reference to W. E. B. DuBois's classic description of black life in the United States as existing "behind the veil" and out of view with respect to the larger American populace.

15. Nina Mjagkij, *Organizing Black America* (London: Routledge, 2013), vi.

16. Johnson, *Along This Way*, 154.

17. Evelyn Brooks Higginbotham, *Righteous Discontent: The Women's Movement in the Black Baptist Church, 1880–1920* (Cambridge, Mass.: Harvard University Press, 1993),

18. "Mme Katherine's Summer School Closes," *Savannah Tribune*, July 30, 1921, 5.

19. See generally Monica Miller, *Slaves to Fashion: Black Dandyism and the Styling of Black Diasporic Identity* (Durham, N.C.: Duke University Press, 2009); and Tanisha Ford, *Liberated Threads: Black Women, Style, and the Global Politics of Soul* (Chapel Hill: University of North Carolina Press, 2015).

20. Ralph Ellison, *Going to the Territory* (New York: Random House, 1987), 136.

21. Ibid., 136–37.

22. Hortense Spillers, "Formalism Comes to Harlem," in *Black, White, and in Color: Essays on American Literature and Culture* (Chicago: University of Chicago Press, 2003).

23. James D. Anderson, "The Historical Context for Understanding the Test Score Gap," *National Journal of Urban Education and Practice* 1, no. 1 (2007): 1–21.

24. Johnson, *Along This Way*.

25. Ibid., 163.

26. See James B. Crooks, *Jacksonville after the Fire, 1901–1919* (Jacksonville, Fla.: Alibris, 1990).

27. Steve Kramer, "Uplifting Our 'Downtrodden Sisterhood': Victoria Earle

Matthews and New York City's White Rose Mission, 1897–1907," *Journal of African American History* 91, no. 3 (Summer 2006): 243–66.

28. See Logan, *The Betrayal of the Negro*.

29. "Victoria Earle Matthews Writes of Two Rising Sons of Florida: The Success of the Johnson Brothers—A Musician and Litterateur," *Colored American*, May 11, 1901, 10.

30. "They Celebrated Emancipation Day," *Atlanta Journal Constitution*, January 2, 1903, 2.

31. See Eddie S. Glaude Jr., *Exodus! Religion, Race, and Nation in Early Nineteenth-Century Black America* (Chicago: University of Chicago Press, 2000), 91, 92.

32. "Colored Commencement Exercises," *El Paso Herald*, May 6, 1905, 8.

33. Keith Cartwright, *Sacral Grooves, Limbo Gateways: Travels in Deep Southern Time, Circum-Caribbean Space, Afro-Creole Authority* (Athens: University of Georgia Press, 2013), 81.

34. Evelyn Fairbanks, *Days of Rondo* (St. Paul: Minnesota Historical Society Press, 1990), 130–31.

35. Written interview with Jason Moran, March 22, 2015.

36. See a discussion of this history in Glaude, *Exodus!*

37. Gwendolyn Brooks, "The Blackstone Rangers," http://www.poetryfounda tion.org/poem/172095 (retrieved December 13, 2015).

38. This analysis of the music of "Lift Every Voice and Sing" was greatly aided by musician Linda Mason Hood's blog, *truffles, turtles & tunes*. While her rendering is far more technically sophisticated than what I can offer, her knowledge was essential for this work. http://truffles-turtles-tunes.blogspot.com/2007/04/musical-analysis-of-lift-evry-voice-and.html.

39. John Rosamond Johnson, "Why They Call American Music Ragtime," reprinted in *The Black Perspective in Music* 4, no. 2, bicentennial number (July 1976): 263.

40. Lynn Abbot and Doug Seroff, *Ragged but Right: Black Traveling Shows, "Coon Songs," and the Dark Pathway to Blues and Jazz* (Oxford: University Press of Mississippi, 2007); "LaVilla: The Rise and Fall of a Great Black Neighborhood," *MetroJacksonville*, December 12, 2014. Also see Paul Oliver, "The Long-Tailed Blue: Songsters of the Road Shows," in *Songsters and Saints: Vocal Traditions on Race Records* (Cambridge: Cambridge University Press, 1984).

41. "How Actors Figured at the Business League," *Freeman* (Indianapolis) 18, no. 35 (1905): 5; a reference to the conference from the *New York Age* on August 2, 1905, 1, refers to "Lift Every Voice and Sing" as "The Negro Anthem."

42. See generally Kathleen Crocker and Jane Currie, *Chautauqua Institution, 1874–1974* (New York: Arcadia, 2001); and Jeffrey Simpson, *Chautauqua: An American Utopia* (New York: Harry N. Abrams, 1999).

43. Nathan B. Young, "A Negro Chautauqua," *Independent*, August 3, 1893; "For a Negro Chautauqua," *Washington Bee*, August 20, 1910, 1.

44. Betsy Riley, "Ladies of the Club," *Atlanta Magazine*, December 2, 2013, http://www.atlantamagazine.com/great-reads/ladies-of-the-club/ (last retrieved December 13, 2015).

45. Oral History Interview with Grace Towns Hamilton, July 19, 1974, interview G-0026, Southern Oral History Program Collection (no. 4007), University of North Carolina at Chapel Hill Library; Thelma D. Perry, *History of the American Teachers Association* (Washington, D.C.: National Educational Association, 1975), 40.

46. Interview with Cheryl Goffney Franklin, Chautauqua Institution, August 5, 2014.

47. Michael C. Dawson, *Behind the Mule: Race and Class in African American Politics* (Princeton, N.J.: Princeton University Press, 1995). Dawson uses "linked fate" to describe the belief among African Americans that their fate is linked to others of their racial group, and that therefore they ought to cast their lots together in political decision making.

CHAPTER TWO

1. Alain Locke, "Enter the New Negro," *Survey Graphic*, March 1925, 631.

2. Manning Marable, *Race, Reform, and Rebellion: The Second Reconstruction and Beyond in Black America, 1945–2006*, 3rd ed. (Oxford: University of Mississippi Press, 2007), 7.

3. Locke, "Enter the New Negro," 631.

4. Marable, *Race, Reform, and Rebellion*, 6.

5. James D. Anderson, *The Education of Blacks in the South, 1860–1935* (Chapel Hill: University of North Carolina Press, 1989).

6. Chi-Yue Chiu and Ying-Yi Hong, *Social Psychology of Culture* (New York: Psychology, 2013), 305.

7. Colin Grant, *Negro with a Hat: The Rise and Fall of Marcus Garvey* (Oxford: Oxford University Press, 2008), 88.

8. Martin Delany (1812–85), an abolitionist, writer, and doctor, is known as the father of black nationalist thought.

9. Rod Bush, *We Are Not What We Seem: Black Nationalism and Class Struggle in the American Century* (New York: New York University Press, 1999), 96.

10. Patricia Sullivan, *Lift Every Voice: The NAACP and the Making of the Civil Rights Movement* (New York: New Press, 2009).

11. Ibid., 103. W. E. B. DuBois, "The Black Star Line," *Crisis*, September 1922, 210–14.

12. Sullivan, *Lift Every Voice*, 34.

13. Ibid., 58.

14. Ibid., 23, 68.

15. Ibid., 60.

16. W. E. B. DuBois, *Dusk of Dawn: An Essay toward an Autobiography of a Race Concept* (Piscataway, N.J.: Transaction, 1968), 244.

17. Sullivan, *Lift Every Voice*, 60.

18. *Florida Times Union*, December 21, 1897, James Weldon Johnson Collection.

19. Lynn Adelman, "A Study of James Weldon Johnson," *Journal of Negro History* 52, no. 2 (April 1967): 141; Walter Francis White, *A Man Called White: The Autobiography of Walter White* (Athens: University of Georgia Press, 1995 [1948]), 33–34.

20. Sean Dennis Cashman, *America Ascendant: From Theodore Roosevelt to FDR in the Century of American Power, 1901–1945* (New York: New York University Press, 1998), 109.

21. Despite her husband's overseas assignments, Ida Gibbs Hunt continued to be active in the civil rights movement. In 1905, she joined a handful of black women in founding the first Young Women's Christian Association (YWCA) for African Americans, in Washington, D.C. She participated in the Niagara Movement, the Femmes de France, the Bethel Literary Society, the National Association for the Advancement of Colored People (NAACP), the Washington Welfare Association, the Women's International League of Peace and Freedom, and the Red Cross. While traveling abroad with her husband, Hunt published various articles and wrote reviews on literary and cultural themes. She also wrote and gave speeches in support of peace, women's suffrage, and civil rights for African Americans. She was able to promote her ideals internationally, an influence no doubt from her husband and father, who had been diplomats. Hunt was the assistant secretary for the Second Pan-African Congress in Paris in 1919. She delivered a paper titled "The Coloured Races and the League of Nations" at the Third Pan-African Congress in London in 1923 and cochaired the conference's executive committee with W. E. B. DuBois. Hunt died in Washington, D.C., on December 19, 1957.

22. Robert A. Hill, ed., *The Marcus Garvey and Universal Negro Improvement Association Papers*, vol. 11, *The Caribbean Diaspora, 1910–1920* (Durham, N.C.: Duke University Press, 2011); Robert A. Hill, ed., *The Marcus Garvey and Universal Negro Improvement Association Papers*, vol. 12, *The Caribbean Diaspora, November 1927–August 1940* (Durham, N.C.: Duke University Press, 2011), 50.

23. Robert A. Hill, ed., *The Marcus Garvey and Universal Negro Improvement Association Papers*, vol. 12, *November 1927–August 1940* (Berkeley: University of California Press, 1991), 50.

24. Robert A. Hill, ed., *The Marcus Garvey and Universal Negro Improvement Association Papers*, vol. 2, *27 August 1919–August 1920* (Berkeley: University of California Press, 1983), 642.

25. Rhonda Y. Williams, *Concrete Demands: The Search for Black Power in the Twentieth Century* (New York: Routledge, 2014), 17.

26. Robert A. Hill, ed., *The Marcus Garvey and Universal Negro Improvement Association Papers*, vol. 1, *1826–August 1919* (Berkeley: University of California Press, 1983), 220.

27. Elliot M. Rudwick, *Race Riot at East St. Louis, July 2, 1917* (Carbondale: Southern Illinois University Press, 1982), 17.

28. Robert A. Hill, ed., *The Marcus Garvey and Universal Negro Improvement Association Papers*, vol. 1, *1826–August 1919*, 376. Article clipping from the *West Indian* (Grenada), February 28, 1919.

29. James Weldon Johnson, "Self-determining Haiti," August 28, 1920, reprinted in www.thenation.com, https://www.thenation.com/article/self-determining -haiti/, March 18, 2004.

30. Carrie Allen McCray, *Freedom's Child: The Life of a Confederate General's Black Daughter* (New York: Algonquin, 1998), 201.

31. Ernest Lyon, "Dr. Lyon Scores Notion of Negro National Anthem in Open Letter to James Weldon Johnson," *Baltimore Afro-American*, June 19, 1926.

32. James Weldon Johnson, "Music of Negro National Anthem More Beautiful Than 'America' or 'The Star Spangled Banner,'" *Baltimore Afro-American*, June 19, 1926.

33. "Missouri Side Notes by Marian," *Plaindealer* (Kansas City, Kans.), March 4, 1949.

34. "Rabbi Stephen S. Wise Lauds Negro Anthem," *Norfolk Journal and Guide*, May 5, 1928.

35. Benedict Anderson, *Imagined Communities: Reflections on the Origins and Spread of Nationalism* (New York: Verso, 1991), 145.

36. Soyica Diggs Colbert, *The African American Theatrical Body: Reception, Performance and the Stage* (Cambridge: Cambridge University Press, 2011), 63.

37. *Crisis*, November 1924, 30. Also Willis Richardson, ed., *Carter G. Woodson, Plays and Pageants from the Life of a Negro* (Oxford: University Press of Mississippi, 1993 [1930]).

38. "The Pageant Proved to Be Greatest in History of Wichita," *Negro Star* (Wichita, Kans.), March 13, 1925; "'Milestones' Musical and Dramatic Pageant: Five Hundred in Cast in Kansas City, Kansas," *Kansas City Advocate*, May 8, 1925, 1.

39. Richardson, *Carter G. Woodson*, 324.

40. Langston Hughes, "Youth," printed in Alain Locke, "Enter the New Negro," *Survey Graphic*, March 1925, 631; Dolan Hubbard, ed., *The Collected Works of Langston Hughes* (Columbia: University of Missouri Press, 2003), 5.

41. Gwendolyn Bennett, "To Usward," *Crisis*, May 1924, 19.

42. Georgia Douglass Johnson, "Homely Philosophy: The Gift of Song," *Pittsburgh Courier*, October 2, 1926.

43. Michael Harper, ed., *The Collected Poems of Sterling A. Brown* (Evanston, Ill.: Northwestern University Press, 1980), 116.

44. Robert B. Stepto, "I Rose and Found My Voice: Narrative, Authentication,

and Authorial Control in Four Slave Narratives," in *From behind the Veil: A Study of Afro-American Narrative* (Urbana: University of Illinois Press, 1991).

45. Countee Cullen, *One Way to Heaven* (New York: Harper & Brothers, 1932), 150.

46. Mrs. Burton Kingsland, *The Book of Good Manners: Etiquette for All Occasions* (New York: Doubleday, 1904), 64.

47. Mason Stokes, "There Is Heterosexuality: Jessie Fauset, W. E. B. DuBois, and the Problem of Desire," *African American Review* 44, no. 1/2 (Spring/Summer 2011): 67–83.

48. Dubose Heyward, "Mamba's Daughters: The Last Installment," *Baltimore Afro-American*, February 1, 1930.

49. Quoted in Julian Bond and Sondra Kathryn Wilson, eds., *Lift Every Voice and Sing: A Celebration of the Negro National Anthem, 100 Years, 100 Voices* (New York: Random House, 2000), 309.

50. "Fredrick [*sic*] Douglass Celebration," *Plaindealer* (Topeka, Kans.), February 18, 1927.

51. W. C. Handy, *Father of the Blues: An Autobiography* (Boston: Da Capo, 1991), 120.

52. Ibid.

53. Ibid., 122.

54. Ibid., 255.

55. Vivian Schuyler, letter to W. E. B. DuBois, August 2, 1927, W. E. B. DuBois Papers, University of Massachusetts Library, http://credo.library.umass.edu/view/pageturn/mums312-b040-i539/#page/1/mode/1up.

56. Vivian Schuyler, letter to W. E. B. DuBois, November 19, 1927, W. E. B. DuBois Papers, University of Massachusetts Library, http://credo.library.umass.edu/view/pageturn/mums312-b177-i235/#page/1/mode/1up.

57. Crystal A. Britton, *Vivian Schuyler Key: One of Many Voices* (Hempstead, N.Y.: Society for the Preservation of Weeksville and Bedford Stuyvesant History, 1990); Amy Helene Kirschke, ed., *Women Artists of the Harlem Renaissance* (Oxford: University Press of Mississippi, 2014).

58. Dina Hampton, *Little Red: Three Passionate Lives through the Sixties and Beyond* (New York: Public Affairs, 2013), 168.

59. Claude McKay, *Harlem Shadows: The Poems of Claude McKay* (New York: Harcourt Brace, 1922), 53.

60. "Labor Chief Pleads Cause of Porters," *Chicago Defender* (national ed.), August 10, 1929, retrieved from http://search.proquest.com/docview/492211044?accountid=13314.

61. An international outcry followed the indictment of nine black teenagers in Scottsboro, Alabama, for allegedly raping two white women, one of whom later recanted her testimony. Eight of the nine received death sentences. They were defended by the International Labor Defense of the Communist Party, although

they were also courted by the NAACP. Although several appeals were unsuccessful, the U.S. Supreme Court, in *Powell v. Alabama*, 87 U.S. 45 (1932), reversed the convictions and remanded the cases to the state for retrial. The state of Alabama then retried one of the accused, Haywood Patterson, and once again convicted him, but Judge James Horton set aside that verdict. Alabama tried him again and sentenced him to seventy-five years. They also retried Clarence Norris and sentenced him to death, but in 1935 the Supreme Court overturned that conviction in *Norris v. Alabama*, 287 U.S. 45. Multiple trials and reconvictions led to such an enormous public outcry that Alabama released the four youngest defendants after they had served six years in prison.

62. Charles Gaines, "Lift Every Voice and Sing" (a parody of the Negro National Anthem), *Afro-American*, November 12, 1932, 6.

63. Community Church of Boston, event program, January 12, 1936, W. E. B. DuBois Papers (MS 312), Special Collections and University Archives, University of Massachusetts, Amherst, Libraries.

64. Walter L. Daykin, "Nationalism as Expressed in Negro History," *Social Forces* 13, no. 2 (December 1934): 257–63.

65. Ibid.

66. T. G. Standing, "Nationalism in Negro Leadership," *American Journal of Sociology* 40, no. 2 (September 1934): 180–92.

67. Ibid.

68. "Will Dies Committee Probe Propaganda Aimed at Negro," *Plaindealer* (Kansas City, Kans.), March 17, 1939.

69. Quoted in Bond and Wilson, *Lift Every Voice and Sing*, 277.

70. Margaret Walker, *This Is My Century: New and Collected Poems* (Athens: University of Georgia Press, 2013), 6.

71. Houston A. Baker, "Modernism and the Harlem Renaissance," in "Modernist Culture in America," special issue, *American Quarterly* 39, no. 1 (Spring 1987): 95.

72. From Richard Powell, "African American Art," in *Africana: The Encyclopedia of the African and African American Experience*, 2nd ed., ed. Henry Louis Gates Jr. and Kwame Anthony Appiah (Oxford: Oxford University Press, 2005).

73. Lisa E. Farrington, *Creating Their Own Image: The History of African American Women Artists* (Oxford: Oxford University Press, 2004), 105.

74. Ibid.

75. Augusta Savage to Grace Nail Johnson, March 21, 1939, James Weldon Johnson Papers.

76. "Protest Name Given Famous Sculpture by New York World's Fair Officials," *Negro Star*, March 31, 1939, 3.

77. Rick Benjamin, liner notes, *From Barrelhouse to Broadway: The Musical Odyssey of Joe Jordan* (New World Records, 2006).

1. Joe R. Feagin, Hernan Vera, and Nikitah Imani, *The Agony of Education: Black Students at a White University* (London: Routledge, 2014), 10.

2. *Proceedings and Debates of the . . . Congress*, 121, part 19, *Congressional Record* (Washington, D.C.: U.S. Government Printing Office, 1975), 218.

3. Betty Jameson Reed, School Segregation in Western North Carolina: A History, 1860s–1970 (Jefferson, N.C.: McFarland, 2011), 24.

4. See generally James D. Anderson, *The Education of Blacks in the South, 1860–1935* (Chapel Hill: University of North Carolina Press, 1989); and Heather Andrea Williams, *Self-Taught: African American Education in Slavery and Freedom* (Chapel Hill: University of North Carolina Press, 2005).

5. Thelma D. Perry, *History of the American Teachers Association* (Washington, D.C.: National Educational Association, 1975), 45.

6. Rudolph Byrd, ed., *The Essential Writings of James Weldon Johnson* (New York: Random House, 2008), xv.

7. G. W. Trenholm, "Status of Negro Education in Alabama," in Perry, *History of the American Teachers Association*, 57.

8. Perry, *History of the American Teachers Association*, 35.

9. Anderson, *The Education of Blacks in the South*; Williams, *Self-Taught*, 95.

10. Ellen Weiss, *Robert R. Taylor and Tuskegee: An Architect Designs for Booker T. Washington* (Montgomery, Ala.: New South, 2012), 122; Clement Richardson, *The National Cyclopedia of the Colored Race*, vol. 1 (Montgomery, Ala.: National, 1919); Macon County, *Alabama Archives and Current History: A Monthly Magazine of the New York Times*, April–September 1922, 232.

11. See Anderson, *The Education of Blacks in the South*.

12. W. E. B. DuBois, *The Common School and the Negro American*, Report of a Social Study Made by Atlanta University under the Patronage of the Trustees of the John F. Slater Fund, with the Proceedings of the Sixteenth Annual Conference for the Study of the Negro Problems, Held at Atlanta University, on Tuesday, May 30, 1911, nos. 15–20 (Atlanta: Atlanta University Press, 1911), nos. 15–20 (Atlanta: Atlanta University Press, 1911), 8.

13. Perry, *History of the American Teachers Association*, 33.

14. Weiss, *Robert R. Taylor and Tuskegee*, 127; Samuel L. Smith, *Builders of Goodwill: The Story of State Agents of Negro Education in the South, 1910–1950* (Nashville: Tennessee Book, 1950), 12.

15. William James Edwards, *Twenty-Five Years in the Black Belt* (Boston: Cornhill, 1918), 54–55.

16. Lance G. E. Jones, *The Jeanes Teacher in the United States, 1908–1933: An Account of Twenty-Five Years' Experience in the Supervision of Negro Rural Schools* (Chapel Hill: University of North Carolina Press, 2011), 22.

17. Ibid., 77.

18. Bonnie J. Krause, "'We Did Move Mountains!' Lucy Saunders Herring, North Carolina Jeanes Supervisor and African American Educator, 1916–1968," *North Carolina Historical Review* 80, no. 2 (April 2003): 188–212.

19. Alice Brown Smith, *Forgotten Foundations: The Role of Jeanes Teachers in Black Education* (New York: Vantage, 1997), 15.

20. Mildred M. Williams and Kara Vaughn Jackson, *The Jeanes Story: A Chapter in the History of American Education, 1908–1958* (Jackson, Miss.: Jackson State University, 1979).

21. Smith, *Forgotten Foundations*, 34–35.

22. "History of Negro Race Compiled by Teachers; Club Studies, Museum Art, and Mural Decorations at Congressional Library," *Washington Post*, May 25, 1924, R3.

23. "Reminiscences of Yesteryear: Roy Hill and Fannie Douglass," *Black Perspective in Music* 2, no. 1 (Spring 1974): 61.

24. Alison Stewart, *First Class: The Legacy of Dunbar, America's First Black Public High School* (Chicago: Chicago Review Press, 2013).

25. *Berea College v. Kentucky*, 211 U.S. 45 (1908).

26. George C. Wright, *A History of Blacks in Kentucky*, vol. 2, *In Pursuit of Equality, 1890–1980* (Frankfort: Kentucky Historical Society, 1992), 137.

27. Stewart, *First Class*, 88.

28. Betty J. Reed, *The Brevard Rosenwald School: Black Education and Community Building in a Southern Appalachian Town, 1920–1966* (Jefferson, N.C.: McFarland, 2004), 90.

29. See Ann Short Chirhart, *Torches of Light: Georgia Teachers and the Coming of the Modern South* (Athens: University of Georgia Press, 2005).

30. Beulah Rucker, *A Rugged Pathway*, quoted in Winfred E. Pitts, *A Victory of Sorts: Desegregation in a Southern Community* (Lanham, Md.: University Press of America, 2003), 18.

31. Albert Murray, *South to a Very Old Place* (New York: Vintage, 1971).

32. Anderson, *The Education of Blacks in the South*, 118.

33. Albert Murray, *Stomping the Blues* (Boston: Da Capo, 1976), 241.

34. Donald L. Maggin, *Dizzy: The Life and Times of John Birks Gillespie* (New York: Harper Collins, 2006), 8.

35. Dizzy Gillespie, *To Be or Not to Bop* (Minneapolis: University of Minnesota Press, 2009), 8.

36. Maggin, *Dizzy*, 9.

37. Mildred J. Hudson, "Finding My Life's Work," in *Multicultural Education: A Reflective Engagement with Race, Class, Gender, and Sexual Orientation*, ed. Carl A. Grant (New York: Routledge, 1999), 120.

38. Quoted in Julian Bond and Sonya Kathryn Wilson, eds., *Lift Every Voice and Sing: A Celebration of the Negro National Anthem, 100 Years, 100 Voices* (New York: Random House, 2000), 158–59.

39. Ibid., 44–45.

40. *Evening Star* (Washington, D.C.), June 16, 1925.

41. Vanessa Siddle Walker, Ninth Annual Brown Lecture in Education Research, "Black Educators as Educational Advocates in the Decades before *Brown v. Board of Education*," *Educational Researcher* 42, no. 4 (May 2013): 20–22.

42. Christine A. Woyshner, *The National PTA, Race, and Civic Engagement, 1897–1970* (Columbus: Ohio State University Press, 2009).

43. *Proceedings of the Kentucky Negro Educational Association*, Louisville, April 21–24, 1926, Kentucky Digital Library, http://kdl.kyvl.org/catalog/xt71891int2s_1.

44. *Kentucky Negro Educational Association Journal* 6, no. 2 (1935): 22.

45. Quoted in Bond and Wilson, *Lift Every Voice and Sing*, 48.

46. Quoted in ibid., 136.

47. *Cleveland Plain Dealer*, February 10, 1986.

48. *Cleveland Plain Dealer*, February 26, 1985.

49. Quoted in Bond and Wilson, *Lift Every Voice and Sing*, 50.

50. Quoted in ibid., 172.

51. "Falls Church Gleanings," *Washington Bee*, August 27, 1921.

52. W. E. B. DuBois, *Dusk of Dawn: An Essay toward an Autobiography of a Race Concept* (Oxford: Oxford University Press, 1940), 102.

53. Jacqueline Goggin, *Carter G. Woodson: A Life in Black History* (Baton Rouge: Louisiana State University Press, 1997), 85.

54. Ibid., 85.

55. Pero Dagbovie, *The Early Black History Movement, Carter G. Woodson, and Lorenzo Johnston Greene* (Urbana: University of Illinois Press, 2007), 55.

56. Houston A. Baker Jr., "Meditation on Tuskegee: Black Studies Stories and Their Imbrication," *Journal of Blacks in Higher Education* 9 (Autumn 1995): 53.

57. "Negro History Week," *Augusta Chronicle*, February 11, 1929.

58. Howard Thurman, *With Head and Heart: The Autobiography of Howard Thurman* (New York: Harcourt Brace, 1979), 23.

59. Charles W. Wadelington and Richard F. Knapp, *Charlotte Hawkins Brown and Palmer Memorial Institute: What One Young African American Woman Could Do* (Chapel Hill: University of North Carolina Press, 1999), 30.

60. Craig Kridel, "Progressive Education in the Black High School: The General Education Board's Black High School Study, 1940–1948" (2013), http://www.rockarch.org/publications/resrep/kridel2.pdf (retrieved December 20, 2015).

61. Quoted in Bond and Wilson, *Lift Every Voice and Sing*, 119.

62. "Negro History Week," *National Notes* 32, no. 6 (March 1, 1930): 11.

63. "Book of the Month," *Negro History Bulletin* 2, no. 1 (October 1, 1938): 8.

64. Ruth White Willis, "Let Our Rejoicings Rise: A Pantomime with Music and Reading," *Negro History Bulletin* 4, no. 8 (May 1, 1941): 187.

65. Quoted in Bond and Wilson, *Lift Every Voice and Sing*, 193.

66. Muriel Wellington, "The Negro Anthem," *Negro History Bulletin* 12, no. 2 (November 1, 1948): 40.

67. Quoted in Bond and Wilson, *Lift Every Voice and Sing*, 147.

68. Quoted in ibid., 102.

69. Quoted in ibid., 105–6.

70. Quoted in ibid., 295.

71. "Ten Years of Bookmobile Service, 1942–1952, Stanford L. Warren Public Library," North Carolina Digital Collections, State Archives of North Carolina, http://digital.ncdcr.gov/cdm/ref/collection/p249901coll36/id/1102 (retrieved December 16, 2015).

72. Gertrude Parthenia McBrown, "History Play," *Negro History Bulletin* 21, no. 5 (February 1, 1958), 113.

73. W. E. B. DuBois, "Does the Negro Need Separate Schools?," in "The Courts and the Negro Separate School," special issue, *Journal of Negro Education* 4, no. 3 (July 1935): 329.

74. "John W. Davis Contends That 'Separate but Equal' Is a Matter for the Legislature Not the Courts to Decide," in *In Our Own Words: Extraordinary Speeches of the American Century*, ed. Senator Robert Toricelli et al. (New York: Washington Square, 1999), 197.

75. Quoted in Carla Kaplan, *Zora Neale Hurston: A Life in Letters* (New York: Doubleday, 2007), 611.

76. Kansas Historical Society, "*Brown v. Board of Education*–Oral History Part 1," https://www.kshs.org/p/brown-v-topeka-board-of-education-oral -history-collection-at-the-kansas-state-historical-society-fin/14000 (retrieved December 15, 2015).

77. Ibid.

78. Scott Baker, "Pedagogies of Protest: African American Teachers and the History of the Civil Rights Movement, 1940–1963," *Teachers College Record* 113, no. 12 (2011): 2778.

79. Greg Toppo, "*Brown v. Board of Education*: Thousands of Black Teachers Lost Jobs," *USA Today*, April 28, 2004 (cites National Education Association, "Horizons of Opportunity: Celebrating 50 Years of *Brown v. Board of Education*, May 17, 1954–2004"). Carol Karpinski, "Faculty Diversity: *Brown* and the Demise of the Black Principal," New York City Department of Education.

80. Lee Ann Caldwell, "Pure in Heart, Brave in Spirit: The Life of Silas X. Floyd," *Augusta Magazine*, February–March 2015, http://www.augustamagazine .com/Augusta-Magazine/February-March-2015/Pure-in-Heart-Brave-in-Spirit- The-Life-of-Silas-X-Floyd/ (retrieved December 20, 2015).

81. Maya Angelou, *I Know Why the Caged Bird Sings*, in *The Collected Autobiographies of Maya Angelou* (New York: Random House, 2012), 132.

82. Ibid., 139.

83. Ibid., 143.

1. Barbara Diane Savage, *Broadcasting Freedom: Radio, War, and the Politics of Race, 1938–1948* (Chapel Hill: University of North Carolina Press, 1999), 64.

2. Ibid., 65.

3. *Evening Star* (Washington, D.C.), March 6, 1940.

4. Savage, *Broadcasting Freedom*, 64.

5. Ibid., 75.

6. "Negro Press Challenges the Nation," *Plaindealer* (Kansas City, Kans.), March 3, 1944.

7. Cited in Charles A. Simmons, *The African American Press: A History of News Coverage during National Crises, with a Special Reference to Four Black Newspapers* (Jefferson, N.C.: McFarland, 2006), 80; and Pat Washburn, "The *Pittsburgh Courier's* Double V Campaign in 1942," paper presented at the Annual Meeting of the Association for Education in Journalism, East Lansing, Mich., August 1981, ed. gov. collection, ED 205 956.

8. "Mass Meeting Monday," *Plaindealer* (Kansas City, Kans.), March 28, 1941.

9. Manning Marable, *Race, Reform, and Rebellion: The Second Reconstruction and Beyond in Black America, 1945–2006*, 3rd ed. (Oxford: University of Mississippi Press, 2007), 12; Alexander Bielakowski, *African American Troops in World War II* (Oxford, UK: Osprey, 2012), 4.

10. Marable, *Race, Reform, and Rebellion*, 13; Brian Greenberg et al., *Social History of the United States* (Santa Barbara, Calif.: ABL-CLIO, 2008), 40.

11. "Lift Every Voice and Sing Said the Poet: Poems from Our Men in the Armed Forces," *Peachite* (Fort Valley, Ga.), December 1, 1944.

12. "Recorded Music," *Dallas Morning News*, January 3, 1943.

13. "Music: Song of Faith," *Time*, September 14, 1942.

14. Peter Dana, "Johnson's Stirring Number Defended," *Atlanta Daily World*, May 11, 1942.

15. "Religion: In Throop Street," *Time*, March 5, 1945.

16. Herbert L. Shore, "The Resurrection and the Life," *Phylon* 22, no. 4 (1961): 386.

17. Diane McWhorter, *Carry Me Home: Birmingham, Alabama, the Cinematic Battle of the Civil Rights Revolution* (New York: Simon and Schuster, 2002), 62.

18. James H. Meriwether, *Proudly We Can Be Africans: Black Americans and Africa, 1935–1961* (Chapel Hill: University of North Carolina Press, 2002), 82.

19. Nell Irvin Painter, *Exodusters: Black Migration to Kansas after Reconstruction* (New York: W. W. Norton, 1992), 247.

20. Harry Reed, "Me and Jackie Robinson: Awakenings as a Historian," *Fourth Genre: Explorations in Nonfiction* 2, no. 2 (Fall 2000): 87.

21. Hearings Regarding Communist Infiltration of Minority Groups, Part 1, Hearings before the Committee on Un-American Activities, House of Repre-

sentatives, 81st Cong., 1st sess., 1949, 479–83 (Joyner Docs CWIS: Y 4: Un 1/2: C 73/11/pt.1).

22. Senator Robert Toricelli et al., eds., *In Our Own Words: Extraordinary Speeches of the American Century* (New York: Washington Square, 1999), 170.

23. Maurine Hoffman Beasley et al., eds., *The Eleanor Roosevelt Encyclopedia* (Westport, Conn.: Greenwood, 2001), 510.

24. Philip S. Foner, "Letter to the Editor," *New York Times*, May 2, 1987.

25. Ibid.

26. Martha Biondi, *The Black Revolution on Campus* (Berkeley: University of California Press, 2012).

27. Penny Von Eschen, *Race against Empire: Black Americans and Anticolonialism, 1937–1957* (Ithaca, N.Y.: Cornell University Press, 1997).

28. Ibid., 57.

29. Quoted in John Oliver Killens, "Charles White, the People's Artist," *Georgia Review* 40, no. 2 (Summer 1986): 453.

CHAPTER FIVE

1. Wanda Lloyd, "Boycott 'Voices' Document History Once Again," *Montgomery Advertiser*, November 27, 2005, 13.

2. *Arkansas State Press* (Little Rock), January 4, 1957.

3. George G. McCray, "Slang in Ghana Eclipses Harlem's 'In New Africa' Column," *Chicago Defender*, April 5, 1958.

4. Homer A. Jack, "Americans at Confab: Attend Event as Observers," *Chicago Defender*, January 10, 1959.

5. "Ex-Chicagoan Praised for TV Show in Ohio," *Daily Defender*, July 3, 1957.

6. Ted Ston, "Heard and Seen," *Chicago Defender*, March 5, 1958.

7. *Sponsor*, March 1948, 93.

8. "Robeson's Singing Wins a Great Ovation out West," *Chicago Defender*, February 27, 1958.

9. Wilson Fallin Jr., *The African American Church in Birmingham, 1815–1963: A Shelter in the Storm* (New York: Routledge, 1997), 84.

10. *Chicago Defender*, March 7, 1959.

11. "Little Rock Central High Student to Speak at First Baptist," *Plaindealer* (Kansas City, Kans.), February 28, 1958.

12. Civil Rights Movement Veterans, "1960," http://www.crmvet.org/tim/timhis 60.htm (retrieved July 9, 2015).

13. Highlander Folk School is a social justice training school founded in 1932 by Myles Horton. In the labor and civil rights movement, Highlander was a critically important training site for organizers.

14. David King Dunaway and Molly Beer, *Singing Out: An Oral History of America's Folk Music Revivals* (Oxford: Oxford University Press, 2010), 141–42.

15. Bernice Johnson Reagon, "A Freedom Singer Shares the Music of the Movement," interview by Neal Conan, *Talk of the Nation*, WBUR and National Public Radio, August 1, 2012.

16. Faith Holsaert, ed., *Hands on the Freedom Plow: Personal Accounts by Women in SNCC* (Urbana: University of Illinois Press, 2010), 182.

17. Interview with Bernice Johnson Reagon by Blackside Inc. for *Eyes on the Prize: America's Civil Rights Years*, Washington University Film and Media Archive, Henry Hampton Collection, camera rolls 589–92, sound rolls 1539–40, http://digital.wustl.edu/cgi/t/text/text-idx?c=eop;cc=eop;rgn=main;view=text;idno=rea0015.0155.086.

18. Pete Seeger, *Everybody Says Freedom: A History of the Civil Rights Movement in Songs and Pictures* (New York: Norton, 2009), 76–77.

19. Interview with Bernice Johnson Reagon conducted by Blackside Inc. for *Eyes on the Prize*.

20. Deborah E. McDowell, *Leaving Pipeshop: Memories of Kin* (New York: W. W. Norton, 1996), 131.

21. Ibid., 132.

22. Ibid., 137.

23. Dave Potter, "'We Shall Overcome' New Negro Anthem," *Daily Defender*, September 17, 1963.

24. University of Georgia, *Freedom on Film: Civil Rights in Georgia*, cities: Rome, 1963, Student Sit-Ins, civilrights.urga.edu/cities/rome/sit-ins.htm.

25. Bessie Hughes, "The People Speak: Deeply Disturbed," *Chicago Defender*, August 8, 1963, 12.

26. Howell Raines, *My Soul Is Rested: The Story of the Civil Rights Movement in the Deep South* (New York: Penguin, 1977), 153.

27. Martin Luther King Jr., "Letter from a Selma Jail," *New York Times*, February 5, 1965.

28. Shana Alexander, "Three Strangers in Selma," *Life*, March 26, 1965, 28.

29. "History Mural for NAACP near Finish," *Atlanta Daily World*, July 4, 1969; "College Plans Art Convo Thursday," *Anderson (Ind.) Herald*, March 5, 1969.

30. Joseph Tirella, *Tomorrow-land: The 1964–65 World's Fair and the Transformation of America* (New York: Rowman and Littlefield, 2013), 160, 197.

31. Ibid.

CHAPTER SIX

1. Herb Aptheker, *A Documentary History of the Negro People in the United States*, vol. 7, *From the Alabama Protests to the Death of Martin Luther King Jr.* (Secaucus, N.J.: Carol, 2010), 431.

2. Sgt. Gerald Westbrook, "The Essence of Soul," *Negro Digest*, May 1964, 12.

3. Ibid., 13.

4. Donald M. Henderson, "Negro Militancy Is Not New: A History of Protest in America," *Negro Digest*, February 1965, 36–42.

5. Quoted in Julian Bond and Sonya Kathryn Wilson, eds., *Lift Every Voice and Sing: A Celebration of the Negro National Anthem, 100 Years, 100 Voices* (New York: Random House, 2000), 199.

6. Martin Luther King Jr., "Where Do We Go from Here?," speech delivered at the Eleventh Annual SCLC Convention, Atlanta, August 16, 1967, http://kingency clopedia.stanford.edu/encyclopedia/documentsentry/where_do_we_go_from_ here_delivered_at_the_11th_annual_sclc_convention/ (retrieved December 20, 2015).

7. Emily Yellin, "The Sanitation Strike, the Assassination and Memphis in 1968," *American Radioworks*, http://americanradioworks.publicradio.org/features/ king/yellin.html (retrieved December 20, 2015).

8. Martin Luther King Jr., excerpted from *The Radical King*, ed. Cornel West (Boston: Beacon, 2015), http://www.truth-out.org/progressivepicks/item/28568-martin-luther-king-jr-all-labor-has-dignity (retrieved December 20, 2015); Martin Luther King Jr., Mason Temple, Memphis, Tennessee, March 18, 1968.

9. Martin Luther King Jr., "I've Been to the Mountaintop," April 3, 1968, http:// kingencyclopedia.stanford.edu/encyclopedia/encyclopedia/enc_ive_been_to_ the_mountaintop_3_april_1968.1.html (retrieved December 20, 2015).

10. Donald Johnson, "Afro-American Flag Raised," *Boston Globe*, April 9, 1968, 13.

11. Adam Fairclough, *A Class of Their Own: Black Teachers in the Segregated South* (Cambridge, Mass.: Harvard University Press, 2007), 389.

12. Educational Broadcasting Corporation, *Assignment America*, air date February 25, 1975.

13. Quoted in Bond and Wilson, *Lift Every Voice and Sing*.

14. Lynn Abbot and Doug Seroff, "Time, Harmony, and Articulation: Quartet Training and the Birmingham Gospel Quartet Style," in *To Do This You Must Know How: Music Pedagogy in the Black Gospel Quartet* (Oxford: University Press of Mississippi, 2013), 141.

15. Quoted in Bond and Wilson, *Lift Every Voice and Sing*, 311.

16. Howell Raines, *My Soul Is Rested: The Story of the Civil Rights Movement in the Deep South* (New York: Penguin, 1977), 107.

17. Quoted in Bond and Wilson, *Lift Every Voice and Sing*, 27–28.

18. Leroi Jones, "Home on the Range," in "Black Theatre," special issue, *Drama Review* 12, no. 4 (Summer 1968): 110.

19. Quoted in Bond and Wilson, *Lift Every Voice and Sing*, 110.

20. Although the official change to Black History Month wouldn't be declared until 1976, some organizations were already designating February Black History Month in the early 1970s.

21. James Thomas Jackson, *Waiting in Line at the Drugstore and Other Writings of James Thomas Jackson* (Denton: University of North Texas Press, 1993), 247–48.

22. Andrea Juliette Lightbourne, "Shining through the Clouds: An Historical Case Study of a Segregated School in Tucson, Arizona" (PhD diss., University of Arizona, 2004), 236, UMI no. 3158122.

23. Adelaide Cromwell, *The Other Brahmins: Boston's Black Upper Class, 1750–1950* (Fayetteville: University of Arkansas Press, 1994).

24. Adelaide Cromwell Hill, "Black Education in the Seventies: A Lesson from the Past," in *The Black Seventies*, ed. Floyd B. Barbour (Boston: Porter Sargent, 1970), 64.

25. Oral History Interview with Joanne Peerman, February 24, 2001, interview K-0557, Southern Oral History Program Collection (no. 4007), Southern Oral History Program Collection, Southern Historical Collection, Wilson Library, University of North Carolina at Chapel Hill.

26. Kenneth L. Fish, "More 'Soul' Needed in White Teachers," *Clearing House* 46, no. 8 (April 1972): 502.

27. Mary Eleanor Rhodes Hoover, "The Nairobi Day School: An African American Independent School, 1966–1984," *Journal of Negro Education* 61, no. 2 (Spring 1992): 203.

28. Ibid.

29. Ibid., 206.

30. Ibid., 205.

31. Orde Coombs, "The Necessity of Excellence: I. Nairobi College," *Change* 5, no. 3 (April 1973): 42.

32. John Egerton, "Success Comes to Nairobi College," *Change* 4 (May 1972): 25–27.

33. Coombs, "The Necessity of Excellence: I. Nairobi College," 44.

34. Ibid.

35. Martha Biondi, *The Black Revolution on Campus* (Berkeley: University of California Press, 2012), 222.

36. Hansonia Caldwell and Hale Smith, "A Man of Many Parts," *Black Perspective in Music* 3, no. 1 (Spring 1975): 74.

37. Angelika Beener, "Five Jazz Songs That Speak of the Freedom Struggle," National Public Radio, June 19, 2012, http://www.npr.org/sections/ablogsupreme/2012/06/18/155318747/five-jazz-songs-which-speak-of-the-freedom-struggle (retrieved December 16, 2015).

38. Willard Jenkins, "Roy Haynes: Force of Nature," *Jazz Times*, November 1997, http://jazztimes.com/articles/24743-roy-haynes-force-of-nature (retrieved December 16, 2015).

39. Vivian Williams, *New York Amsterdam News*, April 26, 1969.

40. Roger Ebert, "*Brewster McCloud* Review," *RogerEbert.com*, December 24,

1970, http://www.rogerebert.com/reviews/brewster-mccloud-1970 (retrieved December 16, 2015).

41. "Lena Horne to Present Black Artists in Tribute to Late Dr. Bethune," *Pittsburgh Courier*, January 8, 1972.

42. Stella G. White, "Negro Anthem Worth Hearing," *Cleveland Plain Dealer*, May 23, 1970.

43. Quoted in Bond and Wilson, *Lift Every Voice and Sing*, 252.

44. John Hope Franklin, Gerald Horne, Harold W. Cruse, Allen B. Ballard, and Reavis L. Mitchell Jr., "Black History Month: Serious Truth Telling or a Triumph in Tokenism?," *Journal of Blacks in Higher Education* 18 (Winter 1997–98): 91.

45. Shana Redmond, *Anthem: Social Movements and the Sound of Solidarity* (New York: New York University Press, 2013), 192.

46. Robert Hayden and Michael Harper, "Robert Hayden and Michael Harper: A Literary Friendship," *Callaloo* 17, no. 4 (Autumn 1994): 980–1016.

47. Paule Marshall, *Triangular Road: A Memoir* (New York: Basic Books, 2010), 157.

CHAPTER SEVEN

1. Cuda Brown, "Meanderings 1.06," June 11, 1994, http://www.newsavanna.com/meanderings/me106/me10602.html (retrieved December 20, 2015).

2. Stella G. White, "New Level of Black Unity," *Cleveland Plain Dealer*, June 28, 1971.

3. *Chicago Metro News*, May 7, 1986, 17.

4. David Schultz, "David's Notes," *Chicago Metro News*, February 1, 1986.

5. Ibid.

6. Ferman Mentrell Beckless, "Bulls Welcome Singing of Negro Anthem," *Chicago Metro News*, February 1, 1986.

7. Sam Attlesley, "Black Voters: Army without General," *Dallas Morning News*, October 29, 1979.

8. Kenneth R. Walker, "Pessimism Running Deep as Urban League Meets: Recuperating Jordan Addresses Members," *Evening Star/Washington (D.C.) Star*, August 4, 1980.

9. Ibid.

10. Nathaniel Clay, Clay Images, "How Blacks Can Get out of Poverty," *Chicago Metro News*, September 7, 1985.

11. Beckless, "Bulls Welcome Singing of Negro Anthem."

12. Quoted in Julian Bond and Sonya Kathryn Wilson, eds., *Lift Every Voice and Sing: A Celebration of the Negro National Anthem, 100 Years, 100 Voices* (New York: Random House, 2000).

13. David Remnick, *The Bridge: The Life and Rise of Barack Obama* (New York: Knopf, 2010).

1. Lara Pellegrinelli, "Poetic License Raises a Star-Spangled Debate," *All Things Considered*, National Public Radio, July 3, 2009.

2. Paul Beatty, *Slumberland* (London: Bloomsbury, 2008), 226.

3. Julie Daunt, "Clifford Owens: Pushing the Boundaries of Performance," *Culture Trip*, https://theculturetrip.com/north-america/usa/new-york/articles/clifford-owens-pushing-the-boundaries-of-performance/ (retrieved April 15, 2017).

Index

122; and SNYC activism, 124; and employment and income gaps between blacks and whites, 144, 206, 214; Martin Luther King Jr. on, 169; economic crisis of 2008 and 2009, 219; protests against, 225

Edwards, Mildred Johnson, 99–100, 106

Edwards, William J., 77

Edwin McMasters Stanton School, Jacksonville, Florida, 3

Egypt, 39, 40, 97

Einstein, Albert, 68

Elisabeth Irwin School, New York, 54

Ellington, Duke, 177, 187–88

Ellison, Ralph, 9–11

Emancipation, process of, 41

Emancipation Day, 15–16, 36, 37, 89, 111, 141, 205

Emancipation Proclamation, 15, 153, 188

Employment: blacks as exploited workers, 2, 27, 161, 169; agricultural labor during Jim Crow, 8; of black women, 68; and NAACP, 122; and gaps between blacks and whites, 206, 214

Enloe Drug Store, 154

Equal Employment Opportunity Commission, 207

Essence, 192

Ethiopia, 39, 40, 60, 97

"Ethiopia, Land of Our Fathers," 32, 33, 34

Ethnic studies programs, 194

Europe, James, 79

Europe, Mary, 79

European cultural forms, 10, 11, 12, 16

European immigrants, access to high school, 73

Evans, Mari, 198

Evanti, Lillian, 115

Evers, Medgar, 166

Evers, Merlie, 203

Fairbanks, Evelyn, 17

Fair Employment Practices Committee (FEPC), 116, 125, 127

Farnham, R. L., 35

Farrakhan, Louis, 216

Fascism: opposition to, 61; Jim Crow compared to, 111, 116; and American racial liberalism, 112; analogies between antifascism and antiracism, 114, 115, 128, 129–30, 136; and World War II, 116, 121, 122, 130, 138–39

Fast, Howard, *Freedom Road*, 125

Fauset, Jessie, 39, 45; *There Is Confusion*, 43

Federal Bureau of Investigation (FBI), 126, 129, 194

Federal Home Loan Bank Board (FHLBB), 59

Federal Housing Administration (FHA), 59

Federal Office of Education, 112

Federal Writers Project, 66

Fellowship of Reconciliation, 116, 162

Feminists, 194, 209

Femmes de France, 233n21

Ferguson, Alice L., 9

Ferguson, Mo., 223–24

Ferguson, Pauline V., 9

FESTAC 77, 200, 222

Fieldston School, New York, 100

"Fight the Power," 212

Fish, Kenneth, "More 'Soul' Needed in White Teachers," 181

Fisk Jubilee Singers, 113

Fisk University, 75, 80, 99, 208

Flack, Roberta, 211

Florida, 2, 3, 4, 74. *See also* Jacksonville, Fla.

Florida Baptist Academy, 4, 38

56, 72–73, 84, 90, 93, 95, 96, 98, 100, 109, 194, 200, 218, 223; and Booker T. Washington's funeral, 28; "Ethiopia, Land of Our Fathers" compared to, 33, 34; Marcus Garvey's use of, 33, 34; James Weldon Johnson's account of writing of, 38; communities choosing as anthem, 38–39; and Pan-African Congress of 1927, 39; and pageantry, 40, 41, 42; and New Negro Era, 42–45; and philosophical argument about black humanity and existence, 44; movement represented in, 45; in secular world, 47–48, 50–51; recordings of, 50, 118, 204, 211, 213, 221–22; as inspiration for visual arts, 51–52; and leftists, 54; poetry paired with, 56; George Gaines's parodic version of, 56–58; symphonic performances of, 60; Walter Daykin on, 62–63; as spiritual bulwark, 66; and black artistic production, 66, 137, 161–62; and ASCAP anniversary celebration of 1939, 71; institutional significance of, 73; and Dunbar High School, Washington, D.C., 78–79; guided group singing as method of socializing children, 84; endurance, striving, and ascent in, 84, 99; prevalence in South compared to North, 88–89; and out-of-school learning communities, 90–91, 101–2; and Negro History Week, 95, 96–98, 105; universal aspirations present in, 97; Mildred Johnson Edwards on, 99–100; and celebration of black achievement, 101, 215, 216, 217, 219, 223; Martin Luther King Jr.'s references to, 111, 112, 169–70; and *Americans All* series, 113;

and representation politics of mass culture, 113; and politics of representation, 113, 114; Americana blended with, 114, 117, 125, 127, 135, 218; and World War II, 118–19; and SNYC conventions, 125; imagery of light and dark in, 134–35; and Montgomery Bus Boycott, 140, 141–42; and civil rights movement, 142, 143, 146, 148, 149, 150–51, 153, 154, 155, 158, 159–60, 168, 174; and Pan-Africanism, 142–43; and black associational life, 145; Gerald Westbrook on, 166; and Martin Luther King Jr.'s assassination, 173; and Black History Month, 177, 211, 215, 222, 224–25; Hale Smith's arrangement of, 186; interpretations of, 186, 187–92, 214, 221–22; Roland Carter's arrangement of, 186–87; children's book versions of, 194; and Kwanzaa, 196; Barbara Jordan's narration of, 204; and Ronald Reagan, 209–10; and advertising campaigns, 211; and black writers, 220; and Ferguson, Missouri, 224; title of, 229n2

Lincoln, Abbey, 188

Lincoln, Abraham, 3, 6, 15, 18, 41, 47, 114, 147

Lincoln Douglass Birthday Banquet, 152–53

Lincoln Institute, Shelby County, Ky., 79–80, 100

Lincoln University, 80, 102, 103

Linked fate concept, 65

Listen Chicago, 144

Literacy: and black formalism, 12; and New Negro, 27; freedom tied to, 45, 138; and rhyming poems, 183

Little Red School House, N.Y., 54, 173

Liuzzo, Viola, 160

60; and black elites, 64–65, 179, 211; and class cleavages in black life, 64–65, 211; and black leadership class, 78; and racial liberalism, 120. *See also* Middle-class blacks; Working-class blacks; Working-class whites

Social democrats, 120

Socialists: and working-class blacks, 52, 54; and Popular Front, 54–55; from West Indies, 55; W. E. B. DuBois identifying as, 60; racial liberalism contrasted with, 120; and Pan-African Congress of 1945, 123; and Henry Wallace, 126; NAACP's disengagement from, 127; and black radicals, 128; and Black Panther Party, 185

Social justice movement, 86, 116

Social Security Act, 59

Solimon, Angelo, 97

Somalia, 136

Sontonga, Enoch, 208

Soul: W. E. B. DuBois on, 44, 189; Gerald Westbrook on, 166–67; Kenneth Fish on, 181

South: public school system introduced in, 2; Radical Republicans in, 2; black associational life in, 8; James Weldon Johnson's NAACP organizing tour of, 31; Communist Party in, 60; Rosenwald school program in, 75; and Anna Jeanes's donations for teachers in black schools, 77; and "Lift Every Voice and Sing" prevalent in school programs, 88; and *Brown v. Board of Education*, 104; school desegregation in, 104–5; oratorical tradition in, 110; legal racial stratification in, 144; cultural resources of, 175

South Africa: racial segregation in, 39, 207, 208–9; Africa National Congress in, 135; boycott of, 206; Ronald Reagan's policies toward, 207, 208, 209; and U.S. student antiapartheid movement, 208–9

South America, 128

Southeast Children's Theater group, 101

Southern Christian Leadership Conference (SCLC): role in civil rights movement, 138, 154, 155; and SNCC, 147, 152; funding of, 148; and freedom songs, 149, 151; and voting rights, 156; and CORE, 163; Freedom Now slogan, 166; Martin Luther King Jr.'s speech at 1967 convention, 169–70; and Andrew Young, 174; and inclusion, 185; and Max Roach, 188; and Jesse Jackson, 192

Southern Negro Youth Congress (SNYC), 124–25, 126, 127, 128, 133, 147, 173

Southern Sons, 118

Southern University, 189, 198–99

Spanish American War, 114

Spanish language, 19

Spelman College, 75, 208

Spencer, Anne, 65–66

Spencer, Chauncey, 65–66

Spillers, Hortense, 11

Spingarn, Joel, 30, 59–60

Spirituals: in pageants, 40–41; and "School Improvement Day" programs, 86; and Negro History Week, 106; and black associational life, 145; and Highlander Folk School, 147; and civil rights movement, 151, 153; and Nairobi Day School, 182–83; recordings of, 204; and black culture, 211. *See also specific spirituals*